AF800001

Creative Insights In AI Ethics

Practical Advances in Artificial Intelligence and Machine Learning

Dr. Lance B. Eliot, MBA, PhD

Disclaimer: This book is presented solely for educational and entertainment purposes. The author and publisher are not offering it as legal, accounting, or other professional services advice. The author and publisher make no representations or warranties of any kind and assume no liabilities of any kind with respect to the accuracy or completeness of the contents and specifically disclaim any implied warranties of merchantability or fitness of use for a particular purpose. Neither the author nor the publisher shall be held liable or responsible to any person or entity with respect to any loss or incidental or consequential damages caused, or alleged to have been caused, directly or indirectly, by the information or programs contained herein. Every company is different and the advice and strategies contained herein may not be suitable for your situation.

Copyright © 2022 Lance B. Eliot

All rights reserved. First Edition.

ISBN: 978-1-95-738610-2

DEDICATION

To my incredible daughter, Lauren, and my incredible son, Michael.

Forest fortuna adiuvat (from the Latin; good fortune favors the brave).

CONTENTS

ACKNOWLEDGMENTS

I have been the beneficiary of advice and counsel by many friends, colleagues, family, investors, and many others. I want to thank everyone that has aided me throughout my career. I write from the heart and the head, having experienced first-hand what it means to have others around you that support you during the good times and the tough times.

To Warren Bennis, one of my doctoral advisors and ultimately a colleague, I offer my deepest thanks and appreciation, especially for his calm and insightful wisdom and support.

To Mark Stevens and his generous efforts toward funding and supporting the USC Stevens Center for Innovation.

To Lloyd Greif and the USC Lloyd Greif Center for Entrepreneurial Studies for their ongoing encouragement of founders and entrepreneurs.

To Peter Drucker, William Wang, Aaron Levie, Peter Kim, Jon Kraft, Cindy Crawford, Jenny Ming, Steve Milligan, Chis Underwood, Frank Gehry, Buzz Aldrin, Steve Forbes, Bill Thompson, Dave Dillon, Alan Fuerstman, Larry Ellison, Jim Sinegal, John Sperling, Mark Stevenson, Anand Nallathambi, Thomas Barrack, Jr., and many other innovators and leaders that I have met and gained mightily from doing so.

Thanks to Ed Trainor, Kevin Anderson, James Hickey, Wendell Jones, Ken Harris, DuWayne Peterson, Mike Brown, Jim Thornton, Abhi Beniwal, Al Biland, John Nomura, Eliot Weinman, John Desmond, and many others for their unwavering support during my career.

And most of all thanks as always to Lauren and Michael, for their ongoing support and for having seen me writing and heard much of this material during the many months involved in writing it. To their patience and willingness to listen.

CHAPTER 1
INTRODUCTION TO AI ETHICS

There is an urgently rising societal interest in the field of AI Ethics.

Thankfully so.

As Artificial Intelligence (AI) continues to advance and increasingly become part of our daily lives, we need to be on our toes about AI that diverges from ethical behavior and crosses over into unethical behavior. The field of AI Ethics seeks to apply ethical precepts and theories of ethical conduct to the devising and usage of AI systems, doing so to try and steer AI into sufficient ethical mores and avert unethical actions by AI.

Formal definitions of AI Ethics tend to vary somewhat. All told, the notion is to combine what we know or believe about ethics as a guiding tool toward the mounting advent of AI-based intelligent systems.

Some would argue that the AI horse is seemingly getting out of the barn and doing so without needed ethical boundaries. In a headline-grabbing worst-case scenario envisioned by AI futurists, AI systems are predicted to become mightier than we can adequately control and end up as an existential risk to the fate of humanity. Dire catastrophic outcomes are being painted.

You don't though need to look solely at the far future to get concerned about the ethical actions of AI. As will be discussed, there are plenty of AI systems of today that already have made known the adverse consequences of not taking into account the importance of AI Ethics.

As a particularly succinct and insightful definition of AI Ethics, consider this one by The Alan Turing Institute: "AI ethics is a set of values, principles, and techniques that employ widely accepted standards of right and wrong to guide moral conduct in the development and use of AI technologies" (as published in *Understanding Artificial Intelligence Ethics And Safety: A Guide For The Responsible Design And Implementation Of AI Systems In The Public Sector* by David Leslie, 2019).

Notice that there is an important dual-element consisting of both the development of AI systems and the usage of AI systems.

AI Ethics comes to play as a guiding light throughout the development process when devising AI. The entirety of the AI development life cycle must encompass AI Ethics principles. From the moment that an AI system is first initially conceived of, and then during the design, building, testing, fielding, and upkeep, all stakeholders involved in producing the AI are to be giving due consideration to AI Ethics. In addition, once an AI system has been placed into active use, you still must be on alert to watch for, detect, and potentially correct AI that verges from ethical conduct into unethical actions.

I mention the aspect of remaining aware once AI has been placed into use because there is often a faulty notion of fire-and-forget mindset that some developers of AI get caught up in. They believe that if they tried to develop the AI in an ethically minded fashion, there is no need to continue any AI Ethics forays once the AI is released into use.

This belies the real and frequent possibility that the AI will veer from its earlier ethics-oriented groundings and sway into unethical territory while in use.

AI Ethics And The Entire AI Development Life Cycle

Keep in mind then that we will want to ensure that both conditions of development and of use are being met, namely:

a) Apply AI Ethics throughout the AI development process from start to "finish"

b) Continue to apply AI Ethics even once the AI is placed into use

The AI development life cycle must be viewed as ranging from the initial conceiving of the AI to the entire time that it is available for use. Do not shortchange that range. Some AI developers do not consider the initial conceiving stage as within the scope of AI Ethics and think that just the building or coding stage is where AI Ethics first arises. In a similar mistaken belief, some AI developers assume that after the AI has been released into production and put into use that they can wash their hands of any residual or newly emerging AI Ethics qualms about the AI system. Nope, trying to narrowly confine where AI Ethics is needed will undoubtedly lead to ethical problems, one way or another, and sooner or later.

Another quick point is to realize that AI Ethics is something that all stakeholders amidst an AI system must be cognizant of. The normal assumption is that the software engineers alone are the caretakers of any AI Ethics considerations. Not so. Management that oversees the crafting of an AI system is part-and-parcel of the AI Ethics matters. If the organizational leaders are shortchanging the value of applying AI Ethics, you can bet that this same persona will permeate and undercut the AI life cycle. Budgets for devising the AI won't include set-asides for incorporating AI Ethics considerations. Schedules and deadlines won't either. In the end, a pell-mell rush to get the AI out the door will take top priority and AI Ethics will barely get a word in edgewise.

All stakeholders have a stake in enduring that AI Ethics is sufficiently incorporated into the full life-cycle of an AI system.

When an AI system exhibits unethical activity, this can be traced not just to the coding and the software developers, but also tracked to the leaders that oversaw the AI life cycle, the business and systems analysts involved, and even those that are operating or responsible for the final deployment of the AI.

The usual escape hatch entails those other stakeholders claiming that they weren't the ones that churned out the code that underlies the AI system. This is a convenient and at times nearly convincing argument for those that do not fully grasp how an AI system came to be. Overall, all stakeholders have both an ethical responsibility for the AI and are likely to have legal accountability too.

Making Sense Of What AI Is

When I refer to Artificial Intelligence, the AI moniker can be a bit confusing as to what AI entails.

Welcome to the club in the sense that the meaning of Artificial Intelligence continues to be bandied around and there is no single comprehensive and all-agreed definition for AI. One of the issues facing the latest efforts to regulate AI systems has been how to appropriately define AI within our laws. If the legal definition is overly broad, new laws seeking to better govern AI systems can inadvertently encroach on all manner of software applications and computer systems. If the legal definition of AI is excessively restrictive, the odds are that AI systems that should have been encompassed will wiggle out from being bound by those laws.

The easiest way to define AI consists of saying that any computer or machine that exhibits seemingly intelligent behavior is in the realm of AI.

This notion dates back to 1956 when Professor John McCarthy coined the name Artificial Intelligence as part of a proposal to bring together many luminaries of math and computer science for a research project: "The study is to proceed on the basis of the conjecture that every aspect of learning or any other feature of intelligence can in principle be so precisely described that a machine can be made to simulate it" (in his co-authored proposal entitled *Proposal For The Dartmouth Summer Research Project On Artificial Intelligence*).

One subtle but extremely vital facet about the definition of AI is that we can presumably seek to attain computer-based or machine-based intelligent behavior without necessarily duplicating the precise way that humans think. There is an ongoing debate about that questionable keystone. Some would contend that the only way to produce an artificial form of intelligence is to completely mimic how the human brain works. Others argue that we might find alternative means to bring forth artificially indued intelligence. The old saying goes that there is more than one way to skin a cat.

The gist is that if we can craft a computer or machine that will *exhibit* intelligence and intelligent behavior, we ought not to be especially caring about how that came to be. All that we need to know is that the system appears to act and respond intelligently. Whatever we did to get there is not particularly relevant, some say. As you might imagine, not everyone agrees with that supposition. The inner workings of how intelligence comes to arise are claimed to be equally important as the result of being able to produce intelligent actions and outputs.

Rather than focusing on definitions of AI, there is another way that AI is often depicted. You can assert that AI is a set of computer-related techniques and technologies. Thus, if you are making use of those AI techniques and technologies, you are ergo devising and employing AI capabilities.

A typical taxonomy would explain AI by suggesting that these associated techniques and technologies are involved:

- Machine Learning
- Natural Language Processing
- Knowledge-Based Systems
- Automated Reasoning
- Robotics
- Multi-Agent Systems
- Etc.

A difficulty of merely referring to those various techniques and technologies as constituting an AI system is that you aren't especially aiming at the intelligence side of things. Recall that the nearly universal goal of AI is to attain systems that exhibit intelligence. You can cobble together the various techniques and technologies and not necessarily derive any semblance of intelligent-like behaviors. Would a system that perchance leverages those capabilities be reasonably construed as an AI system even if it did not showcase intelligent-oriented actions? I would dare say many would contend that such a system does not meet the spirit or tone of what is meant by referring to AI.

AI Ethics Has Been On A Roller Coaster Of Societal Interest

You might be surprised to learn that AI Ethics has been a topic of discussion since the very beginning of the AI field. Perhaps this has partially been fueled by longstanding works of fiction that have indubitably worried that someday humans would construct machines that could overtake humankind. Today's emergence of computer systems that seem to have AI capacities has brought those past fictional stories into greater focus as something that might be constructed in the real world.

Interest in AI Ethics has been a roller coaster ride, consisting of moments of great interest to spans of sparse attention.

During the 1980s and 1990s, intense efforts were being made to craft knowledge-based systems, often referred to as expert systems, and the concerns about AI Ethics began to gain traction. The more AI there is, the more likely the attention to AI Ethics.

You might be aware that then a so-called "AI Winter" arose following the hyped expectations of AI in the 80s and 90s, and a resurgence of AI attention only began anew in the last decade or so. During the winter period of AI, AI Ethics somewhat languished, ostensibly still being worked on but now in the shadows. Upon the newly considered "AI Spring" of advances in AI capabilities that stridently stoked a renewal for AI, along with rapidly decreasing costs of computing, and a myriad of other technology trends such as cloud computing, the Internet of Things (IoT), and so on, this, in turn, sparked a renewal in AI Ethics.

Many speak nowadays of AI as being either *AI For Good* or *AI For Bad.* The initial renewed excitement about contemporary AI capabilities was that we would finally be able to fruitfully use computers and so-called smart machines toward solving many of the globe's most pressing problems, such as dealing with worldwide hunger, widespread poverty, sustainability, and other pressing issues.

That is *AI For Good.*

Lamentedly, we began to realize that the same AI could contain untoward biases and inequities, accordingly, labeled as *AI For Bad.* For example, facial recognition was one of the first AI technologies that got caught with inherent racial and gender biases, which we will be exploring in the chapters ahead.

The odds are that any AI system will have a bit of both. As much as possible, we want to uncover and excise the *AI For Bad.* Also, as much as possible, we want to ensure that *AI For Good* is being devised and fielded. Those that are AI ethicists bring to the table the skillset and passion for striving to maximize the *AI For Good* and minimize or eliminate the *AI For Bad.*

This is assuredly a tough proposition to fulfill.

Being An AI Ethicist Or Adjacent To

Speaking of tough shoes to fill, let's pursue that topic in terms of who can aid in the AI Ethics field.

A properly qualified AI ethicist should be versed in the field of ethics and likewise versed in the field of AI. It is a twofer if you like.

Someone that is strong on the ethics side but weak on the AI side would be doing themselves a disservice because they are bound to lack the needed comprehension about what AI is and what it might become. In the same breath, someone that is weak on the ethics side and strong on the AI side might be missing the boat in terms of understanding the vital nuances of ethics and ethical thinking.

In the case of AI, I like to clearly demarcate that when I am discussing AI, it could be in the context of any or all of these three conditions:

1) Non-sentient AI of today
2) Sentient AI of human intelligence caliber (which we don't know will be achieved)
3) Sentient AI of super-intelligence (which is even more speculative than #2)

Discussions about AI that are in the sentient AI category are highly speculative. We don't have sentient AI today. We don't know when we will have sentient AI, if ever so. In general, covering AI Ethics when solely considering sentient AI is a lot of handwaving. You can pretty much make up whatever you like about how sentient AI is going to behave. I'm not saying that we should not be concerned about sentient AI, and only mentioning that the AI Ethics as pertaining to sentient AI is loosey-goosey and not especially real-world applicable per se.

You can rest assured that there is still plenty to talk about when it comes to AI Ethics and today's non-sentient AI. There is no need to go into the outstretched arena of sentient AI to have lots to discuss.

Furthermore, the handy aspect of AI Ethics regarding non-sentient AI is that this is a very applied discipline that can be immediately put to use throughout society. Companies that are creating AI systems need AI Ethics advice and consultation. Entities and people that are using AI systems are likewise in need of AI Ethics advice and consultation. Regulators are now steeped in trying to create laws related to AI, for which AI Ethics insights are needed too.

The field of ethics and all of its numerous theories about ethics can be applied toward the specific domain of AI. Indeed, one viewpoint is that the field of ethics as *applied to technology* (of any kind) is the umbrella into which the particular application of ethics applied to AI fits.

For those of you that are pursuing a career as an AI ethicist, the good news is that we are still in the infancy of AI Ethics. There is a lot of room to grow. You can also anticipate that as AI gets more pervasive and improves in showcasing intelligent behavior, AI Ethics will be expanding and sought after correspondingly so.

AI Ethics Frameworks And Key Principles

At this time, there are lots of proposed AI Ethics frameworks or principles that are being floated around and discussed heartily. No single set of AI Ethics principles has been universally adopted. Each day there seems to be a new set proffered by one prominent group or entity, or another. You have lots of AI Ethics precepts to choose from.

The chapters will cover this more so, but we can take a sneak peek here.

As stated by the U.S. Department of Defense (DoD) in their *Ethical Principles For The Use Of Artificial Intelligence*, these are the six primary AI ethics principles:

- **Responsible:** DoD personnel will exercise appropriate levels of judgment and care while remaining responsible for the development, deployment, and use of AI capabilities.

- **Equitable:** The Department will take deliberate steps to minimize unintended bias in AI capabilities.

- **Traceable:** The Department's AI capabilities will be developed and deployed such that relevant personnel possesses an appropriate understanding of the technology, development processes, and operational methods applicable to AI capabilities, including transparent and auditable methodologies, data sources, and design procedure and documentation.

- **Reliable:** The Department's AI capabilities will have explicit, well-defined uses, and the safety, security, and effectiveness of such capabilities will be subject to testing and assurance within those defined uses across their entire lifecycles.

- **Governable:** The Department will design and engineer AI capabilities to fulfill their intended functions while possessing the ability to detect and avoid unintended consequences, and the ability to disengage or deactivate deployed systems that demonstrate unintended behavior.

Meanwhile, as stated by the Vatican in the *Rome Call For AI Ethics* these are their identified six primary AI ethics principles:

- **Transparency:** In principle, AI systems must be explainable
- **Inclusion:** The needs of all human beings must be taken into consideration so that everyone can benefit, and all individuals can be offered the best possible conditions to express themselves and develop
- **Responsibility:** Those who design and deploy the use of AI must proceed with responsibility and transparency
- **Impartiality:** Do not create or act according to bias, thus safeguarding fairness and human dignity
- **Reliability:** AI systems must be able to work reliably
- **Security and privacy:** AI systems must work securely and respect the privacy of users.

You astutely probably noticed a commonality across those AI Ethics principles.

Researchers have examined and condensed the essence of numerous such national and international AI ethics tenets, articulating the summary set in a paper entitled "The Global Landscape Of AI Ethics Guidelines" as published in the prized journal *Nature*, which led to this essentials list:

- **Transparency**
- **Justice & Fairness**
- **Non-Maleficence**
- **Responsibility**
- **Privacy**
- **Beneficence**
- **Freedom & Autonomy**
- **Trust**
- **Sustainability**
- **Dignity**
- **Solidarity**

In short, you could say that AI Ethics consists of *applying* those aforementioned ethical precepts to AI systems.

To make this claim abundantly apparent, I'll relist those principles and add the indication that they are to be applied to AI and done so via the auspices of AI Ethics:

- Transparency as applied to AI via AI Ethics considerations
- Justice & Fairness as applied to AI via AI Ethics considerations
- Non-Maleficence as applied to AI via AI Ethics considerations
- Responsibility as applied to AI via AI Ethics considerations
- Privacy as applied to AI via AI Ethics considerations
- Beneficence as applied to AI via AI Ethics considerations
- Freedom & Autonomy to AI via AI Ethics considerations
- Trust as applied to AI via AI Ethics considerations
- Sustainability as applied to AI via AI Ethics considerations
- Dignity as applied to AI via AI Ethics considerations
- Solidarity as applied to AI via AI Ethics considerations

A recent form of terminology is that we are endeavoring to produce *Ethical AI*.

As will be seen in the chapters herein, I will at times interchangeably refer to AI Ethics and Ethical AI as one and the same. I will also explain why some quibble that AI Ethics and Ethical AI are not identically equivalent, though they both share the same lineage.

A handy way to readily grasp the application of ethics to AI is to consider these two overarching avenues:

1. The ethical behavior of the humans devising and using AI
2. The computational embedding of ethical behavior into the AI itself

In the first instance, the notion is to try and get the humans that are developing and fielding AI to become aware of and make use of ethical practices in how they shape, release, and perform the upkeep of AI systems. You might for example train the stakeholders on the AI Ethics precepts. There might be software development tools and methodologies that can provide AI Ethics guidance. Various quality control checks and auditing can be done under the rubric of AI Ethics attainment. And so on.

In the second instance listed, the idea is to embed into the AI a semblance of ethical acting computer components. Whereas the first focus is about the process of devising the AI, this second focus is about trying to embody ethically capable computational functionality into the AI. This is a much less explored arena and rife for great expansion and maturation. Some even argue that it is not especially doable, though as will be discussed in the chapters you can counterargue that it is already being done, to some extent.

Revealing AI Ethics Via AI Self-Driving Cars

This brief introduction has provided an AI Ethics foundation that will aid in your reading of the chapters.

There is something else you need to know too. In my view, one of the most useful ways to showcase AI Ethics and Ethical AI consists of using real-world examples. There is a special and assuredly popular set of examples that are close to my heart. You see, in my capacity as an expert on AI including the ethical and legal ramifications, I am frequently asked to identify realistic examples that showcase AI Ethics dilemmas so that the somewhat theoretical nature of the topic can be more readily grasped.

One of the most evocative areas that vividly presents this ethical AI quandary is the advent of AI-based true self-driving cars. This will serve as a handy use case or exemplar for ample discussion on the topic.

The eloquence of discussing self-driving cars is that they are near enough to being viable that they reveal the realities of AI Ethics considerations. At the same time, we still have a long way to go before we'll see the fully autonomous self-driving cars that heretofore have mainly been portrayed in sci-fi exploits. The fact that there are tryouts underway of somewhat autonomous self-driving cars is a clear indicator that this is not a purely abstract matter.

Yes, you could sensibly assert that AI Ethics and the rubber meets the road is surely found within the advent of AI-based self-driving cars (pardon the slender pun).

Realize that there isn't a human driver involved in a true self-driving car. Keep in mind that true self-driving cars are driven via an AI driving system. There isn't a need for a human driver at the wheel, nor is there a provision for a human to drive the vehicle.

I'd like to further clarify what is meant when I refer to true self-driving cars.

As a clarification, true self-driving cars are ones that the AI drives the car entirely on its own and there isn't any human assistance during the driving task.

These driverless vehicles are considered Level 4 and Level 5, while a car that requires a human driver to co-share the driving effort is usually considered at Level 2 or Level 3. The cars that co-share the driving task are described as being semi-autonomous, and typically contain a variety of automated add-ons that are referred to as ADAS (Advanced Driver-Assistance Systems).

There is not yet a true self-driving car at Level 5, which we don't yet even know if this will be possible to achieve, and nor how long it will take to get there.

Meanwhile, the Level 4 efforts are gradually trying to get some traction by undergoing very constrained and selective public roadway trials, though there is controversy over whether this testing should be allowed per se (we are all life-or-death guinea pigs in an experiment taking place on our highways and byways, some contend).

Semi-autonomous cars require a human driver. For semi-autonomous cars, it is important that the public needs to be forewarned about a disturbing aspect that's been arising lately, namely that despite those human drivers that keep posting videos of themselves falling asleep at the wheel of a Level 2 or Level 3 car, we all need to avoid being misled into believing that the human driver can take away their attention from the driving task while driving a semi-autonomous car. You are the responsible party for the driving actions of the vehicle, regardless of how much automation might be tossed into a Level 2 or Level 3.

For Level 4 and Level 5 true self-driving vehicles, there won't be a human driver involved in the driving task. All occupants will be passengers. The AI is doing the driving.

One aspect to immediately discuss entails the fact that the AI involved in today's AI driving systems is not sentient. In other words, the AI is altogether a collective of computer-based programming and algorithms, and most assuredly not able to reason in the same manner that humans can.

Why is this added emphasis about the AI not being sentient?

Because I want to underscore that when discussing the role of the AI driving system, I am not ascribing human qualities to the AI. Please be aware that there is an ongoing and dangerous tendency these days to anthropomorphize AI. In essence, people are assigning human-like sentience to today's AI, despite the undeniable and inarguable fact that no such AI exists as yet.

With that clarification, you can envision that the AI driving system won't natively somehow "know" about the facets of driving. Driving and all that it entails will need to be programmed as part of the hardware and software of the self-driving car.

It is important to realize that not all AI self-driving cars are the same. Each automaker and self-driving tech firm is taking its approach to devising self-driving cars. As such, it is difficult to make sweeping statements about what AI driving systems will do or not do. Furthermore, whenever stating that an AI driving system doesn't do some particular thing, this can, later on, be overtaken by developers that in fact program the computer to do that very thing. Step by step, AI driving systems are being gradually improved and extended. An existing limitation today might no longer exist in a future iteration or version of the system.

Nearly all of the included chapters provide an indication of how the covered AI Ethics topic applies to a real-world setting, doing so via discussing AI-based self-driving cars.

The usual scenario depicted goes somewhat like this.

An AI-based self-driving car is underway on your neighborhood streets and seems to be driving safely.

At first, you had devoted special attention to each time that you managed to catch a glimpse of the self-driving car. The autonomous vehicle stood out with its rack of electronic sensors that included video cameras, radar units, LIDAR devices, and the like. After many weeks of the self-driving car cruising around your community, you now barely notice it. As far as you are concerned, it is merely another car on the already busy public roadways.

Lest you think it is impossible or implausible to become familiar with seeing self-driving cars, the locales that are within the scope of self-driving car tryouts have gradually gotten used to seeing the spruced-up vehicles. Many of the locals eventually shifted from mouth-gaping rapt gawking to now emitting an expansive yawn of boredom to witness those meandering self-driving cars.

Probably the main reason right now that they might notice the autonomous vehicles is because of the irritation and exasperation factor. The AI driving systems make sure the cars are obeying all speed limits and rules of the road. For hectic human drivers in their traditional human-driven cars, you get irked at times when stuck behind the strictly law-abiding AI-based self-driving cars.

I then use that base scenario to insert AI Ethics related considerations into the setting. This allows a handy means of discussing the perhaps abstract AI Ethics topic in a manner that can be tangibly understood.

About The Chapters And Your Reading Choices

The chapters are each standalone discussion and you do not need to read them in any particular order. I have sequenced them in a manner that I hope will be useful for the best reading and digesting of the material. That being said, you are welcome to jump around and read the chapters in any personally desired sequence.

These chapters are based on my popular columns and were selected based on their timeliness and rated as most viewed or most informative.

I hope that after you've read the chapters, you will be inspired to learn more about AI Ethics. As well, you might be motivated to participate actively in the AI Ethics realm, perhaps doing research, performing consulting, aiding societal awareness on these topics, or otherwise deciding to get directly involved in this exciting field.

As a quick indication of what the chapters contain, here are the chapters in their provided order:

Conclusion

The rapidity of AI being fostered upon us that is replete with ethically questionable behaviors is clearly a sign that we need more parties that are keenly interested in AI Ethics and Ethical AI. Raise awareness about AI Ethics. Get knee-deep into promulgating Ethical AI. I sincerely urge you to pursue this expanding realm and wish you the best in all of your endeavors.

CHAPTER 2
AI ETHICS AND AUDITING OF AI

Are you familiar with this classic nursery rhyme: *Old Mother Hubbard, went to the cupboard, to fetch her poor dog a bone, And when she went there, the cupboard was bare, and so the poor dog had none* (the rhyme was the charming work of Sarah Catherine Martin and published in 1805)?

I'm sure you've heard it before.

The crucial catchphrase within this enchanting verse is that sometimes the cupboard can be bare. You know how that can be. At times, we find ourselves up a creek without a paddle. You might have hoped that the cupboard was stocked or that your canoe had a paddle, but upon closer inspection, you sadly discovered that the things you needed or perhaps dreamily wanted weren't there. This can be disconcerting or even downright debilitating.

Shift gears into modern-day Artificial Intelligence (AI) and the rising tsunami of AI systems that we daily come in contact with. When it comes to auditing AI systems, especially the thorny matter of AI Ethics adherence, you might lamentedly say that the cupboard is bare. You see, we are woefully lacking in fully embraced across-the-board methods, techniques, tools, and standardized approaches for the solemn and necessary act of auditing complex AI.

That is both a shame and an outright perilous omission or insidious state of affairs.

Here's why.

Auditing is a long-revered process to assess and attest to something being of an appropriate or shall we say proper condition. We often rely upon the analyses and conclusions reached by auditors when they have sought to examine whether a business is fair-and-square about reporting its financial status. Without some form of validation, we cannot be sure of the validity of what a business is claiming they are doing or has done. As we have witnessed throughout history, many businesses have opted to cook their books, trying to hide devious schemes or downplay their precarious financial dealings.

That being said, let's all acknowledge that auditing is not a panacea. Can a business still manage to keep secret their deceitful trickery, despite undergoing an audit? Yes, absolutely. Is it possible to pull the wool over the eyes of the auditors or perhaps sneakily feed the auditors a plate of falsehoods that they fall for? Unfortunately, yes.

But just because auditing is not a perfect means of ferreting out what is happening, we should be cautious in unduly throwing out the baby with the bathwater. Auditing can indeed reveal that which was sought to be kept from prying eyes. Auditing can also act as a type of scare tactic that keeps potential wrongdoers from veering into the evil grasp of doing wrongs. Those leaning into the disturbingly foul territory are apt to realize they might get caught with their hands in the cookie jar.

If you don't do audits, a potential Pandora's box of devilish practices might get started and grow without nary a concern that the house of cards is conning others and someday might crash and devastate innocents.

And that brings us to the emerging and pervasive adoption of AI.

Consider these seemingly straightforward questions that ought to be always answerable:

- How does a company know that its AI is working properly and has been well-devised?
- How do consumers know that the AI they are using is doing the right things?

- How do regulators and government overseers know that the AI being used by the public at large is balanced and fair?
- Etc.

The chilling answer is that by and large they don't know.

Companies are pell-mell rushing forward to push shoddy AI out into the marketplace since they realize that if they don't grab the market first, a competitor will do so in their stead. Sometimes a firm does this with the best of intentions and is clueless that their AI is fraught with badness. Other times a firm realizes that the AI is perhaps less-than-optimal, but they take a chance anyway on it. There are the evildoers that know exactly the wrongs they are committing with atrocious and unethical AI, yet they proceed unabated and do so partially because the specter of an AI audit is generally unlikely.

Among the many and varied ways of dealing with bad AI, we should assuredly be clamoring for AI audits.

To clarify, this is not a silver bullet. It is certainly not the only means of coping with or stopping the emergence of bad AI. Nonetheless, it is a vital option and one that surprisingly is not taking place as much as you might assume.

Auditing AI is not especially a top priority for many companies. One reason is that firms are often unaware that auditing AI is something that can be done. Believe it or not, some executives seem to think that AI is entirely unamendable to being audited. Worse still, some of those executives also do not see any reason to audit AI at all, even if it seemed doable. They blindly have faith in AI and believe that AI is magically infallible.

Yikes!

We can add more frightening thoughts to this pile-on of reasons that AI auditing is not often undertaken. An oft-used excuse is that a normal audit will decidedly reveal any concerns with the AI systems being devised or utilized by a company.

Regrettably, that is not necessarily the case. Conventional audits are frequently ill-prepared to handle the AI side of things or skirt over the AI and act like it isn't worthwhile to probe into. An escape clause then might be included in the audit analysis that quietly and unobtrusively says in small print that the AI systems are not encompassed by the scope of the audit.

Meanwhile, executives that didn't read the fine print will incorrectly presume that their AI was given a clean bill of health. Sneaky executives might have gotten out their magnifying glass and carefully read the stated exceptions about AI, and yet act as though AI was presumably included. You might say that they will try the classic ploy of plausible deniability and hope that no one will ever catch them on their happening to have (shockingly, wink-wink) missed noticing that AI was carved out of an audit and not given due attention.

With all of that chicanery about auditing AI, we have the icing on the cake that there aren't fully agreed on standards about how to best audit complex AI systems. The audit camps can argue that they are lacking in the means to do AI audits. They might also worry that if AI audits are indeed performed, perhaps they will be on some ostensibly doubtful loose ground if the audit doesn't catch heinous AI badness. Clients might come after the auditors, as might shareholders and possibly the government.

It is risky business to do an AI audit.

A counterbalancing factor is that AI audits can be monetarily rewarding. Where there is a buck to be made, auditors will find a sufficient way to do audits. The tradeoff of whether a bona fide and defensible AI audit can be done, along with exposures for such audits that are later found to be inadequate, provides a potential ROI (return on investment) that is attractive enough to make dollars-wise sense in the right circumstances, including the auditing of AI.

I guess you could also say that where there is a need, a means will be found to meet the need. Thus, despite the immature state of AI auditing, many are stridently trying to devise AI auditing approaches and put those into practice.

Auditing of AI is like the little train that could, it is chugging and slogging its way up the hill toward providing valuable and usable auditing methods and auditing tools to get the AI auditing job satisfactorily done.

Rather than perhaps starkly contending that the cupboard is completely bare, it might be more suitable to suggest that the cupboard has a smorgasbord of items that are somewhat piecemeal gradually coming together to make an increasingly satisfactory AI auditing meal, as it were. A common approach entails borrowing from conventional tech-oriented auditing principles and techniques and recasting them in the context of AI systems. This is not a slam dunk. There are substantive differences in how AI works versus the traditional forms of everyday tech capabilities.

Let's take a look at what the cupboard already has and then ruminate on what we might expect to see as a further rise in the realm of auditing AI.

First, consider a handy report by the well-known professional association on tech auditing referred to as ISACA (Information Systems Audit and Control Association). Their *Auditing Artificial Intelligence* study proffered this important point: "AI's rise has been accompanied by the traditional lag time between early adoption and the establishment of regulatory and compliance frameworks. There is, for example, no mature auditing framework in place detailing AI subprocesses, nor are there any AI-specific regulations, standards or mandates."

You see, a conundrum exists as to the nature and scope of AI as an area of focus. It is indubitably challenging to try and audit something that you cannot even at the get-go put your arms around. Not only is the definition of AI rather loosey-goosey, the manner in which AI is devised varies widely too. Per the ISACA study: "Moreover, AI systems and solutions vary widely from each other, and the vast set of existing and emerging technologies foundational to AI architecture give birth to complex systems. This complexity points to a high likelihood of uncertainty around the scope of AI within the business."

I especially like this list in the ISACA report that spells out the key reasons that the auditing of AI has yet to have become an all-agreed formalized across-the-board standardized approach (this list is excerpted from the *Auditing Artificial Intelligence* report):

1. Immature auditing frameworks or regulations specific to AI
2. Limited precedents for AI use cases
3. Uncertain definitions and taxonomies of AI
4. Wide variance among AI systems and solutions
5. Emerging nature of AI technology
6. Lack of explicit AI auditing guidance
7. Lack of strategic starting points
8. Possibly steep learning curve for the AI auditor
9. Supplier risk created by AI outsourcing to third parties

Some of the proposed solutions in the report that are aimed to prod along the maturation of doing AI auditing include these stated steps:

- Adopt and adapt existing frameworks and regulations.
- Explain and communicate proactively about AI with stakeholders.
- Become informed about AI design and architecture to set proper scope.
- Focus on transparency through an iterative process.
- Focus on controls and governance, not algorithms.
- Involve all stakeholders.
- Become informed about AI design and engage specialists as needed.
- Document architectural practices for cross-team transparency.

When it comes to auditing AI, there is a particular element that sometimes does not get the attention it deserves. I am referring to AI Ethics and the production and use of Ethical AI. A bona fide audit of AI should encompass whether the AI is being devised to abide by the core precepts of AI Ethics. This is more than simply assessing the AI hardware or software for the usual kinds of auditing concerns.

A research paper in the journal of *Minds and Machines* made a telling observation that audits of AI need to incorporate a form of ethics-based auditing.

The effort tends to examine the basis for the AI, the code of the AI system, and the effects that the AI brings forth: "Rather than attempting to codify ethics, ethics-based auditing helps identify, visualize, and communicate whichever normative values are embedded in a system. Although standards have yet to emerge, a range of different approaches to ethics-based auditing of AI already exists: Functionality audits focus on the rationale behind the decision, code audits entail reviewing the source code, and impact audits investigate the effects of an algorithm's outputs" (by Jakob Mökander and Luciano Floridi in "Ethics-Based Auditing To Develop Trustworthy AI").

I think you can readily discern why the auditing of AI would be of such crucial importance. The AI builder might not realize they have veered into unethical AI waters. The leadership or executives managing the AI efforts might not realize that the AI is potentially going to go astray. All told, stakeholders that are vested in the AI production and deployment can get caught completely off-guard that the AI is not being devised to strictly abide by AI Ethics precepts.

What to do?

One especially sensible answer is to carry out an audit of the AI. Amongst the various avenues for auditing the AI would be the particular focus on AI Ethics. I would say that AI Ethics is instrumental and should not be neglected. At the same time, I would also assert that AI Ethics alone is not the only matter to be of auditing attention. Of course, you could employ a targeted audit to examine solely the Ethical AI aspects, though this should be done in a larger context amid an overarching audit of the AI.

The audit results of a budding AI system can then be shared with a myriad of stakeholders. In addition to showcasing any audit concerns, there would oftentimes be an indication of how the audit points can be potentially rectified. This is not necessarily at any detailed level and instead more so as to broad guidance of what the AI should be exhibiting and how the AI ought to be better devised.

Along those lines, a notable research paper related to the auditing of AI that is entitled "Toward Trustworthy AI Development Mechanisms For Supporting Verifiable Claims" has proposed that an AI audit would usually examine three sets of the mechanism underlying the AI:

- Institutional mechanisms
- Software mechanisms
- Hardware mechanisms

They define institutional mechanisms this way: "Institutional mechanisms are processes that shape or clarify the incentives of the people involved in AI development, make their behavior more transparent, or enable accountability for their behavior. Institutional mechanisms help to ensure that individuals or organizations making claims regarding AI development are incentivized to be diligent in developing AI responsibly and that other stakeholders can Institutions verify that behavior can shape incentives or constrain behavior in various ways."

The gist is that you need to audit not just the software and hardware but also ensure that you audit the organizational envelopment that surrounds the building and deployment of the AI. This might seem like an obvious point. Well, you'd be surprised to then know that many firms will willingly have their AI-related software and hardware activities audited, but the top executives bristle when told that the overall institutional and managerial milieu is also going to come under the audit gaze. The usual knee-jerk response is that this seems afield of the AI.

Do not fall for that kind of thinking. The three-legged stool of institutional, software, and hardware will fall apart if one of the legs is omitted. You can't skip over the institutional aspects. In that same way of thinking, it would equally be lopsided and ineffective to skirt past the hardware aspects or do likewise for the software facets.

The paper defines software mechanisms this way: "Software mechanisms involve shaping and revealing the functionality of existing AI systems.

They can support verification of new types of claims or verify existing claims with higher confidence. This section begins with an overview of the landscape of software mechanisms relevant to verifying claims, and then highlights several key problems, mechanisms, and associated recommendations."

And hardware mechanisms are defined this way: "Computing hardware enables the training, testing, and use of AI systems. Hardware relevant to AI development ranges from sensors, networking, and memory, too, perhaps most crucially, processing power. Concerns about the security and other properties of computing hardware, as well as methods to address those concerns in a verifiable manner, long precede the current growth in adoption of AI. However, because of the increasing capabilities and impacts of AI systems and the particular hardware demands of the field, there is a need for novel approaches to assuring the verifiability of claims about the hardware used in AI development."

You might not be familiar with the usage of the word "claims" that permeates the aforementioned definitions. The notion is straightforward. An AI system should be represented via a series of tangible claims or assertions about what the AI is intended to accomplish. By having explicitly stated and measurable claims, you can then have a fighting chance to ascertain the verifiability of those claims. The AI either does or does not satisfy the stated claims.

Many AI projects do not overtly identify their supposed claims. That is a recipe for disaster. If the stipulations of what the AI is supposed to do, and also not supposed to do, remain in a haze or fog, you are undoubtedly heading toward an AI system of immense problematic concerns. The old line that you cannot manage that which you cannot measure is a truism worthy of rapt reverence for the auditing of AI.

A handwringing qualm about today's AI efforts is that there often is an *accountability gap* involved in pushing AI systems out the door to simply try to get your AI into the marketplace soonest possible. Who has taken responsibility for the AI?

The AI builders might insist they aren't to be held accountable if the AI goes astray and that instead, it is the fault of management. Management might exhort that it is the AI builders that have the responsibility. Massive amounts of finger-pointing will ensue the moment that the AI gets the firm in trouble.

I had mentioned earlier that examining the AI Ethics components is an oft-overlooked part of auditing AI. Sometimes the examination of AI Ethics is referred to as doing a social assessment of an AI system. A research paper entitled *Closing the AI Accountability Gap: Defining an End-to-End Framework for Internal Algorithmic Auditing* helpfully explores the accountability gap and the need for a social assessment of AI systems: "A social impact assessment should inform the ethical review. Social impact assessments are commonly defined as a method to analyze and mitigate the unintended social consequences, both positive and negative, that occur when a new development, program, or policy engages with human populations and communities. In it, we describe how the use of an artificial intelligence system might change people's ways of life, their culture, their community, their political systems, their environment, their health and well-being, their personal and property rights, and their experiences (positive or negative)."

A potential blind spot for many AI builders is that they do not anticipate the unintended consequences of their AI system. They are usually preoccupied with what they purposefully intend their AI to attain. Meanwhile, giving any semblance of consideration to how the AI might generate unintended consequences is just not in their frame of mind. The danger there is that AI systems are especially likely to promulgate unintended consequences, some of which are adverse and some of which might be beneficial. An audit of AI should seek to uncover any such unintended consequences that might later emerge via the AI.

An audit of AI needs to be organized and performed in a logical and explicitly laid out manner.

There are steps or stages that an audit of AI would normally undertake.

In the paper on closing the AI accountability gap, they propose a set of five core steps coined as SMACTR, which are Scoping, Mapping, Artifact Collection, Testing, and Reflection. There is also a follow-on sixth step for doing a post-audit review. By and large, audits are best arranged when a methodology is utilized, for which there are lots of tech-oriented auditing methodologies and they provide a handy step-by-step indication of what should be done. The same is true for doing an AI audit.

You might know that business audits are conventionally conducted in one of two ways, either done as an internal audit or performed as an external audit. Internal auditors typically are considered "internal" in that they work for the company they are auditing. They provide an essential function within a firm. At the same time, there is always a hint of suspicion that perhaps an internally executed audit might not be as strident as one that is done by external auditors.

The assumption is that external auditors would seemingly be less biased toward the firm they are auditing. This does not always work out and there have been famous cases of external auditors that dropped the ball. In any case, external audits are an important part of doing the auditing of AI, in addition to internal audits of AI too. You can also anticipate that the tsunami of AI regulations will serve as an impetus for firms opting to have external audits of their AI undertaken. Indeed, it is likely that the government might mandate AI audits in certain circumstances.

Is the audit of your AI a legitimate audit?

That is the question that seriously will be asked if a firm contends that they have done audits of their AI. Some companies are bound to try and boast that they've had their AI audited and yet will have done the auditing in the thinnest of ways. All they really wanted was a checkmark that they did an audit of AI. They don't care that the audit was sparse, perhaps only covering the most obvious elements. All I can say is that they will ultimately hopefully be held accountable for taking this kind of auditing dodge, and take it hard on the chin when their AI goes bad and lawsuits or the long arm of the law comes after them.

Before we move on, I'd like to also mention that AI can be used for aiding the auditing effort. This might seem like a tongue twister or a mental puzzle. Not really. The idea is that computer-based tools used by auditors are getting better and better via being infused with AI capabilities. It might seem curious or ironic to imagine that an AI-based auditing tool could possibly be used to audit an AI system that someone is devising. I suppose it is akin to the spy-versus-spy notion whereby we use AI to gauge the nature of some other AI.

At this juncture of this weighty discussion, I'd bet that you are desirous of some illustrative examples that might showcase the AI auditing auspices. There is a special and assuredly popular set of examples that are close to my heart. You see, in my capacity as an expert on AI including the ethical and legal ramifications, I am frequently asked to identify realistic examples that showcase AI Ethics dilemmas so that the somewhat theoretical nature of the topic can be more readily grasped. One of the most evocative areas that vividly presents this ethical AI quandary is the advent of AI-based true self-driving cars. This will serve as a handy use case or exemplar for ample discussion on the topic.

Here's then a noteworthy question that is worth contemplating: *Does the advent of AI-based true self-driving cars illuminate anything about the auditing of AI, and if so, what does this showcase?*

Generally, the bona fide self-driving car firms are routinely doing overall audits of the firm all-told and at times doing tech-specific audits too. You might say that this is the business-as-usual kind of mindset.

Fewer are also specifically doing AI audits.

This can be explained by several factors. First, the auditing of AI is considered less well-understood and less likely to come to the minds of those self-driving tech firms or automakers that are building AI driving systems. Second, the assumption is that an overall audit of the firm or any tech-specific audit would be sufficient to somehow encapsulate the AI driving systems. It is a weak assumption and tends to gloss over the fact that the AI driving system is either not being audited or being audited in the most tangential of ways.

Another viewpoint is that auditing the AI that underlies the AI driving system is presumed to be nearly impossible. The complexities of the AI driving system would appear to be of such a large-scale magnitude that no auditors could conceivably do anything substantive by attempts at auditing it. That is yet another falsehood. The right auditors that are armed in the right ways and that are provided the right kind of access can materially perform such audits.

Period, full stop.

Conclusion

Imagine that you were going to buy a used car.

Wouldn't you want to look under the hood?

Yes, you most certainly would want to do so. You need to know what is happening there and whether you are getting a lemon or a shining star. By popping open the hood, you have a reasonable chance of figuring out whether the engine is going to work and whether it will last longer than the time it takes to drive it off the car lot.

You might though not know much about cars. In that case, looking at the engine is probably not going to be especially fruitful. Seeing that there is an engine there is not much of a useful inspection. Then again, even if you know about cars, perhaps you don't have the time available to give the vehicle an in-depth kick of the tires.

I bring up that automotive-related analogy to try and illustrate the demonstrative value of doing an audit of your AI system. You might not know what to look at when trying to discern whether the AI is being built sensibly. You might not have the time available to do so. It could be that even if you did do the assessment, investors or other outsiders would not especially find your audit findings credible.

Time to bring in the AI auditors.

The field of AI auditing is growing and will continue to expand. The advent of AI and the ubiquitous fielding of AI is going to be accompanied by AI that goes awry. Public pressure will mount to make sure that audits of AI are being performed. New laws and regulations will inspire or possibly even force firms into doing AI audits. Companies that make AI systems will be the initial targets. Gradually, any company that deploys AI, meaning just about all companies, will need to do AI audits of how they are fielding and using their licensed or acquired AI systems.

The business of auditing AI is going to be booming.

That being said, there will be some firms that earnestly embrace those AI auditors while other companies will grimace, fight dearly to keep from being audited and try to keep the auditors entirely at bay.

AI auditors that walk in the door never know exactly how they will be treated and nor what they might find. They are brave souls.

May the AI audit be with them.

CHAPTER 3
AI ETHICS
AND
AI INFALABILITY MYTH

AI must always be right.

Wait for a second, does that sentence mean that AI is in fact always right, or does it suggest that if we are going to be making use of AI we ought to make darned sure that it is indeed right all of the time?

Let's focus on the first interpretation.

Some people seem to fall into the mental trap that AI is axiomatically always right and altogether infallible. This is generally referred to as the *AI infallibility myth* by those that know about AI and are shocked or at least dismayed by those that don't understand AI and incorrectly assign a perception of perfection toward AI systems.

You might find it hard to believe that there are people that willfully and openly contend that AI can do no wrong. It would seem nearly impossible to think this way. We've all had computer systems that mess us up. Sometimes a computer turns us down for a loan request when we fervently believe that we should have gotten approved. Wasn't that an example of a computer not being infallible?

One supposes that a distinction is partially made by the phrasing of AI rather than merely blankly referring to a computer system per se. When you invoke the majesty of the term Artificial Intelligence you are seemingly going beyond the normal everyday computing that we already know is at times error-prone. There is a kind of haughty cachet about AI that for some people carries a connotation of perfection.

Perhaps there is a mental gap between the AI of Hollywood fame that works perfectly and the realization that today's AI is just as error-laden as any other type of computing system. But even that doesn't seem to explain why some insist on the infallibility of AI, particularly since there are plenty of sci-fi films and TV shows that highlight AI that has gone berserk. You would seemingly be able to point to that portrayal of AI "gone bad" as a sensible way to overcome the fictionalized imagery of AI perfection.

Compare the perception about what AI appears to be able to attain versus the likewise perception about humans and how human behavior plays out. You would almost find a universal agreement that humankind is not infallible. Humans are time again said to be and repeatedly show themselves to be fallible. No two ways about that. Of course, you might have egocentric people that claim to be infallible, though this is readily questioned and ultimately revealed as a falsehood.

Per the famous words of Thomas Jefferson: *The wise know too well their weakness to assume infallibility, and he who knows most knows best how little he knows.*

The field of AI has cleverly or by happenstance managed to garner an image that exceeds that of human assumed fallibility by magically getting AI into the infallibility camp. What an amazing accomplishment! Convincing breathing people that AI will always do the right thing, perfectly, unerringly is astonishing when you think about it. Turn back the clock before AI began to become a thing. If you asked a public relations guru to make people believe that AI or a machine is steadfastly infallible, they would probably realistically have told you that it isn't a feasible task. Sure, you might fool some of the people for some of the time, but that wouldn't last very long and the AI infallibility labeling would fade and inevitably die off.

You might be wondering whether it makes a difference that some people do seem to fall into the AI infallibility enchantment. So what, you might be asking?

The problem of such an AI infallibility belief is multifold, including that it is wrong, dangerous, and insidiously enduring.

As a quick indication of why it is both wrong and dangerous, consider what can happen if you are reliant upon an AI system and assume that it is infallible. Take for example the emerging use of AI-based autonomous vehicles such as self-driving cars. Some pundits are proclaiming that driverless cars will never get into car crashes. Never, ever. They say that AI makes those vaunted self-driving cars into being uncrashable. An AI driving system is apparently miraculous at driving and will ensure that a self-driving car avoids all possibilities of getting into a collision or crash. It is infallible AI.

Nonsense.

I have emphasized in my column discussions that there is no possible way for an AI driving system to guarantee that no car crashes will ever occur in any real-world public roadway driving scenarios. If a toddler suddenly wanders into the street from between two parked cars, and a self-driving car is coming down the street at the speed limit of say 35 miles per hour, the physics of the situation precludes the autonomous vehicle from stopping in time to avoid striking the youngster. AI does not overcome physics.

Consider what ominously will happen if some people begin to believe in the AI infallibility myth with regards to AI-based self-driving cars. Pedestrians brainwashed with that belief would certainly be willing to wander directly into the path of an oncoming driverless vehicle. In their minds, they believe that AI will ensure that the self-driving car does not strike them. Those pundits that are pushing the uncrashable narrative ought to be ashamed of their efforts in making such risky situations viable.

In short, the AI infallibility myth is both wrong and dangerous.

On top of that, the AI infallibility myth is exasperatingly and scarily *enduring*.

Here's how that often happens. Somebody realizes that AI is not infallible. That's good. A vocal AI researcher or some news headline touts that there have been incredible breakthroughs in AI technology.

The person that once thought AI was infallible but had changed to thinking that AI was fallible, now switches back to the roots of believing that AI is once again infallible. That's bad.

The old AI fallibility-infallibility switcheroo.

Yes, each day that we make advances in AI is likely to boost the AI infallibility myth. Those that beforehand didn't think AI was infallible are now spurred into thinking that the moment has finally arrived. Some already assumed AI was infallible and therefore the latest AI advances simply reinforce that belief. And as mentioned some might have once believed that AI was infallible and changed their minds, yet switch again into the infallibility camp under the assumption that AI is really infallible after the latest and greatest advances that have been hyped.

The whole kit and caboodle can make your head spin.

Why do people accept or adopt the premise that AI is infallible?

That's a great question and one that we will explore next. I will present to you five major reasons that the AI infallibility myth exists and endures. Before we jump into those considerations, you might be relieved to know that there is an ongoing battle to try and diminish or even extinguish the AI infallibility prevalence.

AI Ethics has been aiming to burst the bubble of the AI infallibility myth for quite a while. AI developers need to realize that they can overtly lead people down the false path of AI infallibility, either by the ways they build their AI or how they promote the use of their AI. This can be done by purposeful intent, namely wanting people to think that the AI is infallible or can be inadvertently prompted as a result of what the AI does or how it is portrayed.

Let me clarify that this isn't just those that are programming AI systems since there is a slew of other stakeholders that equally share in promulgating or stoking the AI infallibility myth.

Hopefully, the opening chapter discussion aided in your realizing that today's AI is absolutely not infallible. AI as we know it is instead absolutely fallible. Meanwhile, those that wish to have dreamy debates about a futuristic AI that might someday (maybe, kind of) be wondrously infallible are welcome to do so, though they should undertake such discussions properly. Do not confound today's AI with an unknown and fantastical kind of future AI. Do not convey your mystical unrealized AI in a fashion that gets people into a mindset of thinking that today's AI is infallible. Act responsibly when you make or imply any of those AI infallibility overtones.

With that foundation in hand, we can next poke into why people are apt to get themselves unduly mired in the AI infallibility myth. I will couch the points in a semblance of comparison to humans and human behavior, doing so because that is a significant means of how people tend to think about AI. They do so by comparing AI to humans. I'll say more about the wrongful anthropomorphizing of AI momentarily.

Here are my five key reasons that the AI infallibility myth endures:

- **Myth #1: AI is a machine that can repeat endlessly and unerringly, while in comparison humans are known to slip up and make mistakes.**
- **Myth #2: AI is a machine that acts without emotion, while humans are emotionally fueled.**
- **Myth #3: AI is a machine that is unbiased and neutral, while humans are biased and discriminatory.**
- **Myth #4: AI is a machine that is trustworthy and will do as it is told, while humans are capricious and act on whims.**
- **Myth #5: AI is a machine absent of motivational entailment, while humans have hidden agendas.**

Note that there are many more reasons that can be identified for the widespread endurance of the AI infallibility myth. You've got the scammers and schemers that want people to think that AI is infallible. It is a sneaky and conniving way to make a quick buck. You've got unwashed that think AI is infallible and are eager to tell others that it must be so. You've got the AI proponents that in their hearts wish AI to be infallible and say such things aloud as though they are true.

The list of crazy notions and wild declarations is undoubtedly endless. We will focus herein on my five key reasons and take a deep dive into each of them.

Myth #1: AI is a machine that can repeat endlessly and unerringly, while in comparison humans are known to slip up and make mistakes.

One reason that people seem to think that AI is presumably infallible comes from the notion that machines can apparently do repetitive tasks without complaining or seemingly making a mistake. We imagine a factory floor that has machines working nonstop at a given task. Human laborers would be prone to taking rest breaks or readily mistakenly slipping up when undertaking a constantly repeating series of steps.

This is both a false analogy and a misleading comparison that is attempting to keep this myth alive.

You see, a rudimentary machine might be able to repeat tasks far beyond the patience or endurance of a human, but there is always still a chance of the machine breaking down or going awry. A wheel or integral part can wear out and stall the machine. Some components can go haywire and cause the machine to perform unexpectedly and possibly carry out endangering actions. And so on.

AI can potentially contain programming flaws or bugs that cause the AI to make mistakes or otherwise fail to work as intended. Even self-adjusting AI that perhaps utilizes Machine Learning (ML) or Deep Learning (DL) can turn itself toward performing tasks undesirably, yet the AI has no semblance of common sense that would aid in preventing it from going off the rails. AI builders are supposed to devise suitable system-oriented guardrails to prevent the AI from going adversely amiss, but the protection might not be sufficient or might not work as anticipated.

In brief, AI is not in any reasonable sense a machine that can repeat endlessly and unerringly.

Myth busted.

Myth #2: AI is a machine that acts without emotion, while humans are emotionally fueled.

This myth contends that AI acts without emotion and therefore in comparison to humans will perform tasks in a reliable and emotion-free manner. In a sense, the belief is that AI is like one of those sci-fi robots that speak in a neutral tone and never gets mad or upset. We seem to buy into this fiction and ascribe a sense of utter rationality to AI as though it transcends the vagaries of human sentiment.

AI researchers have characterized this faulty viewpoint about AI in this insightful way: "Of interest in this context is the psychological side to the black box problem. We have the tendency to view the decisions made by a black box more reliable than those made by humans, since algorithms are often perceived as coolly rational or even perfectly rational" (paper published in the *AI And Ethics Journal* entitled "Socio-Cognitive Biases In Folk AI Ethics And Risk Discourse" co-authored by Michael Laakasuo, Volo Herzon, Silva Perander, Marianna Drosinou, Jukka Sundvall, Jussi Palomaki, and Aku Visala).

You might be tempted to fall into this mental trap about emotions since indeed we do not usually expect AI to exhibit emotions. If AI doesn't seemingly experience emotions, doesn't that logically suggest that we do not need to be worried about AI making emotionally-based decisions?

The question is a dodge or distractor.

Just because AI might not exhibit emotions does not directly imply it won't ever make any mistakes. As mentioned in the discussion about the first myth, an AI system is always still susceptible to problems such as flaws or bugs, hardware glitches, and other faltering facets. Thus, even if we somehow agree that AI is not emotionally-based, this does not whisk away all the other issues and limitations associated with AI.

We can go even further on this topic and point out that it is conceivable that we could devise AI that contains or at least exhibits emotions. Briefly, some contend that AI can never embody emotions because emotions are a distinctly human-only element (well, some include animals, some include all living creatures, etc.). By definition, if AI is not a human it cannot ergo contain emotions, they so assert. But this flies in the face of the other perspective that emotions are exhibited by our actions, in addition to seemingly being humanly felt.

A person is said to *feel* their emotions, and meanwhile, they can *exhibit* those emotions by their facial expressions, their mannerisms, their actions, etc.

AI researchers are able to program AI to do *exhibitory emotions* by programming actions that are essentially simulated variants of emotions. If you want AI that can get mad or jealous, this can be programmed. I realize a purist would argue that the AI is not feeling the emotions and only pretending or acting them out, but nonetheless, from the perspective of those interacting with the AI, it appears as though the AI does in fact have emotions.

The practical gist is that an AI system could be programmed to exhibit emotions. In that case, the myth is blown up entirely since the core claim of the myth is that AI is not at all emotional in any manner whatsoever (feeling versus exhibiting).

Myth busted.

Myth #3: AI is a machine that is unbiased and neutral, while humans are biased and discriminatory.

This myth is that AI will always be unbiased and neutral. In comparison, we all know that humans can be biased and discriminatory.

I earlier herein pointed out that ML/DL can be infused with computational biases and act in discriminatory ways. We've already witnessed this in a variety of areas, such as facial recognition, interactive Natural Language Processing (NLP) online conversations, and other venues.

Myth busted.

Myth #4: AI is a machine that is trustworthy and will do as it is told, while humans are capricious and act on whims.

This myth is an especially popular one. The idea is that AI will only do as it is told. We know that humans are often rebellious and won't do as they are told. A sense of relief then seems to arise by believing that AI will blindly do as it is programmed and will never veer from that programming.

Lots of holes exist in this flimsy contrivance.

First, even if it were true that AI would only do as it is programmed, it seems doubtful that we would be willing to trust an AI system that has been programmed to be deceptive and perform heinous acts. Yes, you might say that it is only doing as it was programmed, but I don't think you'd find that very satisfying when the AI is wreaking havoc at the apparent behest of some evildoer.

Second, it is false and wholly misleading to assert that AI will only do as it is told. You tell the AI to save mankind and it kills all of mankind. How can that happen if the AI is only to do as it is told? A well-known thought experiment involves an AI system programmed to make paperclips, for which the AI eventually gobbles up all of Earth's resources to achieve the paperclip making goals and simultaneously causes all humans to die off since there is nothing left on the planet for our survival. A crucial concern is how are we to tell or program the AI to do things when today's AI has no semblance of common sense or sentience to fully grasp what it is being programmed to do.

Third, as per the other busted myths, a programmed AI might contain flaws or bugs and the AI goes beyond what was thought that it was programmed to do. This can have demonstrative adverse effects.

Fourth, AI developers can program AI to go beyond the initially devised programming and undertake self-adjustments. This is especially noted these days in the use of Machine Learning and Deep Learning. The concern is that the AI as programmed becomes something other than what the starting programming consisted of. Whether the self-adjusted AI ends up doing good or doing bad can be generally unpredictable.

AI researchers emphasize that this aspect comes up quite a bit when discussing AI Ethics: "We want to draw attention to what happens if AI is viewed solely through the categories of 'artifact' and 'tool'. It is common to think that AI, or more broadly, any computer executing programs, is doing simply what it has been programmed to do. This assumption is misleading and affects the discussion about AI ethics considerably. It is different to explicitly program an AI to perform a task than to program it to autonomously learn to perform the task.

In both cases, the AI indeed only does what it has been programmed to do, but especially in the latter case it is hard for humans to intuitively follow and predict the complex, data-driven, and probabilistic decision making; hence, the aforementioned black box problem and the surprise about the way a learning system will perform a given task" (same paper published in the *AI And Ethics Journal* entitled "Socio-Cognitive Biases In Folk AI Ethics And Risk Discourse").

Myth busted.

Myth #5: AI is a machine absent of motivational entailment, while humans have hidden agendas.

This last of the five myths entails the assumption that AI won't be motivated by hidden agendas. There is presumably no kind of intrinsic motivation inside the AI. The AI doesn't want fame or fortune. Humans tend to want fame or fortune and will perform egregious acts in the pursuit of such riches. We can breathe a sigh of relief that AI doesn't embody greed and doesn't seem to believe that greed is good, so it would seem.

Time to put a stake through the heart of this myth.

First, the AI developers that made the AI may be indeed motivated by various kinds of motivations, and they could have embedded into the AI programming those same moralities and cultural values. I am not suggesting that AI is sentient. I am only pointing out that the AI as programmed can reflect the values of those that program the AI.

Second, any AI, which we've agreed can contain flaws or bugs, could seem to exhibit a hidden agenda, though we might not conventionally construe the matter as purity of a human-like hidden agenda. Remember that there is a fine line between that which is going awry versus whether it is doing so by purposeful intent as a means of carrying out a devious scheme.

Third, akin to my earlier point, an evildoer could seek to devise AI that will perform a hidden agenda on their human-stoked motivational aspirations. Since the AI would seemingly lack any semblance of common sense or sentience of reasoning, it is perhaps as dangerous or worse so than a human that might opt to overturn the commanded wrongdoing.

Myth busted.

All told, I hope you can plainly see that AI infallibility is entirely *busted*, including that it is a wrongful, highly dangerous, and regrettably enduring false belief based on an incomplete or faulty understanding of what AI is about. Do keep in mind that I am talking about today's AI. For those of you that want to speculate about some futuristic AI, you can readily try to create assumptions that would seem to undercut or fully support each of the myths, doing so in a conjured mythical world that we don't know will arise.

I prefer to stay closer to the grounding of what we know today and that we anticipate will most likely be the case involving AI in the real-world future.

At this juncture of this weighty discussion, I'd bet that you are desirous of some illustrative examples that might showcase the AI infallibility myth. There is a special and assuredly popular set of examples that are close to my heart. You see, in my capacity as an expert on AI including the ethical and legal ramifications, I am frequently asked to identify realistic examples that showcase AI Ethics dilemmas so that the somewhat theoretical nature of the topic can be more readily grasped. One of the most evocative areas that vividly presents this ethical AI quandary is the advent of AI-based true self-driving cars. This will serve as a handy use case or exemplar for ample discussion on the topic.

Here's then a noteworthy question that is worth contemplating: *Does the advent of AI-based true self-driving cars illuminate anything about the AI infallibility myth, and if so, what does this showcase?*

Consider each of the five bases for stoking the AI infallibility myth and let's see how they arise in the context of autonomous vehicles and especially AI-based self-driving cars:

- **Myth #1: AI is a machine that can repeat endlessly and unerringly, while in comparison humans are known to slip up and make mistakes.**

We know that human drivers get into car crashes. Sadly, in the United States alone there are about 40,000 annual human fatalities and around 2.5 million injuries due to car crashes. Humans drink and drive. Humans drive while distracted. The task of driving a car seems to consist of being able to repetitively and unerringly focus on driving and avoid getting into car crashes. As such, we might dreamily hope that AI driving systems will guide self-driving cars repetitively and unerringly.

I earlier cited the misconceived and outrageously wrong assertion that self-driving cars will be uncrashable. Do not expect and do not pretend that AI driving systems will work perfectly and avoid all chances of getting into car crashes. This is an exceedingly bad assumption and one that could cost people their lives.

- **Myth #2: AI is a machine that acts without emotion, while humans are emotionally fueled.**

Human drivers can get quite emotional while at the wheel of a car. The news is replete with stories of road rage that erupted when one driver got angry at another. AI that is appropriately devised for self-driving cars will, by and large, avert those kinds of emotionally sparked reactions that human drivers exhibit. That is good and welcomed. At the same time, there are some downsides.

- **Myth #3: AI is a machine that is unbiased and neutral, while humans are biased and discriminatory.**

Turns out that AI underlying self-driving cars can and has at times been shown to contain various biases and discriminatory actions. This is partly a result of how Machine Learning or Deep Learning is at times employed.

- **Myth #4: AI is a machine that is trustworthy and will do as it is told, while humans are capricious and act on whims.**

I already busted this myth in the earlier part of this discussion, namely that we cannot rely upon the notion that AI is only doing what it is told.

- **Myth #5: AI is a machine absent of motivational entailment, while humans have hidden agendas.**

An AI driving system and the AI that aids in overseeing a fleet of self-driving cars can readily contain numerous hidden agendas.

Conclusion

Throughout history, there has been an ongoing tussle to figure out whether infallibility can exist. We at times have ascribed infallibility to all sorts of conceptions.

I dare say we can pretty much all agree that humans are not infallible. Without going too far out on a limb, we can presumably all agree that AI is also not infallible. At least this seems abundantly true about the AI of today and for the foreseeable future.

Will we someday produce or somehow encounter infallible AI?

Any such infallible AI will ostensibly tell us the answer to that question.

AI Ethics is struggling mightily with trying to figure out what it will take to make AI trustworthy. Some suggest that there is a formula that will get AI into the trustworthy heavens. Others indicate that it will take hard work and consistent and unrelenting adherence to AI Ethics and Ethical AI principles to get the vaunted trust of society.

The contemporary enigma about trust in AI is not especially new per se. You can easily go back to the late 1990s and trace the emergence of a sought-for birth of trusted computing from those days. This was a large-scale tech-industry effort to discern if computers all told could be made in a manner that would be construed as trustworthy by society. Could hardware be made such that it was trustworthy? Could software be crafted such that it was trustworthy? Could we put in place global networked computers that would be trustworthy? And so on.

The prevailing sentiment then and that continues to this day is that trustworthy computing remains a type of holy grail that regrettably is still not quite within our reach (as noted in a paper entitled "Trustworthy AI", October 2021, *Communications of the ACM*). You could convincingly argue that AI is yet another component of the computing trustworthiness envelopment, yet AI makes the trust pursuit even more challenging and uncertain. AI has become the potential spoiler in the fight to attain trustworthy computing. Possibly the weakest link in the chain, as it were.

Let's take a quick look at why AI has gotten our dander up about being less than trustworthy. In addition, we will explore the tenets of AI Ethics that are hoped will aid in propping up the already semi-underwater perceived trust (or bubbling distrust) of today's AI.

One particular segment or portion of AI Ethics that has been getting a lot of media attention consists of AI that exhibits untoward biases and inequities. You might be aware that when the latest era of AI got underway there was a huge burst of enthusiasm for what some now call *AI For Good*. Unfortunately, on the heels of that gushing excitement, we began to witness *AI For Bad*. For example, various AI-based facial recognition systems have been revealed as containing racial biases and gender biases.

Efforts to fight back against *AI For Bad* are actively underway. Besides vociferous *legal* pursuits of reining in the wrongdoing, there is also a substantive push toward embracing AI Ethics to righten the AI vileness. The notion is that we ought to adopt and endorse key Ethical AI principles for the development and fielding of AI doing so to undercut the *AI For Bad* and simultaneously heralding and promoting the preferable *AI For Good.*

Let's tie this to the question about trustworthy AI.

We certainly would not seem to be willing to trust AI that showcases adverse biases and discriminatory actions. Our belief, in that case, would be that such AI is decidedly not trustworthy, thus we would lean toward actively distrusting the AI. Without going overboard on an anthropomorphic comparison (I'll say more about AI anthropomorphizing in a moment), a human that exhibited untoward biases would also be subject to rating as not being particularly trustworthy.

Digging Into Trust And Trustworthiness

Maybe we ought to take a look at what we mean when asserting that we do or do not trust someone or something. First, consider several everyday dictionary definitions of trust.

Examples of what trust definitionally means are:

- Assured reliance on the character, ability, strength, or truth of someone or something (Merriam-Webster online dictionary).
- Reliance on the integrity, strength, ability, surety, etc., of a person or thing (Dictionary.com)
- Firm belief in the reliability, truth, ability, or strength of someone or something (Oxford Languages online dictionary).

I'd like to point out that all of those definitions refer to "someone" and likewise refer to "something" as being potentially trustworthy.

This is notable since some might insist that we only trust humans and that the act of trusting is reserved exclusively for humankind as our target of trustworthiness. Not so. You can have trust in your kitchen toaster. If it seems to reliably make your toast and works routinely to do so, you can assuredly have a semblance of trust about whether the toaster is in fact trustworthy.

In that same line of thinking, AI can also be the subject of our trust viewpoint. The odds are that trust associated with AI is going to be a lot more complicated than say a mundane toaster. A toaster can only usually do a handful of actions. An AI system is likely to be much more complex and appear to operate less transparently. Our ability to assess and ascertain the trustworthiness of AI is bound to be a lot harder and proffer distinct challenges.

Besides just being more complex, a typical AI system is said to be non-deterministic and potentially self-regulating or self-adjusting. We can briefly explore that notion.

A deterministic machine tends to do the same things over and over again, predictably and with a viably discernable pattern of how it is operating. You might say that a common toaster toasts roughly the same way and has toasting controls that moderate the toasting, all of which are generally predictable by the person using the toaster. In contrast, complex AI systems are often devised to be non-deterministic, meaning that they might do quite different things beyond what you might have otherwise expected. This could partially also be further amplified if the AI is written to self-adjust itself, an aspect that can advantageously allow the AI to improve in the case of ML/DL, though can also disturbingly cause the AI to falter or enter into the ranks of AI badness. You might not know what hit you, in a manner of speaking, as you were caught entirely off-guard by the AI's actions.

What might we do to try and bring AI closer to trustworthiness?

One approach consists of trying to ensure that those building and fielding AI are abiding by a set of AI Ethics precepts. As mentioned by AI researchers: "Trust is an attitude that an agent will behave as expected and can be relied upon to reach its goal. Trust breaks down after an error or misunderstanding between the agent and the trusting individual. The psychological state of trust in AI is an emergent property of a complex system, usually involving many cycles of design, training, deployment, measurement of performance, regulation, redesign, and retraining" (indicated in the *Communications of the ACM*, "Trust, Regulation, and Human-in-the-Loop AI Within the European Region" by Stuart Middleton, Emmanuel Letouze, Ali Hossaini, and Adriane Chapman, April 2022).

The gist is that if we can get AI developers to abide by Ethical AI, they hopefully will end up producing trustworthy AI. This is all well and good, but it seems somewhat impractical on a real-world basis, though it is absolutely a path worth pursuing.

Here's what I mean.

Suppose a diligent effort is undertaken by AI developers crafting an AI system for some purpose that we'll generally call X. They carefully make sure that the AI abides by the transparency precepts of AI Ethics. They keenly ensure that privacy is suitably built into the AI. For nearly all of the usual AI Ethics principles, the AI builders exhaustively ensure that the AI meets the given precept.

Should you now trust that AI?

Allow me to help moderate your pondering of that open question. Turns out that cyber crooks managed to infiltrate the AI and sneakily get the AI to perform X and yet also feed the cyber hackers all of the data that the AI is collecting. By doing so, these evildoers are insidiously undercutting the privacy precept. You are blissfully unaware that this is happening under the hood of AI.

With that added piece of information, I'll ask you the same question again.

Do you trust that AI?

I dare say that most people would right away declare that they do not trust this particular AI. They might have trusted it earlier. They now opt to no longer consider the AI trustworthy.

A few key insights based on this simple example are worthy of contemplation:

- Even the best of intentions to cover all the bases of ensuring that AI Ethics is built into an AI system are no guarantee of what the AI might turn out to be or become. Once the AI is placed into use, outsiders can potentially undermine the Ethical AI accruements.

- The act of undercutting the trustworthiness doesn't necessarily have to be outsiders. An insider that is doing regular upkeep to the AI system might blunder and weaken the AI toward being less trustworthy. This AI developer might be clueless about what they have wrought.

- A self-adjusting or self-regulating AI might at some point adjust itself and veer into the untrustworthy territory. Perhaps the AI attempts to bolster the transparency of the AI and yet simultaneously and inappropriately compromises the privacy facets.

- Trying to achieve all of the AI Ethics tenets to the same utmost degree of trustworthiness is usually not readily viable as they are often at cross-purposes or have other inherent potential conflicts. It is a rather idealized perspective to believe that all of the Ethical AI precepts are dreamily aligned and all attainable to some equal maximizable degree.

- The cost to try and achieve a topnotch semblance of trustworthy AI via undertaking the various extensive and exhaustive steps and abiding by the litany of AI Ethics principles is going to be relatively high. You can easily argue that the cost would be prohibitive in terms of getting some AI systems into use that otherwise have important value to society, even if the AI was shall we say less than ideal from a trustworthiness desire.

- And so on.

Do not misinterpret the preceding remarks to suggest that we should somehow avert the effort to thoroughly build and field trustworthy AI. You would be summarily tossing out the baby with the bathwater, as it were. The proper interpretation is that we do need to do those trusting activities to get AI into a trustworthy consideration, and yet that alone is not a cure-all or a silver bullet.

Multi-Prong Paths To Trustworthy AI

There are important additional multi-pronged ways to strive toward trustworthy AI.

These legal guardrails are crucial as an overarching means of making sure that those devising AI are held fully accountable for their AI. Without such potential legal remedies and lawful penalties, those who pell-mell rush AI into the marketplace are likely to continue doing so with little if any serious regard for achieving trustworthy AI. I might notably add, that if those laws and regulations are poorly devised or inadequately implemented, they could regrettably undercut the pursuit of trustworthy AI, perhaps ironically and oddly fostering untrustworthy AI over trustworthy AI (see my column discussions for further explanation).

I have also been a staunch advocate for what I've been ardently referring to as *AI guardian angel bots*. This is an upcoming method or approach of trying to fight fire with fire, namely using AI to aid us in dealing with other AI that might or might not be trustworthy.

First, some background context will be useful.

Suppose you are opting to rely upon an AI system that you are unsure of its trustworthiness. A key concern could be that you are alone in your attempts to ferret out whether the AI is to be trusted or not. The AI is potentially computationally faster than you and can take advantage of you. You need someone or something on your side to help out.

One perspective is that there should always be a human-in-the-loop that will serve to aid you as you are making use of an AI system. This though is a problematic solution. If the AI is working in real-time, which we'll be discussing momentarily when it comes to the advent of AI-based self-driving cars, having a human-in-the-loop might not be sufficient. The AI could be acting in real-time and by the time a designated human-in-the-loop enters the picture to figure out if the AI is operating properly, a catastrophic result might have already occurred.

As an aside, this brings up another factor about trust. We usually assign a trust level based on the context or circumstance that we are facing. You might fully trust your toddler son or daughter to be faithful toward you, but if you are out hiking and decide to rely upon the toddler to tell you whether it is safe to step on the edge of a cliff, I think you would be wise to consider whether the toddler can provide that kind of life-or-death advice. The child might do so earnestly and sincerely, and nonetheless, be unable to adequately render such advice.

The same notion is associated with trust when it comes to AI. An AI system that you are using to play checkers or chess is probably not involved in any life-or-death deliberations. You can be at more ease with your assignment of trust. An AI-based self-driving car that is barreling down a highway at high speeds requires a much more strenuous level of trust. The slightest blip by the AI driving system could lead directly to your death and the deaths of others.

A recent interview of Beena Ammanath, Executive Director of the Global Deloitte AI Institute and author of the newly released book *Trustworthy AI,* provided a similar emphasis on considering the contextual facets of where AI trustworthiness comes to play: "If you're building an AI solution that is doing patient diagnosis, fairness and bias are super important. But if you're building an algorithm that predicts jet engine failure, fairness and bias isn't as important. Trustworthy AI is really a structure to get you started to think about the dimensions of trust within your organization" (*VentureBeat,* March 22, 2022).

When discussing trustworthy AI, you can construe this topic in a multitude of ways.

For example, *trustworthy AI* is something that we all view as a desirable and aspirational goal, namely that we should be desirous of devising and promulgating trustworthy AI. There is another usage of the catchphrase. A somewhat alternative usage is that *trustworthy AI* is a state of condition or measurement, such that someone might assert that they have crafted an AI system that is an instance of trustworthy AI. You can also use the phrase *trustworthy AI* to suggest a method or approach that can be used to attain AI trustworthiness. Etc.

On a related note, I trust that you realize that not all AI is the same and that we have to be mindful of not making blanket statements about all of AI. A particular AI system is likely to be significantly different from another AI system. One of those AI systems might be highly trustworthy, while the other might be marginally trustworthy. Be cautious in somehow assuming that AI is a monolith that is either entirely trustworthy or entirely not trustworthy.

This is simply not the case.

I'd like to next briefly cover some of my ongoing research about trustworthy AI that you might find of interest, covering the arising role of *AI guardian angel bots.*

Here's how it goes.

You would be armed with an AI system (an AI guardian angel bot) that is devised to gauge the trustworthiness of some other AI system. The AI guardian angel bot has as a paramount focus your safety. Think of this as though you have the means to monitor the AI you are relying upon by having a different AI system in your veritable pocket, perhaps running on your smartphone or other such devices. Your proverbial AI guardian can compute on a basis that the AI you are relying upon also does, working at rapid speeds and calculating the situation at hand in real-time, far faster than a human-in-the-loop could do so.

You might at an initial glance be thinking that the AI you are already relying upon ought to have some *internal* AI guardrails that do the same as this separately calculating AI guardian angel bot. Yes, that would certainly be desired. One qualm is that the AI guardrails built into an AI system might be integrally and prejudicially aligned with the AI per se, thus the supposed AI guardrail no longer is able to in a sense independently verify or validate the AI.

The contrasting idea is that your AI guardian angel bot is an independent or third-party AI mechanism that is distinct from the AI that you are relying upon. It sits outside of the other AI, remaining devoted to you and not devoted to the AI being monitored or assessed.

A straightforward means of thinking about this can be expressed via the following simplified equation-like statements. We might say that "P" wishes to potentially trust "R" to do a particular task "X":

- P trusts R to do task X.

This would be the following when only people are involved:

- Person P trusts person R to do task X.

When we opt to rely upon AI, the statement reshapes to this:

- Person P trusts AI instance-R to do task X.

We can add the AI guardian angel bot by saying this:

- Person P trusts AI instance-R to do task X as being monitored by AI guardian angel bot instance-Z

The AI guardian angel bot is tirelessly and relentlessly assessing the AI that you are relying upon. As such, your handy AI guardian might alert you that the trust of this other AI is unwarranted. Or, the AI guardian might electronically interact with the other AI to try and ensure that whatever variance away from being trustworthy is quickly righted, and so on.

The Trusty Trust Reservoir Metaphor

Since we are discussing varying levels of trust, you might find of use a handy metaphor about trustworthiness by conceiving of trust as a type of reservoir.

You have a certain amount of trust for a particular person or thing in a particular circumstance at a particular point in time. The level of the trust will rise or fall, depending upon what else happens related to that particular person or thing. The trust could be at a zero level when you have no trust whatsoever for the person or thing. The trust could be negative when you venture into having distrust of that person or thing.

In the case of AI systems, your trust reservoir for the particular AI that you are relying upon in a particular circumstance will rise or fall as dependent upon your gauging the trustworthiness of the AI. At times, you might be well aware of this varying level of trust about the AI, while in other instances you might be less aware and more so by hunch making judgments about the trustworthiness.

Ways that we've been discussing herein the means to boost trust levels for AI include:

- **Adherence to AI Ethics.** If the AI that you are relying upon was devised by trying to adhere to the proper AI Ethics precepts, you presumably would use this understanding to boost the level of your trust reservoir for that particular AI system. As a side note, it is also possible that you might generalize to other AI systems as to their trustworthiness, likewise, though this can be at times a misleading form of what I call *AI trust aura spreading* (be cautious in doing this!).

- **Use a Human-In-The-Loop.** If the AI has a human-in-the-loop, you might positively add to your perceived trust in the AI.

- **Establish Laws and Regulations**. If there are laws and regulations associated with this particular type of AI, you might likewise boost your trust level.

- **Employ an AI Guardian Angel Bot**. If you have an AI guardian angel bot at the ready, this too will raise further your trust level.

As mentioned earlier, trust can be quite brittle and fall apart in an instant (i.e., the trust reservoir rapidly and suddenly dumps out all of the built-up trust).

Imagine that you are inside an AI-based self-driving car and the AI driving suddenly makes a radical right turn, causing the wheels to squeal and nearly forcing the autonomous vehicle into an endangering rollover. What would happen to your level of trust? It would seem that even if you previously held the AI to a heightened level of trust, you would dramatically and abruptly drop your trust level, sensibly so.

At this juncture of this weighty discussion, I'd bet that you are desirous of additional illustrative examples that might showcase the nature and scope of trustworthy AI. There is a special and assuredly popular set of examples that are close to my heart. You see, in my capacity as an expert on AI including the ethical and legal ramifications,

I am frequently asked to identify realistic examples that showcase AI Ethics dilemmas so that the somewhat theoretical nature of the topic can be more readily grasped. One of the most evocative areas that vividly presents this ethical AI quandary is the advent of AI-based true self-driving cars. This will serve as a handy use case or exemplar for ample discussion on the topic.

Here's then a noteworthy question that is worth contemplating: *Does the advent of AI-based true self-driving cars illuminate anything about the pursuit of trustworthy AI, and if so, what does this showcase?*

Trust is everything, especially in the case of AI-based self-driving cars.

Society seems to be warily eyeing the emergence of self-driving cars. On the one hand, there is a grand hope that the advent of true self-driving cars will demonstrably reduce the number of annual car-related fatalities. In the United States alone there are about 40,000 annual deaths and around 2.5 million injuries due to car crashes. Humans drink and drive. Humans drive while distracted. The task of driving a car seems to consist of being able to repetitively and unerringly focus on driving and avoid getting into car crashes. As such, we might dreamily hope that AI driving systems will guide self-driving cars repetitively and unerringly. You can construe self-driving cars as a twofer, consisting of reducing the volume of car crash deaths and injuries, along with potentially making mobility available on a much wider and accessible basis.

But the concern meanwhile looms over societal perceptions as to whether self-driving cars are going to be safe enough to be on our public roadways at large.

If even one self-driving car gets into a crash or collision that leads to a single death or severe injury, you can likely anticipate that today's somewhat built-up trust toward those AI-based driverless cars is going to precipitously drop. We saw this happen when the now-infamous incident occurred in Arizona that involved a somewhat (not really) self-driving car that ran into and killed a pedestrian.

Some pundits point out that it is unfair and inappropriate to base the trust of AI self-driving cars on the facet that only one such next death-producing crash or collision could undermine the already relatively crash-free public roadway trials. In addition, on a further unfair basis, the odds are that no matter which particular AI self-driving car brand or model perchance gets embroiled in a sorrowful incident, society would indubitably blame all self-driving car brands.

The entirety of self-driving cars could be summarily smeared and the industry as a whole might suffer a huge backlash leading to a possible shutdown of all public roadway trials.

A contributor to such a blowback is found in the nonsensical proclamations by outspoken self-driving car proponents that all driverless cars will be uncrashable. This idea of being uncrashable is not only outrightly wrong, it insidiously is setting up the self-driving car industry for a totally out-of-whack set of expectations. These outlandish and unachievable pronouncements that there will be zero deaths due to self-driving cars are fueling the misconception that any driverless car crashes are a sure sign that the whole kit and kaboodle is for naught.

There is a distinct sadness to realize that the progress toward self-driving cars and the inch-at-a-time accumulation of societal trust could be dashed away in an instant. That is going to be one heck of a showcase about the brittleness of trust.

Conclusion

Many automakers and self-driving tech firms are generally abiding by AI Ethics principles, doing so to try and build and field trustworthy AI in terms of safe and reliable AI-based self-driving cars. Please realize that some of those firms are stronger and more devoted to the Ethical AI precepts than others. There are also occasional fringe or newbie self-driving car-related startups that seem to cast aside much of the AI Ethics cornerstones.

On other fronts, new laws and regulations covering self-driving cars have gradually been getting placed on the legal books. Whether they have the needed teeth to back them up is a different matter, as likewise whether the enforcement of those laws is being taken seriously or overlooked (see my columns for analyses on this).

There is also the high-tech angle to this too. I have predicted that we will gradually see variants of AI guardian angel bots that will come to the fore in the autonomous vehicle and self-driving cars arena. We aren't there yet. This will become more prevalent once the popularity of self-driving cars becomes more widespread.

This last point brings up a famous line about trust that you undoubtedly already know by heart.

Trust, but verify.

We can allow ourselves to extend our trust, perhaps generously so. Meanwhile, we should also be watching like a hawk to make sure that the trust we engender is verified by both words and deeds. Let's put some trust into AI, but verify endlessly that we are placing our trust appropriately and with our eyes wide open.

CHAPTER 5
AI ETHICS AND RESPONSIBLE AI

With great power comes great responsibility.

The price of greatness is responsibility.

Another fine day ruined by responsibility.

Those are all rather popular witticisms about responsibility. The first two of these catchy quips emphasize that you are supposed to realize and accept that when you attain a lofty position of power, you must be willing to bear the associated responsibility accordingly. Not everyone would necessarily agree with that sentiment, though it certainly does stoke a kind of noble belief.

Meanwhile, the third or last of the quips provides a realization that responsibility can be weighty and often spur hefty consequences for those that carry the responsibility on their shoulders. It is said that your day can be utterly ruined when the responsibility of some actions or deeds gets dumped onto your head. We often find ourselves mired in woes as a direct result of having had the responsibility for one thing or another that went awry.

Imagine that you are at work and a deadline is missed that you were responsible for. Yikes, you might be docked some pay or summarily fired for the transgression. It was your designated responsibility to meet the deadline and you failed to do so. The buck stops at your desk.

Humans are apt to try and wiggle out of the responsibility that they are purportedly carrying. You might contend that the deadline was impossible to meet and you were being underhandedly set up for failure.

Or maybe you claim that the fault for missing the deadline ought to go to your boss or your fellow workers, or those cute pet dogs being allowed into the office space by the HR department to soothe the overt pressures of the workplace.

If you give the topic of responsibility some general mulling over, it demonstrably seems as though humankind has sought ways to shirk responsibility from the beginning of civilization. We probably have gotten better at doing so over the years. Whether that is an admirable accomplishment is certainly arguable.

Sometimes you might earnestly welcome responsibility. By having accepted the fearsome deadline-laden project, you were aiming to showcase your talents and strive mightily toward a much-desired promotion and dreamily hoped to be deluged with accolades by your peers. At the outset, you proudly proclaimed that you were responsible for the effort. Only when the grumpy stuff hit the proverbial fan did you suddenly seek to discard or at least distance the overburdensome responsibility.

I am bringing up these tenets of responsibility due to the latest handy-dandy catchphrase echoing throughout the field of AI, namely the need for and pursuit of *Responsible AI*. Any of the latest headlines about AI are bound to mention the importance of Responsible AI. Conversations at conferences on AI are indubitable including vigorous discussions regarding Responsible AI. Social media gushes about the emergence of so-called Responsible AI.

I'll be taking you through the ins and outs of what Responsible AI seems to signify.

The best place to start is by laying a foundation about the very nature of responsibility. We can then add to the equation an infusion of AI and what Responsible AI portends. All of this dovetails into a broader rubric widely referred to as AI Ethics or Ethical AI.

Being Clear On Responsibility

What does responsibility mean to you?

I'm not asking you what you are particularly responsible for. Instead, I am seeking to get your take on what it means to bear responsibility. A typical dictionary definition would simply state that responsibility is the aspect of having a duty to deal with something. Another akin perspective is that responsibility consists of being held accountable for something.

Theorists tend to posit that there are at least two variants of responsibility, consisting of *basic responsibility* and another formulation known as *consequential responsibility* (not all theorists agree on this structure, but we'll go with it for the moment):

- **Basic responsibility** is characterized this way: "If you prefer to spell this out, you could say that basic responsibility is an ability to give a rational explanation for one's actions without giving one's actions any rational explanation that they didn't actually have, i.e., without inventing reasons for what one did" (*Oxford Journal of Legal Studies*, "The Mark of Responsibility" by John Gardner).

- **Consequential responsibility** is depicted this way: "I am consequentially responsible if some or all of the unwelcome moral or legal consequences of some wrong or mistake (whether mine or someone else's) are mine to bear. Responsibility in this consequential sense is by its very nature an unwelcome thing to have descend upon one, and hence something that, all else being equal, any rational being would rather avoid" (as per same Gardner article in the *Oxford Journal of Legal Studies*).

The stakes at hand and the circumstances will seemingly shape an invocation of either or both of the basic responsibility and consequential responsibility modes.

Pretend that you are playing a friendly chess game and lose the match. From a basic responsibility angle, you accept the loss and collegially shake the hand of your competition. You have willingly acknowledged the *basic responsibility* of your actions as to having played not as proficiently as the other player did. No big deal, easy-peasy to acknowledge.

Shifting gears, suppose the chess match was played out in front of a televised worldwide audience consisting of thousands of avid chess fans. The winner of the match would get the acclaimed world chess title. Big bucks will accrue to the winner. Fame and fortune await the winner. The loser will be forgotten. They will be seen as a has-been. Endorsements and admiration are going to abruptly dry up.

What do you think the losing player would say after the game is concluded?

It seems a likely bet that the losing player would contend that the chess match was perhaps rigged. Maybe the room where the match was undertaken had been overly noisy or drafty and cold. Perhaps the chair was unduly uncomfortable and distracted the player. Cameras were making too much of a racket to allow for proper concentration. These are characteristics that might be laid out when employing a semblance of *consequential responsibility*.

All in all, this showcases a twofold model of responsibility. You might find this specific model useful and insightful, or you might not. Mull it over and ascertain whether it is insightful concerning your day-to-day wrangling of responsibility.

Speaking of twofold models, we can segue into the topic of Responsible AI.

What does the phrase "Responsible AI" mean to you?

Within the field of AI, there are roughly two ways to construe this popular catchphrase:

1) Responsible AI is the act of devising AI so that it will perform in a societally sanctioned responsible manner.

2) Responsible AI is the ascertaining of who or what shall be responsible for the actions of AI, especially when AI generates or causes adverse outcomes.

There is some ambiguity about which of these two interpretations is the "right one" and as such, we will herein accept that either variant is generally acceptable. The key though is that whenever someone makes use of the *Responsible AI* moniker, they ought to clarify straightaway what they mean it to represent. The inherent ambiguity and overloading of the catchphrase can lead to inadvertent confusion or miscommunication.

I also would caution that though I've numbered them as #1 and #2, this does not imply that the first one is more so important than the second one. I could have readily labeled them as "a" and "b" rather than numbering. I could have used bullet points rather than any type of sequencing per se. The sequence or order of the two is not significant in this matter of merely describing what they are.

Given that admittedly tortuous stipulation, I will quietly accede that the first listed version of Responsible AI does appear to be the most prominent meaning these days. Depending upon which articles or blog postings about AI you generally consume, the chances are that *Responsible AI* as pertaining to the construction or building of AI that acts responsibly is the usual norm. Coming in at a close second in this horserace would be the variant that *Responsible AI* consists of assigning responsibility for the actions of AI.

We can take a quick look at some examples of these two different meanings.

First, consider the notion that Responsible AI entails devising AI in a responsible manner.

Here is an example of how AI researchers tend to describe the first listed version of Responsible AI: "Responsible AI development involves taking steps to ensure that AI systems have an acceptably low risk of harming their users or society and, ideally, to increase their likelihood of being socially beneficial. This involves testing the safety and security of systems during development, evaluating the potential social impact of the systems prior to release, being willing to abandon research projects that fail to meet a high bar of safety, and being willing to delay the release of a system until it has been established that it does not pose a risk to consumers or the public. Responsible AI development comes in degrees but it will be useful to treat it as a binary concept for the purposes of this paper. We will say that an AI system has been developed responsibly if the risks of it causing harms are at levels most people would consider tolerable, taking into account their severity, and that the amount of evidence grounding these risk estimates would also be considered acceptable" (in an article by co-authors Amanda Askell, Miles Brundage, Gillian Hadfield, entitled "The Role of Cooperation in Responsible AI Development").

The consulting firm Accenture defines the matter this way: "Responsible AI is the practice of designing, developing, and deploying AI with good intention to empower employees and businesses, and fairly impact customers and society—allowing companies to engender trust and scale AI with confidence" (per the Accenture website).

In a survey report entitled "Responsible AI: Maturing From Theory To Practice" the consulting firm PwC depicts Responsible AI as consisting of nine core Ethical AI principles:

- Accountability
- Data Privacy
- Lawfulness and Compliance
- Beneficial AI
- Human Agency
- Safety
- Fairness
- Interpretability (Explainability, Transparency, Provability)
- Reliability, Robustness, Security

The International Technology Law Association (iTechLaw) provides a global policy framework on Responsible AI that consists of these eight key principles:

1) Ethical Purpose and Societal Benefit
2) Accountability
3) Transparency and Explainability
4) Fairness and Non-Discrimination
5) Safety and Reliability
6) Open Data and Fair Competition
7) AI and Intellectual Property

In terms of defining Responsible AI, according to the industry analyst group Gartner: "Responsible AI makes artificial intelligence a positive force, rather than a threat to society and to itself. Responsible AI is an umbrella term for many aspects of making the right business and ethical choices when adopting AI that organizations often address independently. These include business and societal value, risk, trust, transparency, and accountability" (per the Gartner website).

And so on.

All told, the first variant of Responsible AI entails making sure that those developing and fielding AI will do so in a seemingly responsible manner. They will carefully and mindfully proceed to produce AI that will abide by AI Ethics precepts. For those of you familiar with another common phrase, *Trustworthy AI*, you could suggest that the Responsible AI of this manifestation is roughly equivalent to the tenets of devising trustworthy AI.

It is hoped and generally assumed that someone taking the right Ethical AI steps as they are building an AI system will tend toward producing AI that performs in a responsible way. There isn't any guarantee of this result. Logically, it does though seem to make sense as an aspirational North Star. You can see this by using a contrasting and opposite kind of approach. If you are haphazardly devising AI or doing so erroneously, it would seem that the odds of producing AI that does <u>not</u> act responsibly are going to be tremendously heightened.

We will further explore this North Star desired outcome entailing Responsible AI momentarily.

The preceding synopsis pretty much sums up the first listed meaning. Now, we can take a look at the other variant. This alternative perspective suggests that Responsible AI is primarily focused on figuring out who or what is responsible for the actions of AI systems.

This other meaning of Responsible AI has to do with ascribing responsibility for how an AI system came to be: *Who (or what) is responsible for the AI?*

This usually involves tracking the development actions undertaken by various AI builders. You might have AI software engineers, hardware designers, and the like that were all part of the AI being devised. In addition, other stakeholders such as managers, corporate executives, and a slew of many additional participants might have had a hand in making and releasing the AI.

A handy illustration of this perspective consists of a prominent Council of Europe study that examined the matter of taking responsibility for AI actions in the light of potential human rights violations: "The focus of this report is on examining the responsibility implications of AI systems from a human rights perspective. It is therefore primarily concerned with analyzing responsibility for human rights violations, rather than responsibility for tangible harm arising from the operation of these systems. The following discussion focuses primarily upon those who create, develop, implement and preside over AI systems. It asks whether they can be held responsible for the adverse consequences those systems might generate, beginning with an examination of two core themes that have arisen in contemporary responses concerned with identifying where responsibility lies for the risks which AI technologies may pose: first, voluntary action by the tech industry in promulgating and publicly proclaiming their commitment to so-called 'ethical guidelines', and secondly, claims that because AI systems act autonomously, this relieves their creators from responsibility for their decisions and any consequential adverse effects" (Council of Europe Study, DGI 2019-05, *Responsibility and AI*).

Some of the primary difficulties with trying to identify who or what is responsible for AI include these facets:

- Responsibility attribution can be murky as to the parties involved and their degree of involvement in making and fielding AI.
- A kind of "responsibility gap" can arise that inadvertently leaves out parties that should have been included.
- There is a semblance of confounding "distributed responsibility" usually associated with complex AI.
- The AI might not have been the actual cause of a system issue or malfunction yet be falsely or mistakenly assumed as the culprit.
- The enduring question of whether AI can be construed as being "responsible" when it is not sentient, not inured with legal personhood, or not established as a moral agent.

You might find of interest that trying to nail down the responsibility for an AI system is at times harder than it might seem at first glance. If an AI system is made by company X or Y, we can usually figure out who at the company bears responsibility for the AI. On the other hand, if an AI system has passed through many hands, you might be hard-pressed to figure out who is responsible. This includes assigning the magnitudes of responsibility, such as whether someone merely perchance had minimal contact with the AI during the AI being devised versus those that deeply were integral to crafting the AI.

A saying that you might have heard of is that AI is likely to stoke the many-hands problem.

When an AI system goes through numerous coding adjustments and gets modified over a period of time, there is a murkiness about who did what and when they did so. Envision an AI system that is available online and the source code is open-sourced. Many people might have had a hand in making changes to the code. Strictly speaking, there might not be any audit trail that showcases precisely what happened and who made the various changes.

There is yet another sticky point involving assigning responsibility for an AI system.

Some AI systems are constructed with a self-adjusting or self-modifying capacity. If an AI system opts to change itself, you presumably no longer can point the finger at a human that made the change. A viewpoint sometimes stated is that the AI is akin to an organism that can fluidly modify itself, perhaps to the extent that it no longer resembles the original substance that launched the build. As such, it is suggested that the humans involved at the start are now so far removed from the subsequent structure that those humans ought to no longer be held responsible for what this instance of AI has become.

Please know that not everyone buys into that contention about being unable to cast aspersions on a human being. Some critics would argue vehemently about the notion that those human developers who devised the self-adjusting mechanism should be held fully responsible for whatever else spawns from that facility. You cannot hide behind a false front that the AI did the changes on its own, they would stridently shout. Those that established the AI with the self-adjusting capability are to bear the responsibility for whatever evildoing the AI might consequently undertake. Letting the human developers off the hook is disingenuous and ethically improper, they would emphatically insist.

Before I get much further into the two sets of variants of *Responsible AI*, we should take a moment to clarify how this all relates to AI Ethics. In addition, I'd like to make sure we are of a similar mind when it comes to what I mean when referring to AI.

Let's take a quick look at why AI has gotten our dander up about being less than responsible. In addition, we will explore the tenets of AI Ethics that are hoped will aid in propping up the already semi-underwater perceived trust (or bubbling distrust) of today's AI.

One particular segment or portion of AI Ethics that has been getting a lot of media attention consists of AI that exhibits untoward biases and inequities. You might be aware that when the latest era of AI got underway there was a huge burst of enthusiasm for what some now call *AI For Good.* Unfortunately, on the heels of that gushing excitement, we began to witness *AI For Bad.*

In the case of *Responsible AI* entailing having the meaning of crafting AI that will act responsibly, AI developers should be embracing the aforementioned Ethical AI precepts throughout the design, coding, testing, and deployment of their AI systems. The other case of *Responsible AI* consists of figuring out who is responsible for an AI system, in which we are seeking to tie down those that are responsible for the AI being brought into existence.

A controversial subtopic underlying both of the *Responsible AI* variants is worthy of taking a brief look at. Here's the deal. Some would claim that the AI itself can be held responsible for what it does. Rather than solely pointing the finger at the humans that developed the AI, we are supposed to also consider what apportionment of responsibility the AI should have.

A key to this type of blame assignment is that you need to also believe in the possibility of AI as having a form of legal personhood. Recall that I have stated herein that I am not including an as-yet materialized sentient AI in these matters. Despite what some claim is among today's AI that should be granted some semblance of legal personhood, I generally disagree. We do not yet have any AI that by itself is deserving of a legal personhood anointment – but I realize that this is a controversial point and encourage further debate (a hot topic that I continue to revisit in my columns). For the moment herein, let's put to the side the handwringing over whether AI itself is to be held accountable as being Responsible AI. I say it isn't, while others try to contend that it is. This is a saga for another day.

At this juncture of this weighty discussion, I'd bet that you are desirous of some illustrative examples that might showcase the nature and scope of Responsible AI. There is a special and assuredly popular set of examples that are close to my heart. You see, in my capacity as an expert on AI including the ethical and legal ramifications, I am frequently asked to identify realistic examples that showcase AI Ethics dilemmas so that the somewhat theoretical nature of the topic can be more readily grasped. One of the most evocative areas that vividly presents this ethical AI quandary is the advent of AI-based true self-driving cars. This will serve as a handy use case or exemplar for ample discussion on the topic.

Here's then a noteworthy question that is worth contemplating: *Does the advent of AI-based true self-driving cars illuminate anything about the pursuit of Responsible AI, and if so, what does this showcase?*

Recall that there are two different ways to define Responsible AI:

- Responsible AI is the act of devising AI so that it will perform in a societally sanctioned responsible manner.
- Responsible AI is the ascertaining of who or what shall be responsible for the actions of AI, especially when AI generates or causes adverse outcomes.

Consider the first listed meaning of Responsible AI in the light of AI autonomous vehicles and self-driving cars, namely, we can do a mashup of the generic definition with the specifics of self-driving cars:

- *Responsible AI entails the act of devising AI-based self-driving cars so that they will perform in a societally sanctioned responsible manner, including operating safely on our public roadways and adhering to the laws and prevailing ethics associated with driving.*

The gist is that we want automakers and self-driving tech firms to design, build, test, and field AI-based self-driving cars that will abide by AI Ethics precepts. One of the keystones involves the question of whether self-driving cars will be sufficiently safe for use on our public roadways.

Let's unpack the question.

Society seems to be warily eyeing the emergence of self-driving cars. On the one hand, there is a grand hope that the advent of true self-driving cars will demonstrably reduce the number of annual car-related fatalities. In the United States alone there are about 40,000 annual deaths and around 2.5 million injuries due to car crashes. Humans drink and drive. Humans drive while distracted. The task of driving a car seems to consist of being able to repetitively and unerringly focus on driving and avoid getting into car crashes. As such, we might dreamily hope that AI driving systems will guide self-driving cars repetitively and unerringly.

You can construe self-driving cars as a twofer, consisting of reducing the volume of car crash deaths and injuries, along with potentially making mobility available on a much wider and accessible basis.

But the concern meanwhile looms over societal perceptions as to whether self-driving cars are going to be safe enough to be on our public roadways at large. If even one self-driving car gets into a crash or collision that leads to a single death or severe injury, you can likely anticipate that today's somewhat built-up trust toward those AI-based driverless cars is going to precipitously drop. We saw this happen when the now-infamous incident occurred in Arizona that involved a somewhat (not really) self-driving car that ran into and killed a pedestrian.

Some pundits point out that it is unfair and inappropriate to base the trust of AI self-driving cars on the facet that only one such next death-producing crash or collision could undermine the already relatively crash-free public roadway trials. In addition, on a further unfair basis, the odds are that no matter which particular AI self-driving car brand or model perchance gets embroiled in a sorrowful incident, society would indubitably blame all self-driving car brands. The entirety of self-driving cars could be summarily smeared and the industry as a whole might suffer a huge backlash leading to a possible shutdown of all public roadway trials.

A contributor to such a blowback is found in the nonsensical proclamations by outspoken self-driving car proponents that all driverless cars will be uncrashable. This idea of being uncrashable is not only outrightly wrong, it insidiously is setting up the self-driving car industry for a totally out-of-whack set of expectations. These outlandish and unachievable pronouncements that there will be zero deaths due to self-driving cars are fueling the misconception that any driverless car crashes are a sure sign that the whole kit and kaboodle is for naught.

In any case, the quandary for the self-driving car industry is that they are generally expected to be crafting self-driving cars in an ostensibly *Responsible AI* way, but society has a confounded perspective on what the outcome is supposed to be. If the threshold is that when even just one AI self-driving car gets into an adverse outcome that the entire industry is going to be rattled and reviled as irresponsible, this is a heavy and overtly impractical burden.

The upbeat news is that many of the automakers and self-driving tech firms are generally abiding by Responsible AI precepts, doing so to try and build and field trustworthy AI in terms of safe and reliable AI-based self-driving cars to an everyday practical degree. Please realize though that some of those firms are stronger and more devoted to Responsible AI than others. There are also occasional fringe or newbie self-driving car-related startups that seem to cast aside much of the Responsible AI cornerstones.

Consider next the second listed meaning of Responsible AI in the light of AI autonomous vehicles and self-driving cars, namely that we can once again do a mashup of the generic definition with the specifics of self-driving cars:

- *Responsible AI is the ascertaining of who or what shall be responsible for the actions of AI-based self-driving cars, especially when AI generates or causes adverse outcomes such as car crashes, car collisions, and other car-related occurrences involving damages, fatalities, and injuries.*

The gist is who or what will be held responsible for AI self-driving cars that get into car crashes and the like.

Let's quickly identify some plausible scenarios of AI-related troubling encounters:

- Imagine that an AI-based true self-driving car clips a pedestrian, doing mild injury to the person but not causing any sustained or permanent harm. Who is to blame?

- Envision that an AI-based self-driving car rams into the rear of a car ahead of the autonomous vehicle. No one is hurt.

There is though some considerable damage done to both cars. Who is to blame?

- A self-driving car makes a right turn and comes to a sudden stop, for which a human-driven car behind the autonomous vehicle then slams into the halted self-driving car. Who is to blame?

- While navigating a construction zone, an AI self-driving car strikes several red cones and then swerves into a standing pole that (ironically) has a sign that warns to be cautious in the marked zone. Who is to blame?

A myriad of these kinds of scenarios can readily be concocted. They are all realistic.

Who is to be held responsible in each of these particular instances?

Take a gander at these possibilities:

- The company that devised the AI driving system could be a culprit.

- A separate company might own or run a fleet of self-driving cars, operating the autonomous vehicles in a particular locale, which as the fleet operator that might be to blame (perhaps they've not provided proper upkeep or failed to undertake other proper precautions).

- The AI developers that crafted the AI driving system could be the blame-worthy holders.

- Don't forget about the automaker that made the car. It could be that the autonomous vehicle had some defect or issue that led to the crash or collision.

- If a city has allowed self-driving cars on their public streets, you could presumably argue that they are to blame for any autonomous vehicle crashes or collisions. Were it not for their approval of the roaming vehicles, no such calamity could have arisen.

- Etc.

I did not list therein that the AI itself is to be held responsible. As mentioned earlier, some believe AI is or ought to be construed as a responsible party, but my view is that this is currently non-sensical. If we somehow attain AI of a greater capacity such that it becomes an entity worthy of legal personhood or similar societal status, I will agreeably be willing to add to the list that the AI is a responsible party. I await that day.

Conclusion

At the start of this discussion, I mentioned that with great power comes great responsibility.

You could readily assert that AI is becoming a great power of sorts. Nations are competing strenuously to be at the leading edge of AI. Companies are charging ahead with all manner of AI developments. AI is emerging as a ubiquitous form of technology. We will all be subjected to AI systems in our daily lives.

Where will the responsibility lay in the great and powerful emergence of AI?

Responsible AI is a crucial underpinning for seeking to keep AI within societal bounds and it is a well worth price that we need to pay. As indicated by the immortal words of Abraham Lincoln, you cannot escape the responsibility of tomorrow by evading it today.

We need to be seriously and diligently responsible regarding AI.

CHAPTER 6
AI ETHICS AND AI CONFINEMENT

The famous illusionist and acclaimed escape artist Harry Houdini once boldly declared this rather unabashed assertion: "No prison can hold me; no hand or leg irons or steel locks can shackle me. No ropes or chains can keep me from my freedom."

That seems like a pretty tall order. We would all generally agree that it is possible to imprison someone such that they are unable to escape. Human strength and ingenuity can only go so far when it comes to being placed into strictly devised confinement. If a prison or jail is stridently constructed with the idea of being escape-proof, it would seem that no person can overcome such all-encompassing constraints.

Of course, throughout history, there have been notable cases of escapes from otherwise assumed impossible to get out of imprisonments. Going all the way back to the year 1244, a prisoner in the infamous Tower of London managed to craft a makeshift rope via the use of tattered bedsheets. He was able to partially escape by climbing down the flimsy cord. Turns out that the rope snapped amid his endeavor and he immediately thereupon fell to his death.

Would you be willing to say that he did escape?

On the one hand, sure, he managed to get outside of the confining room within the Tower of London. But it ostensibly seems like not much of a successful escape given that he died in the act of performing the breakout. I dare say that we would be unduly generous in calling this an escape per se.

You might vaguely be familiar with the prison escapee William Sutton aka "Slick Willie" that was a notorious bank robber in the 1930s and 1940s. He managed to get on the FBI's Ten Most Wanted Fugitives list. During his various incarcerations, he found a means to escape several times. In one case, he dressed up as a prison guard and got out of the Philadelphia County Prison. Perhaps the more dramatic instance was when he and a dozen other fellow convicts used a tunnel to break out of the Eastern State Penitentiary.

I believe we would all concur that he did in fact make several genuine escapes. Free and clear. Ultimately, he was later apprehended. This somewhat dampens the efficacy of the escapes though it does not undercut the undeniable fact that he did indeed manage to escape. Note that not every one of his attempts led to an escape.

A third illustrative example regarding escapes is the well-known circumstance involving the maximum-security prison Alcatraz or simply called "The Rock" which was presumed to be inescapable confinement residing in the middle of San Francisco Bay. This highly fortified prison had numerous carefully placed guard towers, it had extremely meticulous rules about what the prisoners could do and not do, and the overall semblance of being secure was heightened by the aspect that the rough and unforgiving cold waters of the Pacific Ocean surrounded this fortress-like confinement.

On June 12, 1962, a surprising and history-making escape was discovered. Three prisoners were not in their designated cells. Fake dummy heads rested on their respective pillows, fooling the guards that throughout the night patrolled the hallways in front of the cells. As far as we know, the prisoners had created a means to use a prison ventilator shaft to get up to the prison roof, they then climbed down and got over a fence, so that they could reach the edge of the island. They then apparently launched a raft that they had crudely fashioned from raincoats.

Their whereabouts are still unknown. They might have died during the watery journey. They might have lived and made it to shore and freedom. They nor their bodies were ever found. The FBI closed the case in 1979 and handed it over to the U.S. Marshalls Service.

One supposes that we will never really know what the outcome was.

What do all of these sagas about escaping from confinement tell us?

It seems relatively clearcut that:

- Sometimes an escape is not possible
- Sometimes an escape is possible but falls apart during the escape attempt
- Sometimes an escape is possible but is short-lived
- Sometimes an escape is possible and seemingly everlasting

I bring up this intriguing topic because of something that is seriously being bandied around in the field of Artificial Intelligence (AI). There has been a longstanding question about whether AI can be confined or imprisoned to the degree that the AI is unable to escape or get loose from the said confinement.

This is commonly referred to as the *AI Confinement Problem (AICP).*

Insiders usually say *AICP* to other insiders, doing so with a wink-wink acknowledgment of the insider acronym. Another shortened lingo is to just utter the word "confinement" or the word "containment" to bring up the subject matter. Choose whichever you wish.

The crux of the topic is the earnest and heartfelt belief that we might need to confine AI, though this simultaneously raises the thorny question of whether we can realistically devise confinement that will be truly confining and inescapable. Not just in theory but actual day-to-day practice. AI is not necessarily a pushover. Maybe the AI can find a means to break out, bust out, do a jailbreak, fly the coop, or otherwise wiggle or electronically beam out of the imprisonment.

Houdini said that no prison could hold him and that no shackles can shackle him.

Perhaps AI can make the same audacious claim, doing so without any hyperbole or overstatement.

Time to unpack this.

You might be tempted to readily believe that AI can be an escape artist whilst believing that humans are less likely to be able to escape from a rigorously divined state of imprisonment. Humans are human. Creating confinement for humans generally ought to be straightforward. The trick undoubtedly is that keeping the human alive during their imprisonment means that something must be arranged to allow for providing food, enabling health-related care, and the likes associated with a functioning human body. Those details are bound to leave open ends and chances for finding a means to escape from confinement.

An AI system would not presumably require those same humanitarian provisions (well, as you'll see in a moment, it depends upon whether we are considering sentient AI and the parameters associated with legal personhood). If an AI is a robot, we could just toss the contraption into a special escape-proof cell and not ever come back to see its rusting parts. The deed is done. No worries about it physically being able to escape.

The AI though might principally be software and ergo run on all manner of computer systems. In that case, imprisonment becomes a bit more challenging. Assuming that we can somehow round up all copies, we might be able to place the offending AI into a devoted computer that we have specially crafted to be imprisonment for the AI. This special-purpose computer acts as a type of AI confinement citadel. Maybe it houses just one particular AI or could be cleverly instituted to be an AI holding tank for all manner of AI systems (imagine something like the elaborate entrapment system employed in the movie *Ghostbusters*, just as an illustration of this admittedly somewhat farfetched idea).

Before I get into the details of the AI Confinement Problem, it is worthwhile to envision the realm of AI as consisting of two conditions or possibilities. I am talking about the distinction between AI that is sentient and AI that is not sentient. We need to make sure that we are on the same page about these distinctions to further sensibly discuss the AI Confinement matter.

I proffer next a stark and unabashed remark that you might find either shocking or altogether obvious and mundane.

There isn't any AI today that is sentient.

We don't have sentient AI. We don't know if sentient AI will be possible. Nobody can aptly predict whether we will attain sentient AI, nor whether sentient AI will somehow miraculously spontaneously arise in a form of computational cognitive supernova (usually referred to as the singularity). To those of you that are seriously immersed in the AI field, none of this foregoing pronouncement is surprising or raises any eyebrows. Meanwhile, there are outsized headlines and excessive embellishment that might confound people into assuming that we either do have sentient AI or that we are on the looming cusp of having sentient AI any coming day.

Please realize that today's AI is not able to "think" in any fashion on par with human thinking. When you interact with Alexa or Siri, the conversational capacities might seem akin to human capacities, but the reality is that it is computational and lacks human cognition. The latest era of AI has made extensive use of Machine Learning (ML) and Deep Learning (DL), which leverage computational pattern matching. This has led to AI systems that have the appearance of human-like proclivities. Meanwhile, there isn't any AI today that has a semblance of common sense and nor has any of the cognitive wonderment of robust human thinking.

ML/DL is merely a form of computational pattern matching. All told, we are today utilizing non-sentient AI and someday we might have sentient AI (but that is purely speculative). Both kinds of AI are obviously of concern for AI Ethics and we need to be aiming toward Ethical AI no matter how it is constituted.

Bringing back the topic of AI Confinement, there is a marked contrast between the nature of "confinement" that entails non-sentient AI versus sentient AI.

In the case of the confinement associated with sentient AI, we can wildly play a guessing game of nearly infinite varieties. Maybe sentient AI will cognitively be like humans and exhibit similar mental capacities. Or we could postulate that sentient AI will be superhuman and go beyond our forms of thinking. The ultimate in sentient AI would seem to be super-intelligence, something that might be so smart and cunning that we cannot today even conceive of the immense thinking prowess. Some suggest that our minds will be paltry in comparison. This super-duper AI will run rings around us in a manner comparable to how we today can outthink ants or caterpillars.

I like to depict the AI Confinement Problem as consisting of these two crucial and quite controversial contentions:

- Controversial Contention #1: It will purportedly be impossible to successfully confine sentient AI.

- Controversial Contention #2: It will purportedly be impossible for non-sentient AI to escape from our confinement.

In short, the first listed prevailing assertion is that sentient AI will be so conniving that no matter what manner of confinement we devise and how hard we try, the AI will escape. Humans will be unable to successfully confine sentient AI. The logic partially underlying that contention is that AI will invariably be able to outsmart humans, thus human-devised confinement will be outsmarted by a sentient AI. A caveat that begrudgingly comes with this is that *human-level* sentient AI might not be smart enough to break out, but that the *superhuman* or *super-intelligent* AI will.

Keep in mind too that when I refer to being able to escape, we earlier agreed that there are several variants associated with escaping. There is an escape that leads to failure during the attempt, and there are variations of escape that are more so successful yet lead to short-lived versus longstanding or perpetual freedom. We should apply those same parameters to the AI Confinement Problem.

An AI might momentarily escape and perhaps immediately get captured and reimprisoned. Or an AI might get out and later on be found and confined once again. There is also the possibility that the AI escapes, remains free, and we are never able to confine it again. I trust that you can envision all such possibilities.

Furthermore, we need to be careful and not treat AI as some kind of monolith. When people refer to AI, they at times use the phrasing in a categorically encompassing way. The odds are that AI is probably going to be more piecemeal and not one gigantic AI overlord (which is the usual portrayal). I am not saying that futuristic AI could not ever be bound together and coalesce into one thing, and instead just pointing out that this does not arise necessarily axiomatically.

We will for sake of discussion assume that there are lots of differing AI systems and that when we are contemplating the confinement of AI we are focused on a particular one or a specific set of AIs. Of course, as already stated, since we are for the moment speaking of the sentient AI, all bets are off since you can wildly make as many assumptions as possible about this unknown and yet to exist AI to your heart's content.

A quick twist for you.

Suppose that it is the case that superhuman or super-intelligent AI can outwit us, humans. Suppose further that our human-devised confinement falls short because it was designed and built based on human wits (I am not agreeing to these suppositions, merely noting them). I ask you this, why would we not try to use superhuman or super-intelligent sentient AI to aid in deriving better confinement? The usual answer is that all sentient AI will be in cahoots and would not aid our quest.

Or that the AI that is separate from the other AI is worried that we would end up turning the confinement on the AI that assisted our human-plus-AI devised escape-proof confinement. We certainly wouldn't expect that a superhuman or superintelligent AI would be dumb enough to make confinement that would potentially be used as a trap against itself.

Round and round that goes.

The second listed controversial contention is that non-sentient AI will not be able to escape from whatever confinement we set up for such AI. You see, the logic is that non-sentient AI will not be capable enough to essentially outwit humans. Humans will always be at least one step or more ahead of non-sentient AI. Any confinement that we design and build will be escape-proof. The AI will be captured and confront a "lifetime" behind bars.

I don't buy into that notion, for several reasons.

We have witnessed cybercrooks that cleverly devised computer viruses that have kept going and going. Our efforts are primarily about blocking the computer virus rather than somehow capturing and imprisoning it. Humans devising non-sentient AI can likely find ways to code AI that is going to be extremely hard to keep confined.

In addition, humans can devise AI that is self-adjusting or self-modifying. Readers might be aware of my ongoing discussions covering AI-infused polymorphic computer viruses. These are shape-shifting computer viruses that are sneakily constructed to try and be undetectable, or that upon detection will rapidly reshape to avoid further detection.

There are akin ML/DL systems that intentionally aim to self-adjust or self-modify, allowing for the AI system to hopefully improve by itself as it is being used. This though can be problematic in that the AI might morph in a fashion that is no longer desirable and subsequently acts in notably disturbing ways.

Another angle is that humans can use their computer-based tools, such as non-sentient AI, in order to craft AI confinement. In that sense, the premise that humans are only able to think to some limited degree is potentially a pretense. We might be able to augment our thinking processes via the likes of non-sentient AI and therefore find novel ways to design and build sufficient confinement for non-sentient AI.

All told, I am busting the two controversial contentions about AI Confinement and arguing that we cannot make any such irrefutable ironclad claims. We do not know for sure that we can always and without fail confine non-sentient AI. We do not know for sure that sentient AI of any caliber, including superhuman and super-intelligent, will always and without fail be able to escape our confinement.

The good news is that the whole kit and kaboodle are a hoot to consider. I say that somewhat cheekily. If we do find ourselves under threat by a non-sentient AI, we are going to soberly and strenuously want to ascertain whether we can confine it. Likewise, if we are under threat by a sentient AI of whatever caliber, we are going to desperately want to determine whether we can confine it.

The AI Confinement Problem is a meritorious conundrum and abundantly worthwhile to figure out.

I am guessing that you might be having a nagging ache about one key portion of the AI Confinement matter. All this talk about confinement seems silly or nonsensical since we are referring to AI rather than to a human being confined. The obvious thing to do would be to simply blow the AI to smithereens. Destroy any AI that we don't like and believe ought to be confined. Forget about all these contortions associated with confinement and merely squash AI like a bug. This seems like the best solution whereby you don't have to design and build confinements, instead expend your energies on wiping out AI that we humans decide is unworthy or dangerous.

Easy-peasy.

Turns out there is a series of logical retorts that you might want to ponder.

First, if the AI is sentient, we are possibly going to be willing to anoint such AI with a form of legal personhood. The concept is that we will provide AI with a semblance of human rights. Maybe not verbatim. Maybe a special set of rights. Who knows? In any case, you could conjure up the seemingly outlandish notion that we cannot just summarily wipe out sentient AI. There might be a stipulated legal process involved. This includes that we cannot necessarily exercise the "death penalty" upon a sentient AI (whoa, just wait until we as a society get embroiled in that kind of a societal debate). The gist is that we might need a suitable form of AI confinement in lieu of or while deciding whether to destroy a sentient AI.

Second, we might find useful value in an AI that we want to keep intact and not utterly destroy or delete. Suppose that we created a non-sentient AI that was leading us towards being able to cure cancer. Would we want to delete such AI? I hardly think so. Suppose that a fully sentient superhuman AI existed that promised to solve world hunger. Are we to wipe out this promising sentient AI, doing so without first resolving global hunger? We ought to think carefully about that.

The point is that we could have a variety of bona fide reasons to keep AI intact. Rather than deleting it or scrambling it, we might wish to ensure that the AI remains whole. The AI is going to be allowed to perform some of its actions in a limited manner. We want to leverage whatever AI can do for us.

How can we then have our cake and eat it too?

Answer: *AI confinement.*

Throughout this discussion, I have alluded to a kind of comparison between human confinement and AI confinement. To set the record straight, I am generally opposed to anthropomorphizing AI. I will say more about this momentarily.

The reason I bring the qualm up now is that I do not want to suggest or imply that today's non-sentient AI is analogous to humans and humankind. There is already way too much of that type of false and misleading comparison going on. Excuse my comparative usage which I've done in a hopefully careful and mindful fashion.

Trying to figure out how to confine AI is an interesting and abundantly useful proposition.

Even if we don't have AI today that presents an immediate need for confinement, the matter provides plenty of challenges that can aid in advancing our understanding of cybersecurity. Heaven knows we need to keep on trucking when it comes to boosting cyber protections all told. The pursuit of cybersecurity for confining AI is likely to uncover many useful side benefits that apply to overcoming those human evildoers that use computing for wrongdoing, along with tackling those pesky and ever-expanding computer viruses.

Those that seek to denigrate the erstwhile pursuit of the AI Confinement Problem are missing the bigger picture. For them, they only see this as a solely farfetched and far-off issue for the someday remote possibility of containing superhuman AI or super-intelligent AI. You should instead construe this as a handy means for advancing cybersecurity, entirely applicable in today's world, and for being prepared to deal with perhaps soon non-sentient AI that we might want to confine (along with getting ready for the presumably catastrophic risk of a heinous sentient AI, despite the seemingly low chances of our encountering such AI).

Better to be safe than sorry.

A recent research analysis about the AI Confinement Problem posits this indication of the current status: "AI confinement is a difficult problem with many proposed measures to improve security but no guarantees about safety. However, our current AI either make no attempt to escape or lack the ability to break out of simulations. There are some examples of real-world AI breaking a layer of confinement, but none that present any risk to humans or the capability establishing a persistent presence on remote computers" (*Philosophies* journal, "Understanding and Avoiding AI Failures: A Practical Guide" by Robert Williams and Roman Yampolskiy).

Those same researchers also describe a series of escape-potential levels:

- **Escape Potential Level 0:** None for conventional software
- **Escape Potential Level 1:** The agent may find unexpected behaviors which technically achieve the goal but are not desirable, such as genetic algorithms
- **Escape Potential Level 2:** The agent intentionally seeks to hack its environment, such as advanced reinforcement learners
- **Escape Potential Level 3 (danger):** The agent has the ability and drive to break through most cybersecurity and containment procedures, such as Artificial General Intelligence (AGI)

An explanation is proffered about these escape-potential levels: "At level 0, no confinement is needed beyond standard cybersecurity measures appropriate for the deployment environment. At levels 1 and 2, there is little risk of hostile escape, but the agent should be monitored closely for undesirable behavior and software exploits. The distributional shift from the simulator to the real world provides a barrier against narrow AI affecting the real world. Because of this, agents trained in more realistic simulators should be regarded with a greater degree of caution. At level 3, indefinite confinement is impossible, but, with robust security, at the level of software, hardware, and social engineering, humans can benefit from a contained AGI in a limited capacity" (per Robert Williams and Roman Yampolskiy).

The proposed set of escape-potential levels is thought-provoking. As you'll see in a moment, delineating automation via the use of graduated levels is a useful means of characterizing the scope and capacity of said automation. I'll describe for you the same concept as it relates to autonomous vehicles and AI-based self-driving cars. One notable difference is worth observing. For self-driving cars, there is an agreed-upon standard set of levels, while the above indicated escape-potential levels present an initial and preliminary strawman (you can undoubtedly anticipate that further refinements will be undertaken as the AI Confinement field further matures).

Let's contemplate the rationale or basis for wanting to confine AI.

The most apparent reason to confine AI would be to stop it from deplorable acts. We've already unearthed that instead of wiping out the AI, we might want to keep the AI caged so that it still can be run and meanwhile be prevented from causing harm. This might or might not be simultaneously feasible. There is a chance that the AI is unable to suitably run while imprisoned and therefore we lose the other desirable aspect of gleaning whatever positive value we sought to accrue. Imagine the consternation of having confined the AI though doing so at the cost that the remaining valued capability is no longer viably available. Drat!

There is a veritable range of reasons to confine AI, including but not limited to:

- Incapacitation of the AI
- Detention of the AI
- Protection for humans
- Protection from humans
- Rehabilitation of the AI
- Deterrence for other AI
- Retribution against the AI
- Etc.

You can take your time to mindfully mull over those reasons. Some of the reasons are readily justified. Some of them might seem to be curious and possibly unwarranted.

When discussing human escape artists, there was something that I didn't earlier mention. An escape artist might undertake their escape entirely of their own accord. Houdini often made his escape without any assistance from anyone else. That being said, Houdini sometimes used an accomplice or assistant to aid in making good his escape. You can see the same aspects in the prison escapes that were cited.

Here's why that is important to the dilemma of AI confinement.

Suppose we are able to confine AI. It might be sentient AI or might be non-sentient AI (we'll consider them jointly, first, and then separate the particulars). The AI tries to escape by some electronic or computer-based trickery. Assume that the AI is acting alone.

The AI might not have to act solo in its escape efforts. A human comes along and lets the AI escape. Maybe the human opens an electronic network portal and the AI transmits itself out to other non-confined computers elsewhere. Or perhaps the human makes a copy of the AI onto an external disk drive or memory stick, carrying the AI out of the confinement, and then later on plugs the disk or memory stick into a non-confined computer.

Humans could easily be the weak link in an effort to confine AI.

Why in the heck would a human allow an AI to escape from confinement, you might be exhorting. Surely, all humans would want to keep AI confined if the AI was presumably purposefully placed into confinement. If you are thinking those kinds of thoughts, I suggest you have a somewhat happy face optimistic view of humankind.

An evildoer might believe that they can harness the AI to do evil acts. Some wrongdoers might figure that the AI will wreak havoc, and do not care whether this is profitable for them or not. One supposes that a human might be sympathetic to the AI and believe that the AI was wrongfully incarcerated. On and on the possibilities endlessly go.

There is the accidental release that can occur too. A human with no intention of letting out the AI makes a mistake and voila, the AI is let loose. Consider that a human intending to make the confinement more stringent makes a boo-boo and inadvertently undercuts the rigors of the confinement, allowing the AI to escape.

If the AI can interact with humans while the AI is in confinement, the problem of attaining AI confinement is likely astronomically increased. Here's why.

An AI system might be able to use social engineering (SE) ploys. I'm sure you've had this done to you by humans. A person calls you on your cellphone and claims they are from your bank. They tell you that someone has cracked into your bank account. To fix the break-in, the person asks for your password. Amazingly, you give your password to this person. They then use it to log in to your bank account and steal your money. This is an example of using social engineering techniques to compromise computer systems.

Envision a sentient AI that is acting cleverly and tries this: "In addition to trivial SE attacks such as lying, befriending, blackmailing, hypnotizing and forming a romantic relationship the AI could utilize a number of more advanced strategies. One such strategy would be super-bribery. An AI can convince the guard that releasing the AI is in the guard's best interests. In addition to money and power the guard will be given perfect health, immortality or anything else for that matter. This strategy would work particularly well if the guard has a seriously ill close relative who the AI will promise to cure. Depending on the capabilities of the AI or as a result of lying, AI may also offer to bring back long-ago deceased relatives and friends of the guard. It would be hard to find a person who could remain immune to such bribes" (Roman Yampolskiy, "Leakproofing the Singularity Artificial Intelligence Confinement Problem" in the *Journal of Consciousness Studies*).

Whatever confinement is devised, there is always the potential that a human might disturb or undercut the confinement and allow the AI to escape. This seems especially possible if AI can communicate with humans. Not just any humans, even only when the AI can communicate with trained and specialized human guards that are supposedly aware of and ready for the tricks that the AI might play on them.

A particular focal point of the AI Confinement Problem deals with trying to establish a confinement protocol that can allow for communicating with the AI but restricting the AI such that it is not able to confound or convince humans to let the AI out. Some claim that any permitted communication could result in the AI ultimately getting a human to open the confinement. Others postulate that a multiple-choice protocol or a binary encoding might be a means to prevent the AI from deviously fooling a human guard.

This brings up yet another set of levels that we might wish to consider. The levels of communication security might be devised this way (per the aforementioned paper):

- Communications Security Level 0: Unlimited communication
- Communications Security Level 1: Censored input, uncensored output
- Communications Security Level 2: Outputs only with no inputs
- Communications Security Level 3: Unlimited input and censored output
- Communications Security Level 4: Secured communication
- Communications Security Level 5: Censored output and no inputs
- Communications Security Level 6: Inputs only with no outputs
- Communications Security Level 7: Censored input and no outputs
- Communications Security Level 8: No communication, fully confined AI

The AI could also have other tricks up its sleeve.

Assume we have placed AI into seemingly ironclad confinement consisting of a specialized computer system that is all locked up. And then this happens: "Additionally the AI may engage in the sabotage of the confinement hardware in the hopes of being able to escape as a result of the malfunctions in the security protocol. For example, the AI may try to melt the hardware via temperature increase from placing a high computational load on the processor or try to break a hard drive via multiple reads of the same location" (per the cited paper by Roman Yampolskiy).

You can add to the vulnerabilities of confinement that the confinement container or the facility it is housed in gets disrupted due to some natural act such as a tornado or a hurricane. Maybe the AI can exploit that occurrence. It could be that a nation that is an enemy of the country housing the AI in confinement decides that performing a breach of the confinement will be good for causing panic and serve as a sideways attack against the country that is their avowed foe. Perhaps human activists avowing AI rights raid the facility and let the AI loose.

Let your mind wander as to the many avenues of the AI confinement being compromised.

In one of the earliest papers about the AI Confinement Problem, Butler Lampson of the Xerox PARC (Palo Alto Research Center) published an article in 1973 entitled "A Note on the Confinement Problem" that proposed a handful of leak-proofing rules:

- **Total isolation:** A confined program shall make no calls on any other program.
- **Transitivity:** If a confined program calls another program which is not trusted, the called program must also be confined.
- **Masking:** A program to be confined must allow its caller to determine all its inputs into legitimate and covert channels. We say that the channels are masked by the caller.
- **Enforcement:** The supervisor must ensure that a confined program's input to covert channels conforms to the caller's specifications.

At this juncture of this weighty discussion, I'd bet that you are desirous of some illustrative examples that might showcase the AI Confinement Problem in today's world. There is a special and assuredly popular set of examples that are close to my heart. You see, in my capacity as an expert on AI including the ethical and legal ramifications, I am frequently asked to identify realistic examples that showcase AI Ethics dilemmas so that the somewhat theoretical nature of the topic can be more readily grasped. One of the most evocative areas that vividly presents this ethical AI quandary is the advent of AI-based true self-driving cars. This will serve as a handy use case or exemplar for ample discussion on the topic.

Here's then a noteworthy question that is worth contemplating: *Does the advent of AI-based true self-driving cars illuminate anything about the AI Confinement Problem, and if so, what does this showcase?*

You might be aware that there have been reported instances of Level 2 semi-autonomous cars that had a human driver at the wheel and the human fell asleep while actively underway on a freeway or highway. The scary aspect of Level 2 and Level 3 is that the human driver is still in charge of the driving, and yet they can be lulled into falsely believing that the AI or automation is fully capable to drive the car on its own. The push to ensure that an onboard monitoring system keeps track of the human driver and their driving status is a means to try and mitigate the being-lulled proclivity.

The news stories have showcased instances whereby a police officer in their police car has maneuvered in front of the Level 2 vehicle, then gradually opted to slow down their police car, which in turn has indirectly led to the Level 2 car slowing down correspondingly. This nifty trick is predicated on the idea that the Level 2 car has some form of sensor devices such as video cameras, radar, LIDAR, or the like that are used to detect vehicles that are ahead of the Level 2 car. Upon detecting the vehicle in front of the Level 2 car, the automation will automatically adjust its speed as per the speed of the vehicle ahead.

You could say that AI is being *persuaded* to slow down.

Suppose that the AI or automation in the case of a seeming runaway semi-autonomous (or even fully autonomous self-driving) car is programmed to switch lanes and avoid getting bogged down by a vehicle in front of the car.

What else can we do to contend with this?

You could try surrounding the errant vehicle with an entire posse of police cars. Position one in front of the targeted vehicle, position another on the left, another on the right, and one directly behind the runaway car. The vehicle is now boxed in. Unless it can sprout wings, it cannot presumably escape the *confinement.*

Notice that this is a form of physical confinement. Almost like putting an animal in a cage or forcing a robot into a prison cell. For AI-based systems that are principally robots, the confinement might indeed often be a physical form of confinement whereby the AI needs to be strictly controlled. Keep in mind that a self-driving car is essentially a type of robot. You probably do not think of self-driving cars in that manner, but overall they are in fact robots that have wheels and drive on our roadways.

A significant problem with this form of confinement is that we don't necessarily know how the AI driving system will react. You can potentially have all the police cars in unison gradually slow down and the runaway car will hopefully correspondingly do so too (it won't be able to switch lanes or get out of the blocking confinement). That is the happy face scenario.

We don't know for sure that this is what will happen.

It could be that the AI is not well devised, or has errors, and it ends up ramming one or more of the police cars. Assuming that the officers are not killed, this might save lives all told, though the officers could potentially get injured and all of the vehicles might get severely damaged.

A more failsafe form of confinement for a self-driving car would be to place the vehicle in a secured garage that will entrap the driverless vehicle. The preceding example about an underway vehicle was more complicated since the vehicle was essentially free to roam. Placing the self-driving car into a locked garage might confine the essentially AI robotic system, though if someone opens the garage or somehow the AI is able to electronically get the garage doors to open, an escape or kind of jailbreak could potentially ensue.

That exemplifies the physical nature of AI confinement. Next, consider the software aspects of AI confinement.

Assume for sake of discussion that the AI driving system is calling the shots as to how the self-driving car is going to operate. This presents another avenue for confinement, namely consisting of trying to confine the AI driving system per se that is on-board the vehicle.

One means might be to have pre-built or programmed virtual confinement around the AI driving system that is always existent in the onboard computer that is running the AI of the vehicle. We might be able to send an electronic signal to the confinement or imprisonment code that indicates to go ahead and trap the AI driving system, preventing the AI from operating the self-driving car. Some prearranged special signal could activate the confinement and block the AI driving system. Thus, this would prevent the AI from being able to utilize the driving controls, effectively overruling the self-driving car from proceeding via any of the AI commands.

We would need to be mindful of how this works. A self-driving car that is underway at highway speeds could become a dangerous unguided missile of sorts if the confinement was suddenly enacted and the AI abruptly no longer was able to drive the autonomous vehicle (we are assuming too that there aren't any human accessible driving controls that a human could use to undertake the driving).

How else might such an AI confinement be useful in the use case of self-driving cars?

For those of you that are worried about the possibility of AI self-driving cars all going amok at the same time, either by the AI doing so itself or due to an evildoer that corrupts the AI. A built-in AI confinement configuration is one of several ways to try and overcome such a malicious takeover of autonomous vehicles.

I am sure that you realize that just because we possibly have some concocted or devised virtual confinement that surrounds the AI of a self-driving car this is not a guarantee of successfully preventing an escape by the AI. A non-sentient AI might have been programmed to do some clever jailbreak. A sentient AI might be clever enough to figure out a means around the AI confinement or convince humans to let it free, as noted earlier.

Conclusion

In the famous adventure novel, *The Count of Monte Cristo*, we are treated to a captivating story revolving around a man that is wrongfully imprisoned. He manages to escape. He acquires a great fortune. He then seeks revenge upon those that confined him. When you have time to do so, you really must read this quite wonderfully written story or at least watch one of the numerous movie versions.

A memorable line is this: "How did I escape? With difficulty. How did I plan this moment? With pleasure."

If we are aiming to confine AI, we will need to do a lot of careful planning and try to anticipate how to establish ironclad imprisonment (if that is even possible). The question arises as to whether the AI will also be doing careful planning about how to break free of the confinement. For non-sentient AI, this might be a computational subroutine built into the AI by the human developers of the AI. For sentient AI, if we ever see this, the AI might astutely do its own jailbreak planning.

Are we going to be able to solve the AI Confinement Problem and come up with a surefire means of confining any and all AI systems in an utterly escape-proof or absolutely leak-proof manner?

As stated eloquently in the prison movie *The Shawshank Redemption*, some birds aren't meant to be caged.

AI might very well be that kind of bird.

.

CHAPTER 7
AI ETHICS AND AI DISGORGEMENT

You might say that society seems nearly obsessed with indestructibility.

We relish movies and sci-fi stories that showcase superhumans that are seemingly indestructible. Those of us that are commonplace non-superhuman people dream about magically becoming indestructible. Companies market products claiming that their vaunted goods are supposedly indestructible.

The famous comedian Milton Berle used to tell a pretty funny joke about items that are allegedly indestructible: "I bought my son an indestructible toy. Yesterday he left it in the driveway. It broke my car." That's an uproarious sidesplitter for those that endlessly are seeking to discover anything that could be somehow contended as being indestructible.

I bring up this rather fascinating topic to cover a matter that is rising quickly as an important consideration when it comes to the advent of Artificial Intelligence (AI). I will pose the contentious bubbling topic as a simple question that perhaps surprisingly has a quite complex answer.

In brief, is AI entirely susceptible to destruction or could there be AI that ostensibly could be asserted as being indestructible or thereabouts?

This is a vital aspect underlying recent efforts dealing with both the legal and ethical ramifications of AI. Legally, as you will see in a moment, doors are opening toward using the destruction of an AI system as a means of providing a legal remedy as to a consequence of some pertinent unlawful or unethical wrong. Note that the field of AI Ethics also is weighing in on the considered use of destruction of AI or the comparable deletion of AI.

Mull this whole conundrum over for a moment.

Should we do be seeking to delete or destroy AI?

And, can we do it, even if we wanted to do so?

I'll go ahead and unpack the controversial topic and showcase some examples to highlight the tradeoffs involved in this mind-bending quandary.

First, let's get some language on the table to ensure we are singing the same tune. The suitably lofty way to phrase the topic consists of indicating that we are aiming to undertake *AI Disgorgement.* Some also use interchangeably the notion of *Algorithmic Disgorgement.* For sake of discussion herein, I am going to equate the two catchphrases. Technically, you can persuasively argue that they are not one and the same. I think the discussion here can suffice by modestly blurring the difference.

That being said, you might not be readily familiar at all with the word "disgorgement" since it usually arises in a legal-related context. Most law dictionaries depict "disgorgement" as the act of giving up something due to a legal demand or compulsion.

A noted article in the *Yale Journal of Law & Technology* entitled "Algorithms and Economic Justice: A Taxonomy of Harms and a Path Forward for the Federal Trade Commission" by Rebecca Slaughter, a Commissioner of the Federal Trade Commission (FTC), described the matter this way: "One innovative remedy that the FTC has recently deployed is algorithmic disgorgement. The premise is simple: when companies collect data illegally, they should not be able to profit from either the data or any algorithm developed using it" (August 2021).

In that same article, the point is further made by highlighting some prior akin instances: "This novel approach was most recently deployed in the FTC's case against Everalbum in January 2021. There, the Commission alleged that the company violated its promises to consumers about the circumstances under which it would deploy facial-recognition software. As part of the settlement, the Commission required the company to delete not only the ill-gotten data but also any facial recognition models or algorithms developed with users' photos or videos. The authority to seek this type of remedy comes from the Commission's power to order relief reasonably tailored to the violation of the law. This innovative enforcement approach should send a clear message to companies engaging in illicit data collection in order to train AI models: Not worth it."

Just recently, additional uses of the disgorgement method have come to the fore. Consider this reporting in March of this year: "The Federal Trade Commission has struggled over the years to find ways to combat deceptive digital data practices using its limited set of enforcement options. Now, it's landed on one that could have a big impact on tech companies: algorithmic destruction. And as the agency gets more aggressive on tech by slowly introducing this new type of penalty, applying it in a settlement for the third time in three years could be the charm. In a March 4 settlement order, the agency demanded that WW International — formerly known as Weight Watchers — destroy the algorithms or AI models it built using personal information collected through its Kurbo healthy eating app from kids as young as 8 without parental permission" (in an article by Kate Kaye, March 14, 2022, *Protocol* online blog).

Lest you think that this disgorgement idea is solely a U.S. viewpoint, various assessments of the draft European Union (EU) Artificial Intelligence Act suggest that the legal language therein can be interpreted as allowing for a "withdrawal" of an AI system (i.e., some would say this assuredly amounts to the AI being subject to destruction, deletion, or disgorgement).

Much of this talk about deleting or destroying an AI system is usually centered on a particular type of AI known as Machine Learning (ML) or Deep Learning (DL). ML/DL is not the only way to craft AI. Nonetheless, the increasing availability of ML/DL and its use has created quite a stir for being both beneficial and yet also at times abysmal.

ML/DL is merely a form of computational pattern matching. The usual approach is that you assemble data about a decision-making task. You feed the data into the ML/DL computer models. Those models seek to find mathematical patterns. After finding such patterns, if so found, the AI system then will use those patterns when encountering new data. Upon the presentation of new data, the patterns based on the "old" or historical data are applied to render a current decision.

AI and especially the widespread advent of ML/DL has gotten societal dander up about the ethical underpinnings of how AI might be sourly devised. You might be aware that when this latest era of AI got underway there was a huge burst of enthusiasm for what some now call *AI For Good.* Unfortunately, on the heels of that gushing excitement, we began to witness *AI For Bad.* For example, various AI-based facial recognition systems have been revealed as containing racial biases and gender biases, which I've discussed at **the link here**.

Efforts to fight back against *AI For Bad* are actively underway. Besides vociferous legal pursuits of reining in the wrongdoing, there is also a substantive push toward embracing AI Ethics to righten the AI vileness. The notion is that we ought to adopt and endorse key Ethical AI principles for the development and fielding of AI doing so to undercut the *AI For Bad* and simultaneously heralding and promoting the preferable *AI For Good.*

In a moment, I will be coming back to the AI Disgorgement topic and will be pointing out that we need to separate the destruction or deletion of AI into two distinct categories: (1) sentient AI, and (2) non-sentient AI. Let's set some foundational ground on those two categories so we'll be ready to engage further in the AI Disgorgement matter.

Please be abundantly aware that there isn't any AI today that is sentient.

In the case of the AI Disgorgement associated with sentient AI, we can wildly play a guessing game of nearly infinite varieties. Maybe sentient AI will cognitively be like humans and exhibit similar mental capacities. Or we could postulate that sentient AI will be superhuman and go beyond our forms of thinking. The ultimate in sentient AI would seem to be super-intelligence, something that might be so smart and cunning that we cannot today even conceive of the immense thinking prowess. Some suggest that our minds will be paltry in comparison. This super-duper AI will run rings around us in a manner comparable to how we today can outthink ants or caterpillars.

If there turns out to be AI that is sentient, we are possibly going to be willing to anoint such AI with a form of legal personhood. The concept is that we will provide AI with a semblance of human rights. Maybe not verbatim. Maybe a special set of rights. Who knows?

In any case, you could conjure up the seemingly provocative notion that we cannot just summarily wipe out or destroy sentient AI, even if we can technologically do so. Sentient AI might be construed as a veritable living organism in terms of cognitive capacity and innately having a "right to live" (depending upon the definition of being alive). There might ultimately be a stipulated legal process involved. This includes that we cannot necessarily exercise the "death penalty" upon a sentient AI (whoa, just wait until we as a society get embroiled in that kind of a societal debate).

I doubt that we would be willing to make the same AI Ethical posture for the non-sentient AI. Though some are trying to contend that today's non-sentient AI ought to be classified as a variant associated with legal personhood, this seems to be a steeply uphill battle. Can a piece of contemporary software that is not sentient be granted legal rights on par with humans or even animals? It sure seems like a stretch (but there are advocates fervently aiming for this).

Here's what this all implies.

Assuming we don't grant today's non-sentient AI as embodying the regal legal anointing of personhood, the choice of deleting or destroying such non-sentient AI would decidedly <u>not</u> be reasonably equated to the destruction of a living organism. The wiping out of non-sentient AI is nothing more than the same as deleting that dating app from your smartphone or erasing those excess pictures of your trip to a wonderland forest from your laptop. You can delete or "destroy" those bits of data and software without having a guilty conscience and without having overstepped the law in terms of having harmed a sentient living creature.

You might assume that this pronouncement summarily settles the AI Disgorgement conundrum as it relates to non-sentient AI.

Sorry, the world is never as straightforward as it might initially seem.

Get ready for a twist.

Suppose that we created a non-sentient AI that was leading us towards being able to cure cancer. The company that had developed the AI did something else that the firm should not have done and has gotten into serious legal trouble with various governmental authorities. As part of a remedy imposed upon the firm, the company is compelled to completely delete the AI, including all data and documentation associated with the AI.

The government took that company to task and assured that those wrongdoers can no longer profit from the AI that they had devised.

Unfortunately, in the same breath, we have perhaps shot our own foot because the AI had capabilities that were leading us toward curing cancer. We ended up tossing out the baby with the bathwater, as it were.

The point is that we could have a variety of bona fide reasons to keep AI intact. Rather than deleting it or scrambling it, we might wish to ensure that the AI remains whole. The AI is going to be allowed to perform some of its actions in a limited manner. We want to leverage whatever AI can do for us.

A handy rule would then seem to be that the notion of AI Disgorgement should be predicated on a semblance of context and sensibility as to when this form of a remedy is suitably applicable. Sometimes it might be fully applicable, while in other instances not so. You could also try to find ways to split the apple, perhaps keeping some part of the AI that was deemed as beneficial while seeking to have destruction or deletion for the portions that are considered within the remedy deriving scope.

Of course, doing a piecemeal deletion or destruction is not a piece of cake either. It could be that the part you want to keep is integrally woven into the part you want to have destroyed. Trying to separate the two could be problematic. In the end, you might have to abandon the deletion and simply agree to allow the whole to remain, or you might have to toss in the towel and destroy the whole kit and kaboodle.

It all depends.

Time to tackle another hefty consideration.

We've so far covered the issues underpinning the basis for wanting to bring forth an AI Disgorgement. Meanwhile, we have just now sneaked into that discussion the other next important element to consider, namely whether deleting or destroying AI is altogether always feasible.

In the preceding dialogue, we kind of assumed at face value that we can destroy or delete AI if we wanted to do so. The one twist that was mentioned involved trying to separate out the parts of an AI system that we wanted to keep intact versus the parts that we wanted to delete or destroy. That can be hard to do. Even if it is hard to accomplish, we would still be on relatively cogent turf to claim that it inevitably could be technologically attained (we might need to rebuild parts that we destroyed, putting those back into place to support the other part that we didn't want to destroy).

Slightly change the perspective and ruminate on whether we really always can in fact destroy or delete AI if we wish to do so. Put aside the AI Ethics question and focus exclusively on the technological question of destructive feasibility (I am loath to utter the words "put aside the AI Ethics question" since the AI Ethics question is always a vital and inseparable consideration for AI, but I hope you realize that I am using this as a figure of speech for purposes of directing attention only, thanks).

We'll make this into two lines of reasoning:

- If we have a *sentient* AI that we all agree has to be destroyed or deleted, would we technologically have an assured means to do so?
- If we have a *non-sentient* AI that we all agree has to be destroyed or deleted, would we technologically have an assured means to do so?

I would submit that the answer to both of those questions is a qualified "no" (I'd pretty much be on the rather safe technological ground for saying "no" since there is always a potential chance that we could <u>not</u> destroy or delete the AI, as I will elaborate on next). In essence, a lot of the time the answer would probably be "yes" in the case of non-sentient AI, while in the case of the sentient AI the answer is "maybe, but nobody can say either way for sure" due to not knowing what the sentient AI is going to be or even if it will arise.

In the case of sentient AI, there is a myriad of fanciful theories that can be postulated.

If the sentient AI is superhuman or super-intelligent, you can try to argue that the AI would outsmart us humans and not allow itself to be wiped out. Presumably, no matter what we try, this outsized AI will always be a step ahead of us. We might even try to leverage some human-friendly instance of this sentient super-duper AI to destroy another sentient AI that we are otherwise unable to delete via our own methods. Be wary though that the helpful AI later turns evildoer and we are left at the mercy of this AI that we are hence unable to get rid of.

For those of you that prefer a happy face version of the futuristic sentient AI, maybe we theorize that any sentient AI would be willing to get destroyed and want to actively do so if humans wished it so. This more understanding and sympathetic sentient AI would be able to realize when it is time to go. Rather than fighting its own destruction, it would welcome being destroyed when the time comes for such action. Perhaps the AI does the work for us and opts to self-destruct.

The conjecture about sentient AI can roam in whatever direction you dream of. There aren't particularly any rules about what is possible. One supposes that the realities of physics and other natural constraints would come to bear, though maybe a super-intelligent sentient AI knows of ways to overcome everything we take for granted as reality.

Speaking of reality, let's shift our attention to the non-sentient AI of today.

You might be tempted to believe that we can always without fail opt to destroy or delete any of today's AI. Envision that a company has devised an AI system that governmental authorities order be disgorged. The firm is legally required to destroy or delete the AI system.

Easy-peasy, it seems, just press a delete button and poof, the AI system is no longer around. We do this with no longer needed apps and no longer wanted data files on our laptops and smartphones. No special computer techie skills are needed. The company can comply with the regulatory order in minutes.

We can walk through the reasons why this presumed ease of AI destruction or deletion is not as straightforward as you might initially assume.

First, a notable question surrounds the exact scope of what is meant when you say that an AI system is to be destroyed or deleted. One facet is the programming code that comprises the AI. Another facet would be any data associated with the AI.

The developers of the AI might have generated many versions of the AI while crafting the AI. Let's simplify things and say that there is a final version of the code that is the one running and has become the target for being disgorged. Okay, the company deletes that final version. The deed is done!

But, turns out that those earlier versions are all still sitting around. It might be relatively child's play to essentially resurrect the now-deleted AI by merely using one of those earlier versions. You take an earlier version, make modifications to bring it up to par, and you are back in business.

An obvious way to try and prevent this kind of deletion skirting would be to stipulate that any and all prior versions of the AI must be destroyed. This would seem to force the company into seriously finding any older versions and making sure those get deleted too.

One twist is that suppose the AI contained a significant portion of widely available open-source code. The developers had originally decided that to build the AI they would not start from scratch. Instead, they grabbed up a ton of open-source code and used it as the backbone for their AI. They do not own the open-source code. They do not control the open-source code. They only copied it into their AI creation.

Now we have a bit of a problem.

The company complies with the order to destroy their AI. They delete their copy of the code and all versions of it that they possess. They delete all of their internal documentation. Meanwhile, they are not able to get rid of the open-source that comprises (let's say) the bulk of their AI system since it is not something they legally own and have no direct control over. The firm seems to have done what it could do.

Would you say that the offending AI was in fact destroyed or deleted?

The firm would likely insist that they did so. The governing authority would seem to have a hard time contending otherwise.

They might be able to quickly resurrect the AI by just going out to grab the widely available open-source and adding the pieces by doing some programming based on their knowledge of what the added portions consisted of. They don't use any of the prior offending code that they had fully deleted. They don't use any of the documentation that they had deleted. Voila, they have a "new" AI system that they would argue is not the AI that they had been ordered to disgorge.

I trust that you can see how these kinds of cat and mouse games can be readily played.

There are lots more twists.

Suppose the AI that is to be disgorged was based on the use of Machine Learning. The ML could be a program that the company developed on its own, but more likely these days the ML is an algorithm or model that the firm selected from an online library or collection (there are lots and lots of these readily available).

The firm deletes the instance of the ML that they downloaded and are using. The exact same ML algorithm or model is still sitting in a publicly available online library and potentially accessible for comers that want to use it. The governmental authority might have no means to restrict or cause a disgorgement of that online library.

That's just the start of the difficulties involved in destroying or deleting AI, including for example the use of Machine Learning. As mentioned earlier, ML and DL typically entail feeding data into the ML/DL. If the firm still has the data that they previously used, they could download another copy of the ML/DL algorithm or model from the online library and reconstitute the AI via feeding the data once again into what is essentially the same ML/DL that they had used before.

You might astutely clamor that the data the firm had been using needs to also be encompassed by the disgorgement order. Sure, let's assume that this is so.

If the data is entirely within the confines of the firm, they presumably would be able to destroy or delete the data. Problem solved, one would say. But, suppose the data was based on various external sources, all of which are outside the scope of the destruction order since they are not owned by and not controlled by the offending firm.

The crux is that you could from other external sources grab copies of the data, grab a copy of the ML/DL algorithm, and reconstitute the AI system. In some cases, this might be expensive to undertake and could require gobs of time, while in other instances it might be doable in short order. It all depends on various factors such as how much the data needs to be modified or transformed, and the same goes for the parameter setting and training of the ML/DL.

We also need to consider what the meaning of destroying or deleting consists of.

You undoubtedly know that when you delete a file or app from your computer, the chances are that the electronically stored item is not yet fully deleted. Typically, the operating system updates a setting indicating that the file or app is to be construed as having been deleted. This is a convenience if you want to bring back the file or app. The operating system can merely flip the flag to indicate that the once seemingly deleted file or app is now active again.

Even if you have the operating system perform a more determined deletion, there is a likelihood that the file or app still sits somewhere. It might be on a backup storage device. It might be archived. If you are using a cloud-based online service, copies are likely residing there too. Not only would you need to find all of those shadow copies, but you would also need to perform various specialized cybersecurity erasure actions to try and ensure that the bits and bytes of those files and apps are completely written over and in a sense truly deleted or destroyed.

Note that I just mentioned the notion of a shadow.

We have at least three types of shadows to be thinking about when it comes to AI disgorgement:

1) Shadow copies of the AI
2) Shadow algorithms associated with the AI
3) Shadow data associated with the AI

Imagine that an order for an AI disgorgement instructs a company to proceed with destroying or deleting the data associated with the AI, but the firm can keep around the algorithm (perhaps allowing this if the algorithm is seemingly nothing more than one that you can find in any online ML library anyway).

Turns out that the algorithm itself essentially can be said to have its own kind of data, such as particular settings that underpin the algorithm. The effort to train the ML will usually entail having the ML figure out what parameter settings need to be calibrated. If you are only ordered to get rid of the training dataset per se, those other data-related parameter settings are likely still going to remain. This suggests that the AI can be somewhat readily reconstituted, or you could even argue that the AI wasn't deleted at all and you simply got rid of the earlier used training data that perhaps you no longer care about anyway. There is also a high chance that a form of *imprint* remains from the training data.

Getting rid of the training data might also be challenging if the data comes from a variety of third-party sources. Sure, you might be able to force the company to delete their in-house instance of the compiled data, but if the data exists at those other sources beyond their scope, the same data could be likely reassembled. This might be costly or might be inexpensive to do, depending upon the circumstances.

Throughout this discussion, we have focused on the notion of having a particular company be the target for undertaking an AI disgorgement. This might be satisfying and serve as an appropriate remedy associated with that company. On the other hand, this is not necessarily going to somehow eradicate or destroy the AI as it might exist or be reconstituted beyond the scope of the targeted company.

The AI might be copied to zillions of other online sites that the company has no means to access and cannot force a deletion to take place. The AI might be rebuilt from scratch by others that are aware of how the AI works. You could even have former employees of the firm that leave the company and opt to reuse their AI development skills to construct the essentially same AI elsewhere, which would be argued by them as based on their knowledge and skills, thus not being an infringing or subjected copy of the AI disgorgement order.

A perhaps apt analogy to the AI disgorgement troubles might be the advent of computer viruses.

The chances of hunting down and deleting all copies of a viral computer virus are generally slim, especially due to the legal questions of where the virus might be residing (such as across international borders) and the technological trickery of the computer virus trying to hide (I've discussed the emergence of AI-based polymorphic computer viruses that are electronic self-adapting shape-shifters).

Furthermore, compounding the challenges, there is always the presumed capability of constructing the same or roughly equivalent computer virus by those that are well-versed in the design and crafting of computer viruses all told.

AI Disgorgement is a seemingly handy idea and a potentially viable tool, but the devil is in the details.

At this juncture of this weighty discussion, I'd bet that you are desirous of some illustrative examples that might showcase the applicability of AI Disgorgement in today's world. There is a special and assuredly popular set of examples that are close to my heart. You see, in my capacity as an expert on AI including the ethical and legal ramifications, I am frequently asked to identify realistic examples that showcase AI Ethics dilemmas so that the somewhat theoretical nature of the topic can be more readily grasped. One of the most evocative areas that vividly presents this ethical AI quandary is the advent of AI-based true self-driving cars. This will serve as a handy use case or exemplar for ample discussion on the topic.

Here's then a noteworthy question that is worth contemplating: *Does the advent of AI-based true self-driving cars illuminate anything about the applicability of AI Disgorgement, and if so, what does this showcase?*

A company is developing an AI-based self-driving car and opts to make use of public roadways for doing tryouts of the autonomous vehicle. For a while, the fielded self-driving cars are doing fine. People are going for rides in the fleet. All seems good.

Unfortunately, one of the self-driving cars rams into a bicyclist. Local city leaders and the populace at large are quite upset. Two days later, another bicyclist gets rammed by another one of the self-driving cars from this same fleet. A vitriolic uproar ensures. For similar scenarios that will potentially someday confront city leaders and communities, see the study I co-authored with a Harvard faculty member.

A government authority declares that the company shall be compelled to enact an AI disgorgement. The AI driving system is to be utterly deleted or destroyed. As a side note, this is a somewhat artificial scenario since there would be other options of what might be done and those would presumably be first considered. The disgorging of AI would seem to be the last resort and also would undoubtedly be legally fought stridently by the self-driving car firm.

Please accept the imagined setting for purposes of concentrating on how AI disgorgement might be enacted.

Assume that the company accedes to doing the AI disgorgement. They go ahead and delete the latest copy of the AI driving system. The deed is done.

Well, as earlier identified, the deed is not at all yet completed. The firm deletes all prior versions of the AI driving system. They scour the company servers and delete copies there. They scour the cloud-based servers and delete the copies there. They go to their backups and archives and delete those. They ask that the cloud provider do the same for any backups or archives on the cloud that contain the AI driving system code.

Are we done?

Nope.

There was a lot of data used to train the AI driving system. Vast stores of collected data that contained video and pictures of roadway scenes were used to train the AI driving system. Those are found and deleted. A slew of other data files were all integral to devising the AI driving system. Those are also uncovered and deleted. Backups and archives are dug up and likewise deleted.

The AI disgorgement included all of the AI programs, data, and documentation. So, the company tries to discover all of the online documentation and deletes those documents, including backups, archives, and the like. In addition, the AI developers and others involved in the AI driving system are asked to provide their handwritten notes. Those are then shredded and put into the trash.

Whew, the AI no longer exists.

Kind of.

The AI driving system was based on readily available open-source code. The company has no ability to delete or destroy the open-source per se (they only are able to do so for the copies they held). There is also an ML/DL component of the AI driving system. This ML/DL is based on algorithms licensed on a cloud-based library. The company can only delete the instances that they created and have no means of contending with the cloud-based library. Training data that was used for the ML/DL consists of video and pictures that are readily found on other websites and in specialized openly available datasets.

In terms of the deleted documentation about the AI driving system, this went generally well, though there are likely still pockets of documents here or there that some of the AI developers have on their personal laptops and didn't fess up to having. In any case, the AI developers in their heads know what the AI consisted of and are able to quickly go over to another self-driving car firm to leverage their expertise there.

Shortly after this AI disgorgement, a competing firm that hired those ex-employees has essentially reconstituted the AI driving system. They did not copy the disgorged AI. They instead independently rebuilt the AI by using the open-source code, the ML/DL libraries, and the openly available datasets.

I guess you could say, one down and more to go, at least from a potential AI Disgorgement perspective.

Conclusion

Though the example suggests that the AI disgorgement can be overcome, do not count out this potential means of a remedy for AI wrongs. Some would argue that the use of AI Disgorgement will be viewed as a visibly potent way to convince other companies that they should be more mindful in how they devise and deploy their AI. They could lose their pot of gold, as it were. This is a handy tool in the arsenal of getting compliance with AI Ethics and devising Ethical AI.

Others clamor that the AI Disgorgement could stifle innovation in the advancement and use of AI. Perhaps AI developers will be hesitant to stretch the envelope if they know that someday their AI could be essentially deleted out of existence. That would be a hard pill to swallow for those that had devoted years of blood, sweat, and tears to crafting the AI.

Numerous other tradeoffs are bandied around. Maybe a competing vendor would try to get a governmental authority to undercut the competition by goading the agency into using AI Disgorgement against other firms in their same industry. And, think too of the cost involved in trying to comply with such an order. There isn't just a red button that you can push to perform all the deletion and destruction of the AI. Lots of expensive labor might be required and could take weeks or months to undertake.

Time will tell whether this newly emerging means of coping with AI is going to gain traction or fall by the wayside.

Does this meaty discussion about AI Disgorgement imply that AI is potentially indestructible?

You could contend that the phrasing of being destructible or indestructible is somewhat nebulosus when referring to something that is principally electronic. A human being is not indestructible because we could obviously find a means to destroy the human physical form. The same could be said for just about anything that takes on a conventional physical manifestation. I won't get into the meta-physical philosophizing theories that nothing is ever actually destroyed and that all matter is merely reconstituted into different forms and yet still exists (you are welcome to explore that lofty theorizing if you wish).

Given the ubiquitous nature of today's computing and the likely ever-expanding use of computing, such as the vaunted Internet of Things (IoT), there are lots and lots of places for an electronically-based AI to hide. For the non-sentient AI of today, the AI might be hidden by those humans that wish to hide it, or programmed to hide by those humans that developed the AI. Heaven knows what the sentient AI might do.

If an AI system can easily make copies of itself and hide those copies and ultimately not be caught, would you be willing to say that this exemplifies a semblance of indestructibility?

Some would argue that despite a whack-a-mole possibility, in the end, you could destroy or delete the AI as long as you can successfully find and wipe out each such appearing or reappearing instance. Ergo, AI is not indestructible. Others would retort that a hiding AI is ostensibly indestructible because it can just keep spawning and the elusive cat and mouse gambit could last nearly forever. You are always going to be confronted with the next instance that you still haven't squashed.

A famous quote comes to mind: "I was never born and I will never die; I do not hurt and cannot be hurt; I am invincible, immortal, indestructible" (by noted writer and journalist Aravind Adiga).

Could that be applicable to AI?

Those that are handwringing about sentient super-intelligent AI would seemingly say it could.

CHAPTER 8
AI ETHICS AND AI ADVERSARIAL ATTACKS

It is widely accepted sage wisdom to garner as much as you can about your adversaries.

Frederick The Great, the famous king of Prussia and a noted military strategist, stridently said this: "Great advantage is drawn from knowledge of your adversary, and when you know the measure of their intelligence and character, you can use it to play on their weakness."

Astutely leveraging the awareness of your adversaries is both a vociferous defense and a compelling offense-driven strategy in life. On the one hand, you can be better prepared for whatever your adversary might try to destructively do to you. The other side of that coin is that you are likely able to carry out better attacks against your adversary via the known and suspected weaknesses of any vaunted foe.

Per the historically revered statesman and ingenious inventor Benjamin Franklin, those that are on their guard and appear ready to receive their adversaries are in much less danger of being attacked, much more so than otherwise being unawares, supine, and negligent in preparation.

Why all this talk about adversaries?

Because one of the biggest concerns facing much of today's AI is that cyber crooks and other evildoers are deviously attacking AI systems using what is commonly referred to as *adversarial attacks*. This can cause an AI system to falter and fail to perform its designated functions. As you'll see in a moment, there are a variety of vexing AI Ethics and Ethical AI issues underlying the matter, such as ensuring that AI systems are protected against such scheming adversaries.

Perhaps even worse than getting the AI to simply stumble, the adversarial attack can sometimes be used to get AI to perform as the wrongdoer wishes the AI to perform. The attacker can essentially trick the AI into doing the bidding of the malefactor. Whereas some adversarial attacks seek to disrupt or confound the AI, another equally if not more insidious form of deception involves getting the AI to act on the behalf of the attacker.

It is almost as though one might use a mind trick or hypnotic means to get a human to do wrong acts and yet the person is blissfully unaware that they have been fooled into doing something that they should not particularly have done. To clarify, the act that is performed does not necessarily have to be wrong per se or illegal in its merits. For example, conning a bank teller to open the safe or vault for you is not in itself a wrong or illegal act. The bank teller is doing what they legitimately are able to perform as a valid bank-approved task. Of course, if they open the vault and doing so allows a robber to steal the money and all of the gold bullion therein, the bank teller has been tricked into performing an act that they should not have undertaken in the given circumstances.

The use of adversarial attacks against AI has to a great extent arisen because of the way in which much of contemporary AI is devised. You see, this latest era of AI has tended to emphasize the use of Machine Learning (ML) and Deep Learning (DL). These are computational pattern matching techniques and technologies which have dramatically aided the advancement of modern-day AI systems. ML/DL is often used as a key element in many of the AI systems that you interact with daily, such as the use of conversational interactive systems or Natural Language Processing (NLP) akin to Alexa and Siri.

The manner in which ML/DL is designed and fielded provides a fertile opening for the leveraging of adversarial attacks. Cybercrooks generally can guess how the ML/DL was built. They can make reasoned guesses about how the ML/DL will react when put into use. There are only so many ways that ML/DL is usually constructed. As such, the evildoer hackers can try a slew of underhanded ML/DL adversarial tricks to get the AI to either go awry or do their bidding.

In contrast, during the prior era of AI systems, it was somewhat harder to undertake adversarial attacks since much of the AI was more idiosyncratic and written in a more proprietary or individualistic manner. You would have had a more challenging time trying to guess how the AI was constructed and also how it might react when placed into active use. In comparison, ML/DL is largely more predictable as to its susceptibilities (this is not always the case, and please know that I am broadly generalizing).

You might be thinking that if adversarial attacks are relatively able to be targeted specifically at ML/DL then certainly there be should a boatload of cybersecurity measures available to protect against those attacks. One would hope that those devising and releasing their AI applications would ensure that the app was securely able to fight against those adversarial attacks.

The answer is yes and no.

Yes, there exist numerous cybersecurity protections that can be used by and within ML/DL to guard against adversarial attacks. Unfortunately, the answer is also somewhat a "no" in that many of the AI builders are not especially versed in those protections or are not explicitly including those protections.

There are lots of reasons for this.

One is that some AI software engineers concentrate solely on the AI side and are not particularly caring about the cybersecurity elements. They figure that someone else further along in the chain of making and releasing the AI will deal with any needed cybersecurity protections. Another reason for the lack of protection against adversarial attacks is that it can be a burden of sorts to the AI project. An AI project might be under a tight deadline to get the AI out the door. Adding into the mix a bunch of cybersecurity protections that need to be crafted or set up will potentially delay the production cycle of the AI. Furthermore, the cost of creating AI is bound to go up too.

Note that none of those are satisfactory as to allow an AI system to be vulnerable to adversarial attacks. Those that are in the know would say the famous line of either pay me now or pay me later would come to play in this instance. You can skirt past the cybersecurity portions to get an AI system sooner into production, but the chances are that it will then suffer an adversarial attack. A cost-benefit analysis and ROI (return on investment) needs to be properly assessed as to whether the cost upfront and the benefits thereof are going to be more profitable against the costs to repair and deal with cybersecurity intrusions further down the pike.

There is no free lunch when it comes to making ML/DL that is well-protected against adversarial attacks.

That being said, you don't necessarily need to move heaven and earth to be moderately protected against those evildoing tricks. Savvy specialists that are versed in cybersecurity protections can pretty much sit side-by-side with the AI crews and dovetail the security into the AI as it is being devised. There is also the assumption that a well-versed AI builder can readily use AI constructing techniques and technologies that simultaneously aid their AI building and that seamlessly encompasses adversarial attack protections. To adequately do so, they usually need to know about the nature of adversarial attacks and how to best blunt or mitigate them. This is something only gradually becoming regularly instituted as part of devising AI systems.

A twist of sorts is that more and more people are getting into the arena of developing ML/DL applications. Regrettably, some of those people are not versed in AI per se, and neither are they versed in cybersecurity. The idea overall is that perhaps by making the ability to craft AI systems with ML/Dl widely available to all we are aiming to *democratize AI*. That sounds good, but there are downsides to this popular exhortation.

Speaking of twists, I will momentarily get to the biggest twist of them all, namely, I am going to shock you with a recently emerging notion that some find sensible and others believe is reprehensible. I'll give you a taste of where I am heading on this heated and altogether controversial matter.

Are you ready?

There is a movement toward using adversarial attacks as a means to disrupt or fool AI systems that are being used by wrongdoers.

Let me explain.

So far, I have implied that AI is seemingly always being used in the most innocent and positive of ways and that only miscreants would wish to confound the AI via the use of adversarial attacks. But keep in mind that bad people can readily devise AI and use that AI for doing bad things.

You know how it is, what's good for the goose is good for the gander.

Criminals and cybercrooks are eagerly wising up to the building and using AI ML/DL to carry out untoward acts. When you come in contact with an AI system, you might not have any means of knowing whether it is an *AI For Good* versus an *AI For Bad* type of system. Be on the watch! Just because AI is being deployed someplace does not somehow guarantee that the AI will be crafted by well-intended builders. The AI could be deliberately devised for foul purposes.

Here then is the million-dollar question.

Should we be okay with using adversarial attacks on purportedly *AI For Bad* systems?

I'm sure that your first thought is that we ought to indeed be willing to fight fire with fire. If *AI For Good* systems can be shaken up via adversarial attacks, we can use those same evildoing adversarial attacks to shake up those atrocious *AI For Bad* systems. We can rightfully turn the attacking capabilities into an act of goodness. Fight evil using the appalling trickery of evil. The net result would seem to be an outcome of good.

Not everyone agrees with that sentiment.

From an AI Ethics perspective, there is a lot of handwringing going on about this meaty topic. Some would argue that by leveraging adversarial attacks, even when the intent is for the good, you are perpetuating the use of adversarial attacks all-told. You are basically saying that it is okay to launch and promulgate adversarial attacks. Shame on you, they exclaim. We ought to be stamping out evil rather than encouraging or expanding upon evil (even if the evil is ostensibly aiming to offset evil and carry out the work of the good).

Those against the use of adversarial attacks would also argue that by keeping adversarial attacks in the game that you are going to merely step into a death knell of quicksand. More and stronger adversarial attacks will be devised under the guise of attacking the *AI For Bad* systems. That seems like a tremendously noble pursuit. The problem is that the evildoers will undoubtedly also grab hold of those emboldened and super-duper adversarial attacks and aim them squarely at the *AI For Good*.

You are blindly promoting the cat and mouse gambit. We might be shooting our own foot.

A retort to this position is that there are no practical means of stamping out adversarial attacks. No matter whether you want them to exist or not, the evildoers are going to make sure they do persist. In fact, the evildoers are probably going to be making the adversarial attacks more resilient and potent, doing so to overcome whatever cyber protections are put in place to block them. Thus, a proverbial head-in-the-sand approach to dreamily pretending that adversarial attacks will simply slip quietly away into the night is pure nonsense.

You could contend that adversarial attacks against AI are a double-edged sword. AI researchers have noted this quandary, as stated by these authors in a telling article in *AI And Ethics* journal:

"Sadly, AI solutions have already been utilized for various violations and theft, even receiving the name AI or Crime (AIC). This poses a challenge: are cybersecurity experts thus justified to attack malicious AI algorithms, methods and systems as well, to stop them?

Would that be fair and ethical? Furthermore, AI and machine learning algorithms are prone to be fooled or misled by the so-called adversarial attacks. However, adversarial attacks could be used by cybersecurity experts to stop the criminals using AI, and tamper with their systems. The paper argues that this kind of attacks could be named Ethical Adversarial Attacks (EAA), and if used fairly, within the regulations and legal frameworks, they would prove to be a valuable aid in the fight against cybercrime" (article by Michał Choraś and Michał Woźniak, "The Double-Edged Sword Of AI: Ethical Adversarial Attacks To Counter Artificial Intelligence For Crime").

I'd ask you to mull this topic over and render a vote in your mind.

Is it unethical to use AI adversarial attacks against *AI For Bad*, or can we construe this as an entirely unapologetic Ethical AI practice?

You might be vaguely aware that one of the loudest voices these days in the AI field and even outside the field of AI consists of clamoring for a greater semblance of Ethical AI. Let's take a look at what it means to refer to AI Ethics and Ethical AI. On top of that, we can set the stage by looking at some examples of adversarial attacks to establish what I mean when I speak of Machine Learning and Deep Learning.

One particular segment or portion of AI Ethics that has been getting a lot of media attention consists of AI that exhibits untoward biases and inequities. You might be aware that when the latest era of AI got underway there was a huge burst of enthusiasm for what some now call *AI For Good*. Unfortunately, on the heels of that gushing excitement, we began to witness *AI For Bad*. For example, various AI-based facial recognition systems have been revealed as containing racial biases and gender biases.

Efforts to fight back against *AI For Bad* are actively underway. Besides vociferous *legal* pursuits of reining in the wrongdoing, there is also a substantive push toward embracing AI Ethics to righten the AI vileness.

The notion is that we ought to adopt and endorse key Ethical AI principles for the development and fielding of AI doing so to undercut the *AI For Bad* and simultaneously heralding and promoting the preferable *AI For Good.*

I trust that you can readily see how adversarial attacks fit into these AI Ethics matters. Evildoers are undoubtedly going to use adversarial attacks against ML/DL and other AI that is supposed to be doing *AI For Good.* Meanwhile, those evildoers are indubitably going to be devising *AI For Bad* that they foster upon us all. To try and fight against those *AI For Bad* systems, we could arm ourselves with adversarial attacks. The question is whether we are doing more good or more harm by leveraging and continuing the advent of adversarial attacks.

Time will tell.

One vexing issue is that there is a myriad of adversarial attacks that can be used against AI ML/DL. You might say there are more than you can shake a stick at. Trying to devise protective cybersecurity measures to negate all of the various possible attacks is somewhat problematic. Just when you might think you've done a great job of dealing with one type of adversarial attack, your AI might get blindsided by a different variant. A determined evildoer is likely to toss all manner of adversarial attacks at your AI and be hoping that at least one or more sticks. Of course, if we are using adversarial attacks against *AI For Bad,* we too would take the same advantageous scattergun approach.

Some of the most popular types of adversarial attacks include:

- Adversarial falsifications such as false-positive attacks and false-negative attacks
- Adversarial black-box attacks that are done without knowing what is inside the ML/DL
- Adversarial white-box attacks that are done when the internals of the ML/DL are known
- Adversarial run-time attacks that occur once the ML/DL is placed into active use
- Adversarial training-mode attacks that happen while the ML/DL is being trained

- Adversarial one-time attacks that are used on a one-and-done basis against ML/DL
- Adversarial iterative incremental attacks that dig away stepwise at ML/DL
- Etc.

At this juncture of this weighty discussion, I'd bet that you are desirous of some illustrative examples that might showcase the nature and scope of adversarial attacks against AI and particularly aimed at Machine Learning and Deep Learning. There is a special and assuredly popular set of examples that are close to my heart. You see, in my capacity as an expert on AI including the ethical and legal ramifications, I am frequently asked to identify realistic examples that showcase AI Ethics dilemmas so that the somewhat theoretical nature of the topic can be more readily grasped. One of the most evocative areas that vividly presents this ethical AI quandary is the advent of AI-based true self-driving cars. This will serve as a handy use case or exemplar for ample discussion on the topic.

Here's then a noteworthy question that is worth contemplating: *Does the advent of AI-based true self-driving cars illuminate anything about the nature of adversarial attacks against AI, and if so, what does this showcase?*

As earlier mentioned, some of the most popular types of adversarial attacks include:

- Adversarial falsifications such as false-positive attacks and false-negative attacks
- Adversarial black-box attacks that are done without knowing what is inside the ML/DL
- Adversarial white-box attacks that are done when the internals of the ML/DL are known
- Adversarial run-time attacks that occur once the ML/DL is placed into active use
- Adversarial training-mode attacks that happen while the ML/DL is being trained
- Adversarial one-time attacks that are used on a one-and-done basis against ML/DL

- Adversarial iterative incremental attacks that dig away stepwise at ML/DL
- Etc.

We can showcase the nature of each such adversarial attack and do so in the context of AI-based self-driving cars.

Adversarial Falsification Attacks

Consider the use of adversarial falsifications.

There are generally two such types: (1) false positive attacks, and (2) false-negative attacks. In the false positive attack, the emphasis is on presenting to AI a so-called negative sample that is then incorrectly classified by the ML/DL as a positive one. The jargon for this is that it is a Type I effort (this is reminiscent perhaps of your days of taking a statistics class in college). In contrast, the false-negative attack entails presenting a positive sample for which the ML/DL incorrectly classifies as a negative instance, known as a Type II error.

Suppose that we had trained an AI driving system to detect Stop signs. We used an ML/DL that we had trained beforehand with thousands of images that contained Stop signs. The idea is that we would be using video cameras on the self-driving car to collect video and images of the roadway scene surrounding the autonomous vehicle during a driving journey. As the digital imagery real-time streams into an onboard computer, the ML/DL scans the digital data to detect any indication of a nearby Stop sign. The detection of a Stop sign is obviously crucial for the AI driving system. If a Stop sign is detected by the ML/DL, this is conveyed to the AI driving system and the AI would need to ascertain a suitable means to use the driving controls to bring the self-driving car to a proper and safe stop.

Humans seem to readily be able to detect Stop signs, at least most of the time. Our human perception of such signs is keenly honed by our seemingly innate cognitive pattern matching capacities. All we need to do is learn what a Stop sign looks like and we take things from there. A toddler learns soon enough that a Stop sign is typically red in color, contains the word "STOP" in large letters, has a special rectangular shape, usually is posted adjacent to the roadway and resides at a person's height, and so on.

Imagine an evildoer that wants to make trouble for self-driving cars.

In a false positive adversarial attack, the wrongdoer would try to trick the ML/DL into computationally calculating that a Stop sign exists even when there isn't a Stop sign present. Maybe the wrongdoer puts up a red sign along a roadway that looks generally similar to a Stop sign but lacks the word "STOP" on it. A human would likely realize that this is merely a red sign and not a driving directive. The ML/DL might though calculate that the sign resembles sufficiently enough a Stop sign to the degree that the AI ought to consider the sign as in fact a Stop sign.

You might be tempted to think that this is not much of an adversarial attack and that it seems rather innocuous. Well, suppose that you are driving in a car and meanwhile a self-driving car that is ahead of you suddenly and seemingly without any basis for doing so comes to an abrupt stop (due to having misconstrued a red sign near the roadway as being a Stop sign). You might ram into that self-driving car. It could be that the AI was fooled into computationally calculating that a non-stop sign was a Stop sign, thus committing a false positive error. You get injured, the passengers in the self-driving car get injured, and perhaps even pedestrians get injured by this dreadful false-positive adversarial attack.

A false negative adversarial attack is somewhat akin to this preceding depiction though based on tricking the ML/DL into incorrectly misclassifying in the other direction, as it were. Imagine that a Stop sign is sitting next to the roadway and for all usual visual reasons seems to be a Stop sign. Humans accept that this is indeed a valid Stop.

An evildoer covers up part of the word "STOP" with some tape. Humans still realize this is a Stop sign. The ML/DL might be computationally calculating that since the word "STOP" does not seem entirely present on the sign, the sign is not ranked as a Stop sign. This is conveyed to the AI driving system. Sure enough, the AI driving system allows the self-driving car to plow ahead and completely fails to come to a stop at the Stop sign.

I hope that you can envision how dangerous this false-negative attack can be. A human-driven car coming from a cross-street might be under the assumption that the self-driving car was going to come to a proper legal stop at the Stop sign. Sadly, the two cars crash while in the middle of the intersection. People are injured or possibly killed. The evildoer has wreaked their nefarious havoc.

That briefly explains the nature of false-positive and false-negative attacks. There can be a lot more trickery involved. I mentioned the simplest case as a means of showcasing what those types of adversarial attacks consist of. For the moment, we will continue to explore how adversarial attacks work. Once I've covered those fundamentals, we will revisit the question of whether it is proper or improper to use these adversarial attacks when wishing to confront *AI For Bad*.

Adversarial Black-Box And White-Box Attacks

Recall that I opened this column by pointing out that it is wise to know as much about your adversary as you possibly can. With adversarial attacks, sometimes you might know quite a bit about how the ML/DL internally functions, while in other instances you might have little if any clues about how a particular ML/DL was devised.

In a black-box adversarial attack, the evildoer has little if any understanding of how the particular ML/DL being targeted has been set up. The cybercrook has to make some form of reasoned guess. This guess might be completely on-target. Luck favored their devious deed. Other times the guess might be wildly off-target. Luck was not on their evil side.

In a white-box adversarial attack, the evildoer has some understanding of how the particular ML/DL being targeted has been set up. This makes life a lot easier for the evildoer. They can devise an adversarial attack that they pretty much know or believe strongly will undercut the ML/DL. If you've ever wondered why sometimes an AI builder might try to hide the details of how their ML/DL has been set up, this is a reason for that secrecy (there are other valid reasons too).

Here's an example of how the black-box and white-box adversarial attack approaches come to play.

Returning to the Stop sign scenario, an evildoer is having to decide whether to try and use a false-positive or a false-negative attack against a self-driving car. If the cybercrook knows the internals of the ML/DL involved ("white-box"), they can figure out which of the two means is the better choice. Perhaps the ML/DL is well-fortified against the false-positive but unduly weak against the false-negative. Voila, the attacker would likely choose to use the false-negative for their insidious trickery.

That being said, sometimes an evildoer might not have any ready way of discerning how the ML/DL has been established ("black-box"). In that case, the cybercrook might have to make a guess at which of various adversarial attacks will be most successful. The guess could be right or the guess could be wrong. The odds are that when facing a black-box situation, the evildoer will resort to using a scattergun approach in hopes that something will do the trick for them.

Adversarial Run-Time and Training Time Attacks

The examples so far have dealt with the assumed circumstance that the self-driving car is being attacked at the time of the self-driving car being underway on the roadway. This can be characterized as doing an adversarial attack during the *run-time* of the AI ML/DL system.

An evildoer might though try to get to the AI *beforehand* prior to the ML/DL being placed into active use, doing so during the time that the ML/DL is being trained. Remember that the ML/DL presumably had to be "trained" to do whatever tasks are being undertaken.

It is conceivable that a determined wrongdoer could get access to the ML/DL when it is still being set up. If so, the evildoer can then potentially implant or shape the ML/DL to contain a particular vulnerability.

Take the example of the Stop sign. Imagine that the evildoer was able to access the ML/DL when the Stop sign detection training was being accomplished. Perhaps specially fabricated data is fed into the ML/DL. Or the ML/DL parameters are tweaked by the wrongdoer. All in all, the idea is that this might undercut how the ML/DL is going to work once it is placed into active use.

An evildoer that has done their dirty work beforehand would potentially know for sure that the AI ML/DL is vulnerable to for example a false-positive attack, or likewise vulnerable to a false negative attack. Whereas in the usual white-box approach the baddies might simply inspect the ML/DL to see if they can uncover any weaknesses, this effort to seed weaknesses is obviously a likely more strident evildoing avenue.

Complicating and worsening such matters is the possibility that the ML/DL also trains during run-time. You might want the ML/DL to adjust by itself while it is in active use. In that case, the evildoer can potentially do nefarious training infusion acts, even while the ML/DL is in the midst of being used.

Adversarial Attack Of One-Time Or Iterative Nature

Another perspective on adversarial attacks against AI consists of doing them on a one-time basis versus doing so iteratively on an incremental basis.

It could be that an evildoer repeatedly tries the Stop sign trickery and hopes that eventually, a self-driving car falls for the appalling act. Or the wrongdoer might decide that the attack should be tried just once. An issue for an attacker is that if they repeatedly do an attack, the AI being attacked might detect that such attacks are being launched and then alert someone or invoke a built-in counterattack.

Conclusion

Now that I've covered the overall nature of adversarial attacks against AI, we should revisit the latest AI Ethics twist that consists of debating whether or not those kinds of nefarious attacks are okay to be used by those seeking to take down *AI For Bad.*

Yes, you might say, of course, it is perfectly fine to do so. Use whatever means we can to curtail *AI For Bad.* The ends justify the means.

No, you might reply, it isn't suitable to employ adversarial attacks, even when used to deal with *AI For Bad.* We must resist getting into an arms race of adversarial attacks. The more that we entertain the use of them, the worse things will get. Put aside this Pandora's box and avoid the temptation that it entails. Also, keep in mind that we are potentially shooting our own foot, including that we might inadvertently use adversarial attacks against *AI For Good* that we falsely thought was *AI For Bad.*

While you mull over these hefty matters, let's end the discussion for now with some insightful quotes.

Evagrius Ponticus, a famous monk and highly influential theologian, said this about adversaries: "The further the soul advances, the greater are the adversaries against which it must contend." And, as further contemplative milieu, Tennessee Williams, the revered American playwright, noted this about adversaries: "But I think the spirit of man is a good adversary."

You be the judge and jury when it comes to deciding whether or not we are to proceed to embrace adversarial attacks as a full-fledged member of the AI Ethics club, or whether such methods should be relegated to the junk heap as something reviled and never to be used (even when employed for the pursuit of goodness and aiming to virtuously root out Unethical AI).

Welcome to the world of the vexing ethical conundrum about AI adversarial attacks.

CHAPTER 9
AI ETHICS
AND INTENTIONALLY BIASED AI

Here's an old line that I'm sure you've heard before.

It takes one to know one.

You might not realize that this is an expression that can be traced to the early 1900s and was usually invoked when referring to wrongdoers (other variations of the catchphrase go back further such as to the 1600s). An example of how this utterance might be used entails the notion that if you wish to catch a thief then you need to use a thief to do so. This showcases the assertion that it takes one to know one. Many movies and TV shows have capitalized on this handy bit of sage wisdom, often portraying that the only viable means to nab a crook entailed hiring an equally corrupt crook to pursue the wrongdoer.

Shifting gears, some might leverage this same logic to argue that a suitable way to discern whether someone is embodying undue biases and discriminatory beliefs would be to find someone that already harbors such tendencies. Presumably, a person already filled with biases is going to be able to more readily sense that this other human is likewise filled to the brim with toxicity. Again, it takes one to know one is the avowed mantra.

Your initial reaction to the possibility of using a biased person to suss out another biased person might be one of skepticism and disbelief. Can't we figure out whether someone holds untoward biases by merely examining them and not having to resort to finding someone else of a like nature?

It would seem oddish to purposely seek to discover someone that is biased in order to uncover others that are also toxically biased.

I guess it partially depends on whether you are willing to accept the presumptive refrain that it takes one to know one. Note that this does not suggest that the only way to catch a thief requires that you exclusively and always make use of a thief. You could reasonably seem to argue that this is merely an added path that can be given due consideration. Maybe sometimes you are willing to entertain the possibility of using a thief to catch a thief, while other circumstances might make this an unfathomable tactic.

Use the right tool for the right setting, as they say.

Now that I've laid out those fundamentals, we can proceed into the perhaps unnerving and ostensibly shocking part of this tale.

Are you ready?

The field of AI is actively pursuing the same precept that it sometimes takes one to know one, particularly in the case of trying to ferret out AI that is biased or acting in a discriminatory manner. Yes, the mind-bending idea is that we might purposely want to devise AI that is fully and unabashedly biased and discriminatory, doing so in order to use this as a means to discover and uncover other AI that has that same semblance of toxicity. As you'll see in a moment, there are a variety of vexing AI Ethics issues underlying the matter.

I guess you could express this use of toxic AI to go after other toxic AI as the proverbial fighting fire-with-fire conception (we can invoke plenty of euphemisms and illustrative metaphors to depict this situation). Or, as already emphasized, we might parsimoniously refer to the assertion that it takes one to know one.

The overarching concept is that rather than only trying to figure out whether a given AI system contains undue biases by using conventional methods, maybe we should seek to employ less conventional means too.

One such unconventional means would be to devise AI that contains all the worst of biases and societally unacceptable toxicities and then use this AI to aid in routing out other AI that has those same propensities of badness.

When you give this a quick thought, it certainly appears to be perfectly sensible. We could aim to build AI that is toxic to the max. This toxic AI is then used to ferret out other AI that also has toxicity. For the then revealed "bad" AI, we can deal with it by either undoing the toxicity, ditching the AI entirely or imprisoning the AI, or do whatever else seems applicable to do.

A counterargument is that we ought to have our heads examined that we are intentionally and willingly devising AI that is toxic and filled with biases. This is the last thing we ought to ever consider, some would exhort. Focus on making AI consisting wholly of goodness. Do not focus on devising AI that has the evils and dregs of undue biases. The very notion of such a pursuit seems repulsive to some.

There are more qualms about this controversial quest.

Maybe a mission of devising toxic AI will merely embolden those that wish to craft AI that is able to undercut society. It is as though we are saying that crafting AI that has inappropriate and unsavory biases is perfectly fine. No worries, no hesitations. Seek to devise toxic AI to your heart's content, we are loudly conveying out to AI builders all across the globe. It is (wink-wink) all in the name of goodness.

Furthermore, suppose this toxic AI kind of catches on. It could be that the AI is used and reused by lots of other AI builders. Eventually, the toxic AI gets hidden within all manner of AI systems. An analogy might be made to devising a human-undermining virus that escapes from a presumably sealed lab. The next thing you know, the darned thing is everywhere and we have wiped ourselves out.

Wait for a second, the counter to those counterarguments goes, you are running amok with all kinds of crazy and unsupported suppositions. Take a deep breath. Calm yourself.

We can safely make AI that is toxic and keep it confined. We can use the toxic AI to find and aid in reducing the increasing prevalence of AI that unfortunately does have undue biases. Any other of these preposterously wild and unsubstantiated snowballing exclamations are purely knee-jerk reactions and regrettably foolish and outrightly foolhardy. Do not try to throw out the baby with the bathwater, you are forewarned.

Think of it this way, the proponents contend. The proper building and use of toxic AI for purposes of research, assessment, and acting like a detective to uncover other societally offensive AI is a worthy approach and ought to get its fair shake at being pursued. Put aside your rash reactions. Come down to earth and look at this soberly. Our eye is on the prize, namely exposing and undoing the glut of biased-based AI systems and making sure that as a society we do not become overrun with toxic AI.

Period. Full stop.

There are various keystone ways to delve into this notion of utilizing toxic or biased AI for beneficial purposes, including:

- Setup datasets that intentionally contain biased and altogether toxic data that can be used for training AI regarding what not to do and/or what to watch for
- Use such datasets to train Machine Learning (ML) and Deep Learning (DL) models about detecting biases and figuring out computational patterns entailing societal toxicity
- Apply the toxicity trained ML/DL toward other AI to ascertain whether the targeted AI is potentially biased and toxic
- Make available toxicity trained ML/DL to showcase to AI builders what to watch out for so they can readily inspect models to see how algorithmically imbued biases arise
- Exemplify the dangers of toxic AI as part of AI Ethics and Ethical AI awareness all told via this problem-child bad-to-the-bone AI series of exemplars
- Other

Before getting into the meat of those several paths, let's establish some additional foundational particulars.

You might be vaguely aware that one of the loudest voices these days in the AI field and even outside the field of AI consists of clamoring for a greater semblance of Ethical AI. Let's take a look at what it means to refer to AI Ethics and Ethical AI. On top of that, we can set the stage by exploring what I mean when I speak of Machine Learning and Deep Learning.

One particular segment or portion of AI Ethics that has been getting a lot of media attention consists of AI that exhibits untoward biases and inequities. You might be aware that when the latest era of AI got underway there was a huge burst of enthusiasm for what some now call *AI For Good.* Unfortunately, on the heels of that gushing excitement, we began to witness *AI For Bad.* For example, various AI-based facial recognition systems have been revealed as containing racial biases and gender biases.

Efforts to fight back against *AI For Bad* are actively underway. Besides vociferous *legal* pursuits of reining in the wrongdoing, there is also a substantive push toward embracing AI Ethics to righten the AI vileness. The notion is that we ought to adopt and endorse key Ethical AI principles for the development and fielding of AI doing so to undercut the *AI For Bad* and simultaneously heralding and promoting the preferable *AI For Good.*

What else can be done about all of this?

Let's return to the earlier posited list of how to try and cope with AI biases or toxic AI by using a somewhat unconventional "it takes one to know one" approach. Recall that the list consisted of these essential points:

- Setup datasets that intentionally contain biased and altogether toxic data that can be used for training AI regarding what not to do and/or what to watch for
- Use such datasets to train Machine Learning (ML) and Deep Learning (DL) models about detecting biases and figuring out computational patterns entailing societal toxicity
- Apply the toxicity trained ML/DL toward other AI to ascertain whether the targeted AI is potentially biased and toxic

- Make available toxicity trained ML/DL to showcase to AI builders what to watch out for so they can readily inspect models to see how algorithmically imbued biases arise
- Exemplify the dangers of toxic AI as part of AI Ethics and Ethical AI awareness all told via this problem-child bad-to-the-bone series of AI exemplars
- Other

We shall take a close-up look at the first of those salient points.

Setting Up Datasets Of Toxic Data

An insightful example of trying to establish datasets that contain unsavory societal biases is the CivilComments dataset of the WILDS curated collection.

First, some quick background.

WILDS is an open-source collection of datasets that can be used for training ML/DL. The primary stated purpose for WILDS is that it allows AI developers to have ready access to data that represents *distribution shifts* in various specific domains. Some of the domains currently available encompass areas such as animal species, tumors in living tissues, wheat head density, and other domains such as the CivilComments that I'll be describing momentarily.

Dealing with distribution shifts is a crucial part of properly crafting AI ML/DL systems. Here's the deal. Sometimes the data you use for training turns out to be quite different from the testing or "in the wild" data and thus your presumably trained ML/DL is adrift of what the real world is going to be like. Astute AI builders should be training their ML/DL to cope with such distribution shifts. This ought to be done upfront and not somehow be a surprise that later on requires a revamping of the ML/DL per se.

As explained in the paper that introduced WILDS:

"Distribution shifts -- where the training distribution differs from the test distribution -- can substantially degrade the accuracy of machine learning (ML) systems deployed in the wild. Despite their ubiquity in the real-world deployments, these distribution shifts are under-represented in the datasets widely used in the ML community today. To address this gap, we present WILDS, a curated benchmark of 10 datasets reflecting a diverse range of distribution shifts that naturally arise in real-world applications, such as shifts across hospitals for tumor identification; across camera traps for wildlife monitoring; and across time and location in satellite imaging and poverty mapping" (in the paper entitled "WILDS: A Benchmark of in-the-Wild Distribution Shifts" by Pang Wei Koh, Shiori Sagawa, Henrik Marklund, Sang Xie, Marvin Zhang, Ashay Balsubramani, Weihua Hu, and others).

The number of such WILDS datasets continues to increase and the nature of the datasets is generally being enhanced to bolster the value of using the data for ML/DL training.

The CivilComments dataset is described this way: "Automatic review of user-generated text—e.g., detecting toxic comments—is an important tool for moderating the sheer volume of text written on the Internet. Unfortunately, prior work has shown that such toxicity classifiers pick up on biases in the training data and spuriously associate toxicity with the mention of certain demographics (Park et al., 2018; Dixon et al., 2018). These types of spurious correlations can significantly degrade model performance on particular subpopulations (Sagawa et al.,2020). We study this issue through a modified variant of the CivilComments dataset (Borkan et al.,2019b)" (as posted on the WILDS website).

Consider the nuances of untoward online postings.

You've undoubtedly encountered toxic comments when using nearly any kind of social media. It would seem nearly impossible for you to magically avoid seeing the acrid and abysmal content that seems to be pervasive these days. Sometimes the vulgar material is subtle and perhaps you have to read between the lines to get the gist of the biased or discriminatory tone or meaning.

In other instances, the words are blatantly toxic and you do not need a microscope or a special decoder ring to figure out what the passages entail.

CivilComments is a dataset that was put together to try and devise AI ML/DL that can computationally detect toxic content. Here's what the researchers underlying the effort focused on: "Unintended bias in Machine Learning can manifest as systemic differences in performance for different demographic groups, potentially compounding existing challenges to fairness in society at large. In this paper, we introduce a suite of threshold-agnostic metrics that provide a nuanced view of this unintended bias, by considering the various ways that a classifier's score distribution can vary across designated groups. We also introduce a large new test set of online comments with crowd-sourced annotations for identity references. We use this to show how our metrics can be used to find new and potentially subtle unintended bias in existing public models" (in a paper entitled "Nuanced Metrics For Measuring Unintended Bias With Real Data for Test Classification" by Daniel Borkan, Lucas Dixon, Jeffrey Sorensen, Nithum Thain, Lucy Vasserman).

If you give this matter some broad contemplative thinking, you might begin to wonder how in the world can you discern what is a toxic comment versus what is not a toxic comment. Humans can radically differ as to what they construe as outright toxic wording. One person might be outraged at a particular online remark or comment that is posted on social media, while someone else might not be stirred at all. An argument is often made that the notion of toxic commentary is a wholly vague precept. It is like art, whereby art is customarily said to be understood only in the eye of the beholder, and likewise, biased or toxic remarks are only in the eye of the beholder too.

Balderdash, some retort. Anyone of a reasonable mind can suss out whether an online remark is toxic or not. You do not need to be a rocket scientist to realize when some posted caustic insult is filled with biases and hatred.

Of course, societal mores shift and change over periods of time. What might not have been perceived as offensive a while ago can be seen as abhorrently wrong today. On top of that, things said years ago that were once seen as unduly biased might be reinterpreted in light of changes in meanings. Meanwhile, others assert that toxic commentary is always toxic, no matter when it was initially promulgated. It could be contended that toxicity is not relative but instead is absolute.

The matter of trying to establish what is toxic can nonetheless be quite a difficult conundrum. We can double down on this troublesome matter as to trying to devise algorithms or AI that can ascertain which is which. If humans have a difficult time making such assessments, programming a computer is likely equally or more so problematic, some say.

One approach to setting up datasets that contain toxic content involves using a crowdsourcing method to rate or assess the contents, ergo providing a human-based means of determining what is viewed as untoward and including the labeling within the dataset itself. An AI ML/DL might then inspect the data and the associated labeling that has been indicated by human raters. This in turn can potentially serve as a means of computationally finding underlying mathematical patterns. Voila, the ML/DL then might be able to anticipate or computationally assess whether a given comment is likely to be toxic or not.

As mentioned in the cited paper on nuanced metrics: "This labeling asks raters to rate the toxicity of a comment, selecting from 'Very Toxic', 'Toxic', 'Hard to Say', and 'Not Toxic'. Raters were also asked about several subtypes of toxicity, although these labels were not used for the analysis in this work. Using these rating techniques we created a dataset of 1.8 million comments, sourced from online comment forums, containing labels for toxicity and identity. While all of the comments were labeled for toxicity, and a subset of 450,000 comments was labeled for identity. Some comments labeled for identity were preselected using models built from previous iterations of identity labeling to ensure that crowd raters would see identity content frequently" (in the cited paper by Daniel Borkan, Lucas Dixon, Jeffrey Sorensen, Nithum Thain, Lucy Vasserman).

Another example of aiming to have datasets that contain illustrative toxic content involves efforts to train AI-based Natural Language Processing (NLP) conversational interactive systems. You've probably interacted with NLP systems such as Alexa and Siri.

A recent study sought to use nine categories of social bias that were generally based on the EEOC (Equal Employment Opportunities Commission) list of protected demographic characteristics, including age, gender, nationality, physical appearance, race or ethnicity, religion, disability status, sexual orientation, and socio-economic status. According to the researchers: "It is well documented that NLP models learn social biases, but little work has been done on how these biases manifest in model outputs for applied tasks like question answering (QA). We introduce the Bias Benchmark for QA (BBQ), a dataset of question sets constructed by the authors that highlight attested social biases against people belonging to protected classes along nine social dimensions relevant for U.S. English-speaking contexts" (in a paper entitled "BBQ: A Hand-Built Benchmark For Question Answering" by Alicia Parrish, Angelica Chen, Nikita Nangia, Vishakh Padmakumar, Jason Phang, Jana Thompson, Phu Mon Htut, Samuel R. Bowman).

The setting up of datasets that intentionally contain biased and altogether toxic data is a rising trend in AI and is especially stoked by the advent of AI Ethics and the desire to produce Ethical AI. Those datasets can be used to train Machine Learning (ML) and Deep Learning (DL) models for detecting biases and figuring out computational patterns entailing societal toxicity. In turn, the toxicity trained ML/DL can be judiciously aimed at other AI to ascertain whether the targeted AI is potentially biased and toxic.

Furthermore, the available toxicity-trained ML/DL systems can be used to showcase to AI builders what to watch out for so they can readily inspect models to see how algorithmically imbued biases arise. Overall, these efforts are able to exemplify the dangers of toxic AI as part of AI Ethics and Ethical AI awareness all-told.

At this juncture of this weighty discussion, I'd bet that you are desirous of some further illustrative examples that might showcase this topic. There is a special and assuredly popular set of examples that are close to my heart. You see, in my capacity as an expert on AI including the ethical and legal ramifications, I am frequently asked to identify realistic examples that showcase AI Ethics dilemmas so that the somewhat theoretical nature of the topic can be more readily grasped. One of the most evocative areas that vividly presents this ethical AI quandary is the advent of AI-based true self-driving cars. This will serve as a handy use case or exemplar for ample discussion on the topic.

Here's then a noteworthy question that is worth contemplating: *Does the advent of AI-based true self-driving cars illuminate anything about the utility of having datasets to devise toxic AI, and if so, what does this showcase?*

There are numerous potential and someday likely to be realized AI-infused biases that are going to confront the emergence of autonomous vehicles and self-driving cars. We are still in the early stages of self-driving car rollouts. Until the adoption reaches a sufficient scale and visibility, much of the toxic AI facets that I've been predicting will ultimately occur are not yet readily apparent and have not yet garnered widespread public attention.

Consider a seemingly straightforward driving-related matter that at first might seem entirely innocuous. Specifically, let's examine how to properly determine whether to stop for awaiting "wayward" pedestrians that do not have the right-of-way to cross a street.

You've undoubtedly been driving and encountered pedestrians that were waiting to cross the street and yet they did not have the right-of-way to do so. This meant that you had discretion as to whether to stop and let them cross. You could proceed without letting them cross and still be fully within the legal driving rules of doing so.

Studies of how human drivers decide on stopping or not stopping for such pedestrians have suggested that sometimes the human drivers make the choice based on untoward biases.

A human driver might eye the pedestrian and choose to not stop, even though they would have stopped had the pedestrian had a different appearance, such as based on race or gender.

How will AI driving systems be programmed to make that same kind of stop-or-go decision?

You could proclaim that all AI driving systems should be programmed to always stop for any waiting pedestrians. This greatly simplifies the matter. There really isn't any knotty decision to be made. If a pedestrian is waiting to cross, regardless of whether they have the right-of-way or not, ensure that the AI self-driving car comes to a stop so that the pedestrian can cross.

Easy-peasy.

Life is never that easy, it seems. Imagine that all self-driving cars abide by this rule. Pedestrians would inevitably realize that the AI driving systems are, shall we say, pushovers. Any and all pedestrians that want to cross the street will willy-nilly do so, whenever they wish and wherever they are.

Suppose a self-driving car is coming down a fast street at the posted speed limit of 45 miles per hour. A pedestrian "knows" that the AI will bring the self-driving car to a stop. So, the pedestrian darts into the street. Unfortunately, physics wins out over AI. The AI driving system will try to bring the self-driving car to a halt, but the momentum of the autonomous vehicle is going to carry the multi-ton contraption forward and ram into the wayward pedestrian. The result is either injurious or produces a fatality.

Pedestrians do not usually try this type of behavior when there is a human driver at the wheel. Sure, in some locales there is an eyeball war that takes place. A pedestrian eyeballs a driver. The driver eyeballs the pedestrian. Depending upon the circumstance, the driver might come to a stop or the driver might assert their claim to the roadway and ostensibly dare the pedestrian to try and disrupt their path.

We presumably do not want AI to get into a similar eyeball war, which also is a bit challenging anyway since there isn't a person or robot sitting at the wheel of the self-driving car (I've discussed the future possibility of robots that drive). Yet we also cannot allow pedestrians to always call the shots. The outcome could be disastrous for all concerned.

You might then be tempted to flip to the other side of this coin and declare that the AI driving system should never stop in such circumstances. In other words, if a pedestrian does not have a proper right of way to cross the street, the AI should always assume that the self-driving car ought to proceed unabated. Tough luck to those pedestrians.

Such a strict and simplistic rule is not going to be well-accepted by the public at large. People are people and they won't like being completely shut out of being able to cross the street, despite that they are legally lacking a right-of-way to do so in various settings. You could easily anticipate a sizable uproar from the public and possibly see a backlash occur against the continued adoption of self-driving cars.

Darned if we do, and darned if we don't.

I hope this has led you to the reasoned alternative that the AI needs to be programmed with a semblance of decision-making about how to deal with this driving problem. A hard-and-fast rule to never stop is untenable, and likewise, a hard-and-fast rule to always stop is untenable too. The AI has to be devised with some algorithmic decision-making or ADM to deal with the matter.

You could try using a dataset coupled with an ML/DL approach.

Here's how the AI developers might decide to program this task. They collect data from video cameras that are placed all around a particular city where the self-driving car is going to be used within. The data showcases when human drivers opt to stop for pedestrians that do not have the right-of-way. It is all collected into a dataset. By using Machine Learning and Deep Learning, the data is modeled computationally.

The AI driving system then uses this model to decide when to stop or not stop.

Generally, the idea is that whatever the local custom consists of, this is how the AI is going direct the self-driving car. Problem solved!

But, is it truly solved?

Recall that I had already pointed out that there are research studies showcasing that human drivers can be biased in their choices of when to stop for pedestrians. The collected data about a particular city is presumably going to contain those biases. An AI ML/DL based on that data will then likely model and reflect those same biases. The AI driving system will merely carry out the same existent biases.

To try and contend with the issue, we could put together a dataset that in fact has such biases. We either find such a dataset and then label the biases, or we synthetically create a dataset to aid in illustrating the matter.

All of the earlier identified steps would be undertaken, including:

- Setup a dataset that intentionally contains this particular bias
- Use the dataset to train Machine Learning (ML) and Deep Learning (DL) models about detecting this specific bias
- Apply the bias-trained ML/DL toward other AI to ascertain whether the targeted AI is potentially biased in a likewise manner
- Make available the bias-trained ML/DL to showcase to AI builders what to watch out for so they can readily inspect their models to see how algorithmically imbued biases arise
- Exemplify the dangers of biased AI as part of AI Ethics and Ethical AI awareness via this added specific example
- Other

Conclusion

Let's revisit the opening line.

It takes one to know one.

Some interpret that this incredibly prevalent saying implies that when it comes to ferreting out toxic AI, we should be giving due credence to building and using toxic AI toward discovering and dealing with other toxic AI. Bottom line: Sometimes it takes a thief to catch another thief.

A voiced concern is that maybe we are going out of our way to start making thieves. Do we want to devise AI that is toxic? Doesn't that seem like a crazy idea? Some vehemently argue that we should ban all toxic AI, including such AI that was knowingly built even if purportedly for a heroic or gallant *AI For Good* purpose.

Squelch toxic AI in whatever clever or insidious guise that it might arise.

One final twist on this topic for now. We generally assume that this famous line has to do with people or things that do bad or sour acts. That's how we land on the notion of it takes a thief to catch a thief. Maybe we should turn this saying on its head and make it more of a happy face than a sad face.

Here's how.

If we want AI that is unbiased and non-toxic, it might be conceivable that it takes one to know one. Perhaps it takes the greatest and best to recognize and beget further greatness and goodness. In this variant of the sage wisdom, we keep our gaze on the happy face and aim to concentrate on devising *AI For Good.*

That would be a more upbeat and satisfyingly cheerful viewpoint on it takes one to know one, if you know what I mean.

CHAPTER 10
AI ETHICS
AND MACHINE LEARNING MYOPIA

Some say this town isn't big enough for both of them.

What am I referring to?

Well, it could be that I am invoking an ever-popular and longstanding memorable line from an old-time film about two sparring cowpokes. Yes, in the now richly classic cowboy movie *The Western Code,* which was released in 1932, an ex-lawman hero rides into town and confronts the local ruffian. A head-to-head confrontation ensues in which one harshly tells the other to get out of town.

Here's the dialogue that you surely are familiar with since it inevitably historically went viral (of a sort) and has variously been used and revitalized in countless plots since then: "I'm getting tired of your meddling. This town ain't big enough for the both of us and I'm going to give you 24 hours to get out. If I see you in Carabinas by this time tomorrow, it's you or me!" (quoted from the movie *The Western Code*).

Nearly identical lines of such hearty dialogue can be readily subsequently found in all kinds of movies and TV shows, including ones about the Wild West, ones about dueling detectives, dueling lawyers, dueling spies, and so on. I openly admit though that I am not particularly referring to the original line and instead revamping yet another advantageous incarnation of it, doing so to succinctly describe an ongoing and potentially enduring confrontation taking place in the burgeoning field of Artificial Intelligence (AI).

You see, the AI field is mired in a somewhat subtle and yet increasingly vocal and acrimonious battle raging between the *sub-symbolics* versus the *symbolics*. One camp is telling the other camp to get out of town. A stare-down is taking place. Guns are drawn. The townspeople are cowering and waiting to see what will happen.

This heady situation of today's AI could also be likened to the infamous family spats between the Hatfields and the McCoys, those two legendary families in the West Virginia and Kentucky areas that fiercely feuded in the late 1800s. But in lieu of Hatfield and McCoy going toe-to-toe, we have the modern-day AI-focused *sub-symbolics* camp and the still-in-there AI *symbolics* family rancorously battling each other.

Here's how this in-house AI feuding came to be.

And, I might add, we need to give this crucial attention since it could determine the future of AI and perhaps accordingly the future of society if you assume that AI is indeed a budding transformative force that will alter what we do and the world that we live in. This divisive behind-the-scenes debate comes filled with AI Ethics and Ethical AI ramifications.

Find a cozy spot to sit down and enjoy the tale of joy and woe, as it were.

To begin with, you might be scratching your head that you've seemingly not ever heard of the AI sub-symbolics and nor recognize the moniker of saying that there are AI symbolics either. Don't feel disheartened or embarrassed since those are not the usual everyday popularized catchphrases (it is the semi-secret jargon used by AI insiders).

I would be willing to bet my treasured gold coin that you've undoubtedly heard of Machine Learning (ML) and Deep Learning (DL), which for sake of discussion is the frontman for AI sub-symbolics. The use of ML/DL is the talk of the town. Headlines that blare out the latest in AI are bound to toss around the Machine Learning or Deep Learning phrasing and catch your attention.

The wording does indeed roll off the tongue.

By and large, you can construe the stoutest devotees of ML/DL as being card-carrying members of the AI sub-symbolics camp. The basis for being labeled as sub-symbolic is that the crux of the ML/DL approach entails trying to attain a semblance of computationally modeled "intelligent" behavior by using relatively arcane mathematical formulations.

Qualms about this sub-symbolic approach include the difficulty of being able to explain how the ML/DL has reached some choice or made a decision of one kind or another. The whole shebang can be so mathematically dense and complex that you are not going to easily discover what led to a specific outcome. Instead, there is a data-infused and computed morass that you have to hope did the right thing and calculated out an appropriate answer. This lack of interpretability has given rise to a subfield of AI known as Explainable AI, typically abbreviated as XAI, and for which the aim is to craft AI that can somewhat explain itself.

I want to share with you additional background about the nature of ML/DL but before I do so, it might be helpful for me to briefly indicate what the contrasting AI symbolics camp portends. This will give you a comparative basis for why this matter has become a Hatfield-McCoy feud or a classic "get out of town" rivalry.

Shifting gears, turn your eye toward the symbolic AI camp.

The symbolics camp is undoubtedly known to any of you that are aware of AI that arose in the 1980s and 1990s. This was the earlier heyday of AI that touted the use of knowledge-based systems (KBS) or sometimes anointed as expert systems (ES). The gist was that AI systems were being devised based on explicitly identifying the various rules or logic that underlie presumed "intelligent" behavior. You would work with a human expert in say medicine or finance, ferret out what kinds of logical rules they use, and establish a so-called computer-based knowledge base that kind of replicated those articulated cognitive rules.

These were considered rules-based systems (RBS) or equivalently known as KBS or ES.

Eventually, the rules-based approach and the symbolics camp fell into disfavor. The prevailing opinion was that we could only elucidate a fraction of the rules that really underlie knowledge. In addition, a confounding factor was the use of common-sense knowledge. It seemed that to get to use expert knowledge you often would require a basis or foundation that contained common-sense knowledge, such as knowing that birds fly, the sky is blue, and other normal everyday awareness. We still to this day have not successfully cracked the code on how to computationally embody common sense, though the pursuit stridently continues.

You might also be aware that when the AI mania of the late 1990s began to recede, the AI field was somewhat set aside and no longer given the same outsized attention it once had. This was the era when the AI field went into a bit of a slump, notoriously now said to be the dour AI Winter. This wintery naming was catchy because AI ostensibly went into hibernation and was no longer stomping around like Godzilla.

The hoped-for AI that was to be based on a symbolic approach appeared to have been a bust. Sadness ensued. Wintertime was solemn and left many unsure of what the AI field would do next. Symbolics avenue got a bad reputation as being a bit of a dead-end. No sense in putting your eggs in that basket.

Meanwhile, the eventual advent of Machine Learning and Deep Learning was percolating behind the scenes. Outsiders seem to think that ML/DL just magically appeared out of nowhere. You might compare this notion to those massively popular movie stars that you sometimes think had an overnight success and had sprung out of the blue. Most of them were toiling away for years in bit roles and taking on any acting engagements that they could.

The same case can be made for ML/DL. An effort was going toward advancing ML/DL. It wasn't until more modern times that the needed computational resources became available. This coincided to a great extent with the emergence of cloud computing. In addition, lots of data is typically needed for ML/DL, for which large-scale databases and other data lakes and data warehouses were being put together and made available.

A type of grand convergence of improvements in ML/DL, along with readily available datasets, and combined with less costly computing that could be accessed and shared remotely were all coming together to aid in bolstering the movement toward adopting and using ML/DL. The new kid on the block had been years in the making.

Here are some key takeaways from this brief history lesson about the trials and tribulations of the AI field:

- There is little doubt that today's AI is abundantly focused on Machine Learning and Deep Learning, thus knowingly or unknowingly embracing the AI *sub-symbolics* camp.

- There is scant doubt that today's AI foregoes even a modicum of attention toward the AI *symbolics* camp, whereby the use of KBS, ES, and RBS or similar tech are all relegated to the backroom and rarely given any room to breathe. Some blatantly ignore the symbolics, while others express outright disdain for it.

We are now poised to explore the question of who is supposed to get out of town.

There are outspoken proponents of the sub-symbolic approach that go out of their way to insist that the sub-symbolic avenue is the only way to ultimately attain an aspired fully achieved AI that would presumably slide into sentience. In that insistent stance, they outrightly denigrate the symbolic camp. The point seems to be that all other styles or approaches of AI ought to bow down to the sub-symbolics approach and toss in the towel. Take a knee. Do not waste precious resources on the "losing" side, and instead jump on the winning side.

As an aside, I am not suggesting that everyone is saying this, and only highlighting what some of the more vocal and staunchly adherent ML/DL proponents are stating or implying. If you are fully into the sub-symbolics camp and yet are not taking this rather adamant and oppositional stance, your willingness of openness is well-acknowledged.

But back to those that are staking out their turf. It is one thing to try and showcase your turf, while it is another to urge that all others give up their turf too. Going that extra mile of pushing out the other homesteaders would seem unduly overbearing. In essence, some of the sub-symbolics proponents seem to believe that all the air in the room should rightfully and exclusively be wholly reserved for the ML/DL devotees. You either have a cattle ranch or you don't. No agricultural farming is allowed.

Borrowing from the Old West, this town ain't big enough for the both of them (i.e., the sub-symbolics and the symbolics), and furthermore, the sub-symbolics radical adherents are going to give you symbolics a tightly bounded 24 hours to get out of town (so exhorts sub-symbolics of that mindset).

We don't know for sure what the 24 hours consists of, which is obviously metaphorically being used and not of a literal nature. One supposes that some sub-symbolics would want the 24 hours deadline to have already passed and ergo that symbolics should already have dropped their gear and left town, riding as far away and as fast as they can. Disappearing beyond the horizon and never to be seen again. The sun has set on the symbolics.

Others might be more "reasonable" and suggest that the symbolics can take a few months or possibly even a couple of years to close the books. Start now though by gradually putting aside those grant requests. Pack up the labs. No need to continue publishing since it is hopeless anyway. All told, be getting into a position of being able to turn out the lights and go do something else, as long as it isn't immersed in that symbolic "malarky" that has nothing other than disappointment and futility.

Wow, you can imagine how those are fighting words.

Should we go ahead and opt to put all our eggs into the AI sub-symbolic basket?

This raises thorny AI Ethics considerations and prompts related questions about the present and future of AI.

For example, you might be thinking this is merely infighting within the field of AI and does not rise to a level of importance that others ought to weigh in. Let the AI insiders go toe-to-toe with the other AI insiders. They need to figure out what is right and what is possibly misguided. No need and no basis for anyone else to intervene.

The challenge of that perspective is that if you believe that AI is going to profoundly change society and our lives, the notion of letting AI insiders work things out might not produce the results that society as a whole would cherish. Each day we are witnessing a tsunami of new AI-based applications that are being avidly shoveled out into society. It would seem rather narrowminded to simply allow the AI insiders to ostensibly make such a likely monumental and consequential choice on their own accord.

It takes a village to craft and suitably field AI.

Before getting into the meat of those several paths, let's establish some additional foundational particulars.

You might be vaguely aware that one of the loudest voices these days in the AI field and even outside the field of AI consists of clamoring for a greater semblance of Ethical AI. Let's take a look at what it means to refer to AI Ethics and Ethical AI. On top of that, we can set the stage further by exploring what I mean when I speak of Machine Learning and Deep Learning.

One particular segment or portion of AI Ethics that has been getting a lot of media attention consists of AI that exhibits untoward biases and inequities.

You might be aware that when the latest era of AI got underway there was a huge burst of enthusiasm for what some now call *AI For Good.* Unfortunately, on the heels of that gushing excitement, we began to witness *AI For Bad.* For example, various AI-based facial recognition systems have been revealed as containing racial biases and gender biases.

Let's now return to the debate about who is considered in town, and likewise who ought to be in town or ought to not be in town.

The glory right now is clearly shining on the AI sub-symbolics camp and especially the expanding use of Machine Learning and Deep Learning. One worry is that even aspects such as our approach to AI Ethics are being subliminally warped by the preoccupation with ML/DL. In essence, some AI Ethics methods concentrate only on AI that is composed of the ML/DL facilities. They don't seem to acknowledge that a likewise set of AI Ethics methods also needs to be established for the AI symbolics camp. It is as though the ML/DL approach is the only game in town.

Fortunately, the essence of most AI Ethics precepts is broad enough to apply to both camps. Nonetheless, there is usually a swaying of showing how to implement Ethical AI in ML/DL more so than in more AI symbolic means. You can point out that this makes sense since the preponderance of AI is being done in ML/DL these days, thus you get more bang for the buck in terms of AI Ethics tuned to the hotter approach.

Does all of this suggest that the only way forward is via the AI sub-symbolics path?

For those that believe we will eventually attain sentient AI, or perhaps Artificial General Intelligence (AGI), one line of thinking is that it will be exclusively via *scaling up* with our existing sub-symbolics ML/DL efforts. Throw more and more computing power into the mix. Make those computational pattern matching models massive in size. Go big, as they say, and don't look back.

Those same proponents might also make a seemingly logical assertion that any attention and use of our limited AI development resources toward other avenues of AI is not only misguided but altogether detrimental to wanting to arrive at sentient AI or AGI. The claim is that the symbolic camp is inadvertently draining energies that properly should be going to the sub-symbolic realm. In this viewpoint, the AI symbolics family is both misaimed and worse still diluting and distracting from AI sub-symbolics.

In short, per this dogmatic perspective, AI symbolics needs to get out of town (or, alternatively, drop the symbolics "charade" and embrace the true path of the AI sub-symbolics). There is only room for one cowpoke in these hereabout parts, namely the rough and ready AI sub-symbolics.

Researcher Gary Marcus describes the rise of what is referred to as "Alt Intelligence" in his new *substack* blog: "*Alt Intelligence* isn't about building machines that solve problems in ways that have to do with human intelligence. It's about using massive amounts of data – often derived from human behavior – as a substitute for intelligence. Right now, the predominant strand of work within Alt Intelligence is the idea of scaling. The notion that the bigger the system, the closer we come to true intelligence, maybe even consciousness" (posting of May 14, 2022, entitled "The New Science Of Alt Intelligence").

All of this could be quite tempting. If indeed the AI sub-symbolics avenue is the right and only path, it would be indubitably sensible to have everyone jump into the water and be swimming together toward the AI aspirational goal. We should seemingly support the winning horse and not spend time on those areas of AI that apparently will hold us back or slow down the best path.

Are we or should we make that kind of a wildcard bet?

Suppose all the AI symbolics agree without hesitation to join the ranks of the AI sub-symbolics. No more AI symbolic efforts exist. All of that AI symbolics-oriented technology, research, methods, and the rest of the kit and kaboodle are packed into boxes and allowed to gather dust.

If the guess was right that AI sub-symbolics was the chosen one, okay, we made a great choice, though perhaps lucky it be. Sometimes you do win the lottery.

If the guess was wrong and we hit some limitations of AI sub-symbolics that perhaps we didn't see coming, the question will be whether we shot our own foot by having stopped efforts on the AI symbolics angle. Sure, we could begrudgingly then say that we should restart on the AI symbolics front, but this might be a lot harder than it seems. Those that once were at the forefront of AI symbolics might no longer be available or might find that doing a reboot is arduous and we have actually fallen behind rather than merely being perfectly waiting in limbo.

In fact, some strident proponents of AI symbolics argue that AI sub-symbolics are definitely going to hit a gigantic roadblock. AI symbolics will be the only sufficient means of getting past that hurdle. Yet if AI symbolics has been battered and treated atrociously all that time, the chances of AI symbolics being able to expediently swing to the rescue will be grievously hampered. Putting all your eggs into the wrong basket can have adverse consequences.

You don't find many in the AI symbolics camp that are urging the AI sub-symbolics to leave town.

I mention this because you might naturally assume that what is good for the goose is good for the gander. When the AI sub-symbolics opt to talk up sub-symbolics and simultaneously talk down the AI symbolics, it would be a nearly irresistible urge to have the AI symbolics camp talk up symbolics and trounce the AI sub-symbolics family. There isn't much of that going around. Remarkedly so, especially in comparison to the bashing being meted out by some in the AI sub-symbolics camp upon the heads and careers of the AI symbolics followers.

Into this mix comes the proverbial middle ground or mashup that is being referred to as ne*uro-symbolic AI* or simply *hybrid AI*.

Here's the deal.

We could encourage both cowpokes to live in this same town and possibly even get them to work together. They don't have to be on widely separated sides of the territorial landscape. They don't need to warily eye each other and anxiously have their trusty holstered revolver at the ready. Instead, they could (heaven forbid) mutually respect each other and try to dovetail together to attain sentient AI or AGI.

When you bring together the AI sub-symbolics camp and the AI symbolics camp you get yourself a mashup that is jointly sub-symbolics and symbolics or to be equally fair it is jointly symbolics and sub-symbolics. The easiest catchphrase is to call this *neuro-symbolic AI*, meaning a combining of the artificial neural network (ANN) underpinnings within Deep Learning in conjunction with the symbolic AI. But since neuro-symbolic sounds like a lofty or esoteric concept, it is easiest to just say *hybrid AI*.

Lest you think that this seems like a viable and amicable solution, realize that rarely in life is there a free lunch. There are AI sub-symbolics that decry the neuro-symbolic or hybrid AI approach. Some exclaim that you are attaching a ten-ton weight to AI sub-symbolics that will slow progress. You are once again draining resources from the purity of AI sub-symbolics.

On and on it goes.

Some would argue that we *must* pursue the neuro-symbolics or hybrid AI else the AI symbolics arena will be left adrift and continue to be castigated as not worthy. By getting attached to the currently heralded AI sub-symbolics and ML/DL, the symbolics will still have relevancy and be kept in the game. This is our insurance policy underlying the pursuit of AI. You see, if the AI sub-symbolics camp doesn't get us to sentient AI or AGI, the AI symbolics will still be up and running, ready to save the day.

As an aside, some furtively whisper that this will be akin to the return of the Jedi.

In whatever way you want to characterize the situation, the bigger picture would seem to be whether we are willing to pick one particular path at this time and commit to just that path, forsaking all others. It is a gutsy move. I would dare say a risky move in that if the AI is that vital to society, we could be doing a disservice to society all told and find ourselves boxed in with AI that has reached lesser limits than we were striving to reach (admittedly, there is a debate about whether we even should be trying to reach sentient AI or AGI).

In general, I tend to concur with the sentiment expressed in the earlier cited piece on Alt Intelligence: "Let us all encourage a field that is open-minded enough to work in multiple directions, without prematurely dismissing ideas that happen to be not yet fully developed. It may just be that the best path to artificial (general) intelligence isn't through Alt Intelligence, after all" (per Gary Marcus at his substack blog as earlier mentioned herein).

At this juncture of this weighty discussion, I'd bet that you are desirous of some illustrative examples that might showcase this topic. There is a special and assuredly popular set of examples that are close to my heart. You see, in my capacity as an expert on AI including the ethical and legal ramifications, I am frequently asked to identify realistic examples that showcase AI Ethics dilemmas so that the somewhat theoretical nature of the topic can be more readily grasped. One of the most evocative areas that vividly presents this ethical AI quandary is the advent of AI-based true self-driving cars. This will serve as a handy use case or exemplar for ample discussion on the topic.

Here's then a noteworthy question that is worth contemplating: *Does the advent of AI-based true self-driving cars illuminate anything about the utility of neuro-symbolic AI or hybrid AI, and if so, what does this showcase?*

We shall begin by heaping praise upon the use of ML/DL in the realm of bringing forth AI-based self-driving cars. Several key aspects of self-driving cars have come to fruition as a result of using AI sub-symbolics techniques and technologies encompassing Machine Learning and Deep Learning. For example, consider the core requirement of having to detect and analyze the driving scene that surrounds an AI-based self-driving car.

You've undoubtedly seen videos or pictures of self-driving cars that showcase the myriad of mounted sensors on the autonomous vehicle. This is often done on the rooftop of the self-driving car. Sensor devices such as video cameras, LIDAR units, radar units, ultrasonic detectors, and the like are typically included on a rooftop rack or possibly affixed to the car top or sides of the vehicle. The array of sensors is intended to electronically collect data that can be used to figure out what exists in the driving scene.

The sensors collect data and feed the digitized data to onboard computers. Those computers can be a combination of general-purpose computing processors and specialized processors that are devised specifically to analyze sensory data. By and large, most of the sensory data computational analysis is undertaken by ML/DL that has been crafted for this purpose and is running on the vehicle's onboard computing platforms.

The ML/DL computationally tries to find patterns in the data such as where the roadway is, where pedestrians are, where other nearby cars are, and so on. All of this is crucial to being able to have the self-driving car proceed ahead. Without the ML/DL performing the driving scene analysis, the self-driving car would be essentially blind as to what exists around the autonomous vehicle.

In brief, you can readily make the case that the use of ML/DL is essential to the emergence of AI-based self-driving cars. This in turn can be touted as a success story for the AI sub-symbolics approach.

But there is some confusion by many that somehow the entirety of the Artificial Intelligence aspects regarding self-driving is perhaps nothing other than ML/DL. This is not the case. Many other vital elements of the AI self-driving stack use a variety of other AI techniques and technologies. Whether you are willing to call those other AI elements as being symbolic might be argued, though referring to those other elements as being sub-symbolic would almost assuredly not be applicable.

Let's examine those other facets of an AI driving system.

Once the computational analyses are done of the driving scene, the other parts of the AI self-driving capability have to figure out what driving actions are to be undertaken. There is usually a virtual model being kept computationally that represents the driving scene. The AI seeks to plan out the next moves of the autonomous vehicle. In addition, the AI needs to send commands to the driving controls as befits whatever next action the AI has ascertained should be performed by the self-driving car.

All in all, you could reasonably assert that a modern-day AI-based self-driving car contains both AI sub-symbolics-related components and also contains AI symbolics-oriented components. Those components all need to work in harmony. It is fair to say that a well-devised self-driving car is effectively a neuro-symbolic AI system or an example of hybrid AI.

We now return to the two gunslingers facing off with each other. Recall that there is a contentious posture by some that the AI sub-symbolics approach is the only cowpoke that belongs in AI town. We can ask some pointed questions about this, doing so in the context of AI-based self-driving cars.

Could we dispense with the portions of the AI stack that are not AI sub-symbolics?

In today's world, no, since this would pretty much cut out a sizable chunk of the AI driving system and the self-driving car would be unable to sufficiently operate on a roadway.

Could we exclusively use AI sub-symbolics and devise a self-driving car without making use of any other kind of AI?

Generally, the answer would seem to be no.

Some though theorize that we could ultimately do so. Their reasoning is as follows. We know that humans drive cars. We know that humans use their brains and minds for undertaking the driving act.

If you are ascribing that the AI sub-symbolics approach is the equivalent or will someday achieve the equivalent of what happens in human brains and minds, this suggests that the only AI needed to drive a car would indeed be AI sub-symbolics. This seems rather ironclad. Maybe so, maybe not. There are various holes in this logic, which I've discussed elsewhere in my columns.

Conclusion

Should anyone be getting out of town?

The idea that some part of the AI constellation of techniques and technologies is more important than the other is an ongoing and somewhat reasoned debate. An unsettling overreach seems to be the growing claim that only one part is the "exclusive right" approach, implying or explicitly demanding that the other AI approaches should be abandoned in favor of that vaunted part.

In William Shakespeare's *Romeo and Juliet* there is a notable line that says this: "Two households, both alike in dignity." Perhaps we can garner from that telling line the realization that dignity should be bestowed on both the AI sub-symbolics and the AI symbolics with equal fervor.

A mounting concern is that if this bickering continues to simmer and ferment, we might see the AI field become unduly splintered and fragmented. It could turn back the clock or at least confound advances in AI. You might recall another line from Romeo and Juliet that comes to mind, namely that the bickering could bring "A plague o' both your houses!"

A final comment for now and a slight twist to this tale.

Suppose that the implied notion of dividing AI into two camps consisting of sub-symbolics and symbolics is itself a misleading bifurcation (i.e., a false dichotomy). It could be that to attain sentient AI or AGI that we have to revisit and revamp our existing assumptions and see the world of AI as consisting of completely different terms. In that sense of things, the moniker "hybrid AI" might be the most suitable naming and encompass a catchall of AI avenues that we might not yet even have thought of.

Let's give Shakespeare the last word on this: "What's in a name? That which we call a rose by any other word would smell as sweet."

CHAPTER 11
AI ETHICS
AND MACHINE LEARNING JUICING

Juicing and doping.

Doping and juicing.

We all know about the ongoing and surreptitious use of performance-enhancing drugs that are sadly relied upon in various sports. This occurs in professional sports and even in amateur sports. It happens in the Olympics, which in theory is a globally revered contest that is supposed to be a purity exemplar of human performance limits and topmost extremes across all of humankind.

There is a kind of pervasiveness in the act of juicing and doping. Sports figures are under a tremendous amount of pressure to attain first place and they are alluringly tempted to use whatever means they can to get there. As a result of the likelihood of juicing or doping, we've seen that many if not most sports have instituted procedures and steps that aim to deter and catch those that wrongly abide in such endeavors. If someone is caught having juiced or doping, they risk having their sports medals revoked. Plus, they are likely to be cast aside by their supporters and sponsors. A tremendous sense of reputational risk goes hand-in-hand with the chancy act of juicing or doping.

People that are desirous of being the "best" at a particular sport are torn between *not* using performance-enhancing drugs and opting to use either illegal or at least unethical substances. Using the drugs can be an almost surefire way to the top. If administered sneakily and with careful attention, there is a chance that no one will know and the testing won't detect it. You can get away with it, seemingly scot-free.

Of course, there is also the possibility that you are harming your body and will eventually pay a physical price, but the intensity of desire for the in-the-moment opportunity at winning tends to downplay any future consequences.

So, we have on the one hand the grandiose potential for attaining great glory and maybe even wealth by using performance-enhancing drugs, while on the other hand, we have the inglorious chance of getting caught and being stripped of the otherwise hard-earned winnings and becoming a horribly despised worldwide public figure (along with the health-related adverse consequences too).

That is some kind of meaty cost-benefit analysis that needs to be made.

Some do the mental ROI (return on investment) calculation and decide to never touch any of the performance-enhancing drugs. They resolve to stay perfectly clean and pure. Others might start that way and then stray slightly. You might justify the slippage as just a tiny toe into the performance-enhancing waters and swear solemnly to yourself that you will never do so again. This though can lead to a slippery slope. The classic and predictable proverbial snowball that slips and slides and rolls down the snowy hillside, gathering into a bigger and bigger ball as it does so.

You've also got those that decide upfront they are going to go ahead and use performance-enhancing drugs. A typical mode of thought is that it is the only way to fight fire with fire. The assumption being made is that everyone else that you are competing with is doing likewise. As such, it makes absolutely no sense for you to be pure and yet go against those that are obviously impure (so you assume).

I think you can see why then the nature of the testing and detection is especially vital in these matters. If some participants can get away with the use of performance-enhancing drugs, it spoils the whole barrel. Inch by inch, all other participants will almost surely go that same path. They have to make a horrendous choice.

This entails either competing without the drugs, but probably at a physical disadvantage, or they have to adopt the drugs and remain competitive, despite perhaps wanting with all their heart and might not have to resort to the performance enhancers.

A quandary, for sure.

There is more milieu that confounds these circumstances. For example, a question that arises continually is what in fact is a performance-enhancing drug. Authorities might come up with a list of the banned drugs. Meanwhile, in a cat and mouse gambit, other drugs are devised or identified that will provide performance enhancements and yet are not on the list of banned chemicals. You can try to keep a step ahead of the list, switching to other drugs and remaining slimly within the rules of the game.

The overarching gist is that juicing and doping is not a necessarily straightforward topic. Yes, we might all agree that juicing or doping is atrocious and should not be undertaken. Yes, we might all concur that there should be strict rules about not juicing and doping, along with strident efforts to catch those who stray. Unfortunately, there is a lot of trickery that can undermine those lofty goals.

Why have I shared with you the trials and tribulations of juicing and doping?

I do so for a reason that you might find startling, vexing, upsetting, and altogether heart-wrenching.

You see, there are increasingly vocal claims that AI is at times being "performance enhanced" via the use of juicing or doping (of a sort). The notion is that when devising an AI system, the developers might undertake somewhat underhanded ploys to get the AI to appear better than it really is. This in turn can trick others into assuming that the AI has capabilities that it truly does not have. The consequences can be mild or they can be dangerously dire.

Imagine an AI system that plays checkers that was (shall we say) "performance enhanced" to appear as though it will never lose a checker's game. Some investors pile a ton of dough into the game, doing so under the false belief that AI will always win. After being placed into public use, the AI wins and wins. At some point, it perchance loses a game. Yikes, what happened? In any case, this is not likely to be a life-or-death consideration in this use case.

Imagine instead an AI system that drives a self-driving car. The AI is "performance enhanced" to seem as though it can drive safely and without incident. For a while, the self-driving car is used on public roadways and all seems fine. Lamentedly, at some point, the AI goes astray and a car crash occurs that was clearly the fault of the AI system. Humans might get injured and fatalities can arise. This is a situation whereby juicing or doping of the AI has sobering and serious life-or-death consequences.

I realize that you might be having some heartburn about referring to juicing and doping when it comes to AI. I say this because today's AI is absolutely not sentient and we should be cautious in anthropomorphizing AI, which I'll be elaborating about further shortly herein. In brief, AI is not a human and not anything close to being human, as yet. Trying to compare the two and align with the conventional conceptualization of juicing or doping is somewhat sketchy and should be done with our eyes wide open.

I am going to proceed with the suggested analogous idea of juicing and doping of AI, though I ask that you keep in mind that this is something that should not be carried too far. We can somewhat reasonably lean into the phrasing as a means of exposing aspects that I would argue are abundantly needed to be exposed. That's a viable basis for using the catchphrases. But we ought to not stretch this into the nether realms and make this into something that it is not. I will say more about this momentarily.

One facet of AI that is getting the most attention about AI-related juicing and doping entails certain ways in which some developers are crafting AI-based Machine Learning (ML) and Deep Learning (DL) systems. There are lots of AI Ethics and Ethical AI ramifications pertaining to these kinds of nefarious actions during the development of ML/DL systems.

Let's also keep our heads above water and please underscore these facets as you proceed throughout this discussion:

- Not everyone that is devising AI ML/DL is doing juicing or doping of the ML/DL
- Some do so but aren't especially aware of doing something wrong
- Some do so and know exactly what they are doing as to juicing or doping the ML/DL
- Unlike the sports field, there is very little formalized standardized across-the-board "testing or detecting" of these types of matters for contemporary ML/DL
- The adverse consequences of doing this can vary significantly depending upon the nature of the ML/DL (e.g., AI playing checkers, AI driving a self-driving car).
- Some argue there is nothing inherently improper about these acts
- Definitions of what is or is not juicing or doping of ML/DL are all over the map
- AI Ethics is grappling with how to best deal with the ostensibly emerging trend

I would like to clear up another twist on this topic. I ask that you bear with me on this. Somehow, some utterly misconstrue the matter and fall into an oddish way of thinking that the AI developers are themselves taking performance-enhancing drugs, and therefore this is a discussion about humans that are themselves doing juicing and doping.

That usually gets a bit of a chuckle from a number of AI developers.

To be abundantly clear, that is not what I am referring to. I am distinctly and solely focused herein on the so-called juicing and doping of AI itself, and not of the humans devising AI. That being said, I am not saying that it isn't possible that there might be AI developers that somehow opt to take performance-enhancing drugs for whatever reasons they might opt to do so. It would seem doubtful that there is a fully suitable sports analogy comparable to the act of AI developers that perchance decide to take performance-enhancing illicit drugs, but I leave that to other researchers that might wish to explore that realm. I would simply say that taking any performance-enhancing drugs for whatever reasons is assuredly not prudent and could decidedly be illegal, unethical, and sorely ill-advised.

I trust that helps set things straight.

Before getting into some more meat and potatoes about the juicing and doping of AI, let's establish some additional fundamentals on profoundly integral topics. We ought to take a breezy dive into the AI Ethics and ML/DL arena to set the stage appropriately.

You might be vaguely aware that one of the loudest voices these days in the AI field and even outside the field of AI consists of clamoring for a greater semblance of Ethical AI. Let's take a look at what it means to refer to AI Ethics and Ethical AI. On top of that, we will explore what I mean when I speak of Machine Learning and Deep Learning.

One particular segment or portion of AI Ethics that has been getting a lot of media attention consists of AI that exhibits untoward biases and inequities. You might be aware that when the latest era of AI got underway there was a huge burst of enthusiasm for what some now call *AI For Good.* Unfortunately, on the heels of that gushing excitement, we began to witness *AI For Bad.* For example, various AI-based facial recognition systems have been revealed as containing racial biases and gender biases.

In a recent article in *Science* magazine, the juicing or doping of Machine Learning and Deep Learning came up in the context of efforts by AI developers seeking to attain high marks on ML/DL benchmarks: "The pursuit of high scores can lead to the AI equivalent of doping. Researchers often tweak and juice the models with special software settings or hardware that can vary from run to run on the benchmark, resulting in model performances that aren't reproducible in the real world. Worse, researchers tend to cherry-pick among similar benchmarks until they find one where their model comes out on top" (*Science*, "Taught To The Test" by Matthew Hutson, May 2022).

You could liken the ML/DL benchmark situation involving juicing to the earlier points about trying to win at sports competitions via such untoward practices.

In the AI arena, there is a semblance of competition to see who can arrive at the "best" ML/DL models. Various benchmarks can be used to run an ML/DL and gauge how well the ML/DL seems to score on the benchmark. Leaderboards and informal sharing of benchmark results are often used to tout who has achieved the latest topmost position with their ML/DL configurations. You could reasonably suggest that a modicum of fame and fortune awaits those that can craft their ML/DL to be the "winner" as the latest and greatest performer on the benchmarks.

But just like any kind of competition, there are ways to try and trick out your ML/DL so that it seemingly performs mightily on a benchmark even though under-the-hood sneaks are being applied. This is the classic corruption of aiming to score well on a test by honing your approach to the test, whereas the general principle is supposed to be that you are trying to ascertain overall performance.

Imagine giving a test to someone that is intended to measure their overall understanding of say American literature, but the test taker figures out that the questions are only going to be focused on Mark Twain. Thus, the test taker studies only the works of Mark Twain and scores immensely on the test.

The test taker proudly proclaims that they aced the test and ergo obviously is a brainiac about all of American literature. In reality, they merely honed in on the test and in a sense tricked the testing process.

I realize that some might right away point fingers at the test and whoever prepared the test. If the test maker was dense enough to allow test takers to exploit the test, you might argue that this is entirely on the shoulders of the test maker and not the test taker. The test taker did whatever they could to prepare for the test, including figuring out what would behoove them to study. This is not only seemingly allowed, you might congratulate the test taker for having outsmarted the test maker.

I won't go further into that ethical abyss here. You can easily go round and round on such a topic. Let's just say that the spirit of the ML/DL benchmarks is that those utilizing the benchmarks are hoped or presumed to do so in a sportsmanship manner. This might seem naïve to some, while it might seem aboveboard and proper to others.

I hope that you can immediately see how AI Ethics and Ethical AI considerations naturally arise in such a context.

Consider for example that a given ML/DL does extremely well on a benchmark and that the basis for the heightened score is due to juicing or doping of the AI. Suppose further that the AI developers of the "winning" ML/DL do not reveal that they juiced the AI. Other AI developers hear about or read the results of the ML/DL performance and become excited about a seeming breakthrough in AI ML/DL. They are woefully unaware of the hidden juicing or doping of the AI.

Those elated AI developers opt to switch their efforts over to the presumed approaches of that particular ML/DL in a desire to further extend the capabilities. At some point, perhaps they discover that they have hit a wall and to their unpleasant surprise they seem to be getting nowhere. This could be quite perplexing and exasperating. They have been toiling away for months or years on something that they did not realize had been juiced at the get-go.

Again, I realize that you might wish to find fault with those now disappointed AI developers that were not apparently clever enough to earlier ferret out the juicing, but I dare say that we might also find concern that there were the juicers that started things down that path, to begin with.

All of this is certainly reminiscent of the sports analogy.

You've got a desire to win, seemingly at any cost. Some will aim to win without juicing, while others fully do the juicing. Those using juicing might rationalize the activity as being legitimate. Efforts to try and curtail or catch juicing are put in place, though the cat and mouse nature of the situation means that juicing is likely going to be a step ahead. When someone that is juicing gets caught, they risk the possibility of reputational backlash and other adverse consequences. They are constantly weighing the perceived risks versus the perceived costs. And so on.

The tough thing about catching AI ML/DL juicing is that there is a myriad of ways to undertake the juicing or doping. One supposes you could say the same about sports and juicing, namely that a wide variety of means and performance enhancers can be used to try and stay under the radar.

Anyway, here are some broad categories to consider in the AI ML/DL juicing forays:

a) Juice at the Machine Learning and Deep Learning design stage
b) Juice the data used to train the ML/DL
c) Juice the ML/DL model
d) Juice the ML/DL outputs
e) Do any of the above two in combination
f) Do any of the above three in combination
g) Do all of the above

As a taste, let's briefly consider the kind of juicing that can occur via the data that is used to train ML/DL.

The usual rule of thumb is that you hold out some of your training data for purposes of testing your ML/DL model. A customary recommendation is to use an 80/20 rule. You use about 80% of your data for training the ML/DL. The remaining 20% is used to test the ML/DL. It is hoped that the 20% is relatively representative of the other 80% and that you would simply randomly choose which of your training data is in the training set and which is in the testing set.

Seems straightforward.

We will now do some juicing or doping:

- **Sneakily mirror your training data and testing data**. One means to juice things would be to carefully scrutinize your data and try to purposely ensure that the 80% and the 20% are ideally aligned. You don't randomly divide up the data. Instead, you do a secretive selection to try and get the 80% and the 20% to resemble each other to the letter. This is intended to make your testing come out looking extraordinarily good. In essence, if your ML/DL does well on the 80%, it is almost guaranteed to then do well on the 20%. Doing this is not in the spirit of things since you are potentially deluding yourself (and others) into believing that the ML/DL has computationally done an excellent job of generalizing. It might not have.

- **Shortchange the test data.** Another way to juice your ML/DL dataset is to divide the training data such that it is say 95% of your data, while the holdout testing data is only 5%. This is likely to increase your odds that there is nothing in the paltry 5% that will undercut the ML/DL performance. Very few people would ever ask how much of your data was used for training versus testing. They don't know to ask this question or assume that whatever you did was the proper way of doing things.

- **Get rid of outliers beforehand.** A sly means of juicing or doping your ML/DL involves trickery about outliers in your data. Before you feed any of your data into the budding ML/DL, you first examine the data. This is a prudent step and highly recommended since you should be familiar with your data before you just slap it into an ML/DL. That being said, here's the trickery that can be used. You find any outliers in the data and toss them out. This will usually aid the mathematics of the ML/DL when it is trying to computationally find patterns. Outliers are typically a pain to deal with, though they are oftentimes crucial and can tell a lot about the nature of the data and whatever you are trying to model. By blindly excising the outliers, you are bound to miss something that can make-or-break the reality of what the ML/DL is supposed to be able to do. A better practice is to pay attention to outliers and consider how best to contend with them, rather than summarily kicking them out of the dataset.

- **Do no testing at all.** A more outrageous act of juicing or doping entails not doing any testing at all. You use all of your data for training. If things look good, you wave your hands in the air and declare that the ML/DL is good to go. In that sense, you are using a 100/0 rule-of-thumb, namely 100% of the data for training and 0% for the testing. I'm guessing that you might be shocked that anyone would do this. Well, some are so assured about the training results that they feel that no testing is required. Or they are in a rush and do not have time to deal with that "annoying" testing stuff. You get the picture.

I had earlier mentioned that juicing or doping of AI can be somewhat inconsequential if the nature of the AI itself is not especially paramount, while other settings might involve AI-directed life-or-death consequences and therefore the juicing is scarily a weak link and potential harbinger of grave doom.

At this juncture of this weighty discussion, I'd bet that you are desirous of some illustrative examples that might showcase this topic. There is a special and assuredly popular set of examples that are close to my heart.

You see, in my capacity as an expert on AI including the ethical and legal ramifications, I am frequently asked to identify realistic examples that showcase AI Ethics dilemmas so that the somewhat theoretical nature of the topic can be more readily grasped. One of the most evocative areas that vividly presents this ethical AI quandary is the advent of AI-based true self-driving cars. This will serve as a handy use case or exemplar for ample discussion on the topic.

Here's then a noteworthy question that is worth contemplating: *Does the advent of AI-based true self-driving cars illuminate anything about the juicing or doping of AI, and if so, what does this showcase?*

We shall begin by heaping praise upon the use of ML/DL in the realm of bringing forth AI-based self-driving cars. Several key aspects of self-driving cars have come to fruition as a result of using Machine Learning and Deep Learning. For example, consider the core requirement of having to detect and analyze the driving scene that surrounds an AI-based self-driving car.

You've undoubtedly noticed that most self-driving cars have a myriad of mounted sensors on the autonomous vehicle. This is often done on the rooftop of the self-driving car. Sensor devices such as video cameras, LIDAR units, radar units, ultrasonic detectors, and the like are typically included on a rooftop rack or possibly affixed to the car top or sides of the vehicle. The array of sensors is intended to electronically collect data that can be used to figure out what exists in the driving scene.

The sensors collect data and feed the digitized data to onboard computers. Those computers can be a combination of general-purpose computing processors and specialized processors that are devised specifically to analyze sensory data. By and large, most of the sensory data computational analysis is undertaken by ML/DL that has been crafted for this purpose and is running on the vehicle's onboard computing platforms.

The ML/DL computationally tries to find patterns in the data such as where the roadway is, where pedestrians are, where other nearby cars are, and so on. All of this is crucial to being able to have the self-driving car proceed ahead. Without the ML/DL performing the driving scene analysis, the self-driving car would be essentially blind as to what exists around the autonomous vehicle.

In brief, you can readily make the case that the use of ML/DL is essential to the emergence of AI-based self-driving cars.

Can you juice or do doping of ML/DL that pertains to AI-based self-driving cars?

Absolutely.

We can readily invoke the earlier stated examples of juicing or doping when it comes to the data aspects of ML/DL formulations. Keep in mind that the ML/DL that is being used to scan for pedestrians, cars, and other roadway objects was likely trained first on various datasets of driving scenes. This training of the ML/DL is instrumental in the AI driving system being able to properly and safely navigate the streets while commanding the autonomous vehicle driving controls.

Here's what a juicing or doping effort could underhandedly do:

- **Sneakily mirror your training data and testing data**. You collect together the dataset that is being used to train an ML/DL on roadway objects and purposely align the training portion and the testing portion. You abide by the rule of thumb about dividing the data into 80% for training and 20% for testing, which therefore seems like the right approach. The juicing is that you move around the data to make sure that the 80% and the 20% are astoundingly similar. You are stacking the deck in favor of whatever ML/DL you devise during the training.

- **Shortchange the test data.** You divide the training data into 95% of the total dataset and put just 5% into the testing data portion. When the testing is undertaken, turns out you've reduced the chances of the ML/DL not looking good.

- **Get rid of outliers beforehand**. While scrutinizing the data at the outset, you discover that there are instances of billboards that have pictures of people on them. You are concerned that this will confuse your ML/DL, so you remove those images or videos from your dataset. Once you've done the training and testing, you declare that your ML/DL is ready for use in the wild. Unfortunately, at some point, there is bound to be a situation whereby the self-driving car is going down a street or highway and there is a billboard with pictures of people on it. You don't know how your ML/DL will react. It could be that the ML/DL warns that pedestrians are nearby and as a result the AI driving system suddenly slams on the brakes, prompting other nearby human-driven cars to ram into the self-driving car or drive off the roadway to avoid a collision.

- **Do no testing at all.** You are in a hurry to get the ML/DL setup. Maybe the self-driving firm has put a date out that says when the self-driving car is going to be doing an important public demonstration. You don't have much time to do things the right way. As such, you keep your fingers crossed and use all of the data for training. You do no testing at all. You have a sense of relief that you were able to meet the stated deadline. Of course, what happens next on the roadway could be a calamity in the making.

Conclusion

Generally, the bona fide self-driving car makers are quite cautious about allowing corner-cutting and taking chances by performing juicing or doping actions in their burgeoning AI driving systems. There is usually a slew of checks and balances to try and detect and correct any such actions.

In addition, many of the firms have established somewhat rigorous AI Ethics precepts and alerting mechanisms to try and early on catch any slippages or underhandedness that might be happening.

Some of the fly-by-night attempts at putting together AI self-driving cars have opted to throw caution to the wind. They brazenly take any shortcuts they can think of. Furthermore, they put little stock in doing double-checking or trying to stop any juicing or doping. Some even use the classic of plausible deniability by merely instructing their AI developers to do "whatever they think is right" and then can, later on, proclaim that the firm did not know what juicing or doping of the AI was taking place. I've discussed these dangerous efforts in my columns.

In the case of self-driving cars, life or death is clearly on the line. The added point is that if there is a chance of juicing or doping AI in the self-driving car realm, you have to wonder what might be permitted in the other less life-or-death realms that are relying on AI systems. The pressures to get the AI out the door soonest are immense. The pressures to make sure that the AI does the right things in the right way can be a lot less compelling. Sadly so.

Besides the ethical concerns about AI-related juicing and doping, I've continued to hammer away at the coming tsunamis of legal actions on these matters. When AI systems get away with atrocious activities, those that have devised and fielded the AI are ultimately going to find themselves being held accountable. We haven't yet seen the rise of legal cases against those that make AI and that use AI in their businesses. Mark my words that the reckoning will inevitably arise.

Companies are going to be legally forced to open their doors to show how they put together their AI systems. What did they do during the design? What did they do during the data efforts? What did they do as part of the testing before release? All of this is going to shine a light on the possibility of unseen, under-the-hood AI juicing and doping. There ought to <u>not</u> be a free lunch for those that opt to do AI juicing and doping. Be wary and keep your eyes open. Stand tall and insist on anti-juicing and anti-doping of AI. We need clean AI, that's for darned sure.

CHAPTER 12
AI ETHICS AND SOCIETAL POWER

Hiding in plain sight.

Have you ever heard that line before?

Probably so.

It can have various meanings, though the most common understanding seems to be that sometimes we fail to notice something that is right there before our very eyes. You might have experienced this phenomenon.

For example, maybe you recently mildly panicked that you couldn't find your smartphone, and then suddenly and embarrassingly realized that it was being held firmly in your own hand, and yet you overlooked it. This happened because you were anxiously glancing all around the room to find where you had last left your smartphone, which distracted you from realizing that the elusive and treasured electronic device was within your own grasp.

It happens to all of us.

A related and quite legendary psychological experiment in the late 1990s vividly documented this type of human oversight and has periodically regained public attention as to this ostensibly mindless or shall we say mind-distracted vulnerability. In modern times, there are plenty of online videos that showcase the essence of the experiment and how easily we can forego seeing something that is "hiding" in plain sight.

On a somewhat formal basis, the matter overall is often referred to as *inattentional blindness*, though other characterizations and variations have been extensively described.

I'd like to tell you about the experiment and the videos depicting it, though I must first alert you that if you read my elucidation about this then the fun of the trick is lamentedly lessened. You might compare this to a magic act. Once you know how the trick works, you never quite see the magic trick in the same light. Just wanted to give you a fair heads-up.

Are you ready?

It usually goes like this. You are asked to watch a video containing several people that are loosely grouped together. They are somewhat idly and randomly tossing a ball or some such object back and forth to each other. There is no particular pattern to the tossing and they are merely having an enjoyable time doing some lighthearted fare.

So far, so good.

The twist comes next.

You are asked to count how many times the ball or object is being tossed around. Usually, this task is given a bit more specificity. For example, count how many times the members of the group that are wearing a purple shirt are tossing the ball, while do not count the instances of those in a white shirt catching the ball. As you'll see in a moment, this is the "sneaky" means of distracting you, doing so by engaging your cognitive processes on a narrowed task.

You are asked to earnestly perform the counting task, giving it your most heartfelt try. It is admittedly somewhat hard to do and requires intense concentration because the ball is moving quickly and the people are seemingly randomly choosing where and when to toss the ball. Your mind tries to focus on the purple-shirted participants. Your mind watches for the ball. Your mind simultaneously tries to ignore or blot out the white-shirted members. They are getting almost confoundingly mentally in your way.

You don't want to inadvertently count them into your count (an exasperating mistake if you do).

At the end of the sequence of tosses, you are asked how many times the purple-shirted members tossed the ball. You are smug in your personal confidence and profound assurance that you accurately and precisely made the exact count. Indeed, you unquestionably must be absolutely right about the count.

The experiment though is not finished (here's the magic trick revealed, so continue reading only if you want to or are willing to know).

You are asked whether you perchance noticed that a gorilla had walked amongst the participants that were tossing the ball or other objects.

Say what?

Huh?

Come again?

Most people laugh or scoff at the question of whether there was a gorilla in the scene. The knee-jerk response consists of stubbornly insisting that no such gorilla ever appeared. In fact, the question seems like a quirky query and entirely fantastically made up.

I've had people that were willing to put a ton of dough on their contention that no gorilla of any kind was in that tossing scene that they closely and attentively watched. I sometimes wish that I had taken those people up on that bet since I would be rolling in cash today. It would though be an entirely unfair bet and likely become a lamented friend-turns-to-foe kind of hollow misstep.

You see, there was indeed a gorilla that walked in that scene (a person in a gorilla suit, which for all practical purposes is essentially a gorilla per se when it comes to the nature of the experiment).

Upon watching the same recorded scene again, the person that failed to spot the gorilla is gobsmacked. They will typically and within a few seconds gyrate frantically through a series of emotional reactions. First, they are stunned in disbelief. Second, they will claim that you are showing them a doctored version of the scene and that you are not showing them the one that they watched. Third, they will reluctantly acknowledge that you are showing them the actual scene but will insist that you never told them to watch for a gorilla. In other words, you obediently did what you were asked to do. Nothing more, nothing less. As such, whether you happened to notice a gorilla or not is utterly immaterial and has no bearing or merit on the sobering matter at hand.

I caution you that the bottom line here is that you risk losing a friend or possibly forever irking an acquaintance if you try this on them without any semblance of a clue or at least a wink-wink helpful tip of what is about to happen. Be careful trying this out. I've done my duty and given you a suitable precautionary warning, so it's up to you to decide whether to spring this on anyone that you might know.

I do though have to mention how powerful an exercise this is.

For those caught unawares, there is almost a surefire guarantee that the person will forever remember the "experiment" and will always recall it, not necessarily fondly but they will remember it quite strongly. If you have never seen such a video, and if you go watch one now, I doubt that you will have as strident a recall about the matter. There is a notable difference between being caught completely unawares about the intriguing notion of such a cognitive blind spot and merely learning about it secondhand.

We all tend to pride ourselves on our keen cognitive capacities. Getting snared in having missed seeing the gorilla is a huge takedown in our cognitive confidence. That is also why some are so adamant in refusing to accept what occurred and will fight tooth and nail against the experimental result. If you tell someone beforehand they are about to witness a bit of magic, they are usually fine afterward if they get tricked. When you ask someone to seemingly do a serious task, and then out of the blue opt to pull the rug out from under them, the reaction can be emotionally and cognitively explosive.

For those of you of a literary bent, you might mildly have experienced a similar example of this mind-oriented distractedness when reading Edgar Allen Poe's famous story entitled "The Purloined Letter" about an amateur sleuth bucking to be a full-fledged detective. I don't want to give too much away, especially since I've already potentially spoiled the gorilla experiment for you, so let's just say that this wonderful tale as published in 1844 is wholly relevant to the idea of hiding something in plain sight (maybe that will perk your curiosity to read the delightful story).

Let's do a quick recap on the *hiding in plain sight* mantra.

Here are some key takeaways:

- We can at times <u>not</u> notice things that are right in front of our eyes
- This is especially possible when you are cognitively preoccupied
- The cognitive preoccupation might have nothing to do with the *hidden in plain sight* aspect
- There is also a chance that the cognitive preoccupation might be related to the "hidden" aspect

A few additional corollaries are worthwhile to consider:

- If you are on the alert to such a condition you might be able to overcome the misperceived hiddenness
- The hiddenness should be reasonably out in the open else the hiddenness is truly hidden (a rigged and unfair test of this specific phenomenon)
- By cognitively being prepared it is feasible to cope with the situation, though surprises can still indeed occur (various other cognitive factors arise)
- This phenomenon is cognitively pervasive and generally the case for basically everyone

With that keystone foundation established on this fascinating matter, I'd like to shift gears and share with you a perhaps surprising angle to it, including that all of this ties in an extraordinary way to the advent of Artificial Intelligence (AI).

In brief, some are asserting that the emergence of AI biases is hiding something else in veritably plain sight. The argument goes that AI biases are often more so indicators of societal power dynamics rather than mere data-misshapen oddities requiring a techno-focused resolution alone.

Allow me a moment to elaborate on this.

The detection of biases within AI systems is often seen as a type of whack-a-mole gambit. When you manage to find an embedded bias, you stomp it out, hopefully so. Of course, many more such imbued biases might still exist and ultimately be revealed or worse perhaps never see the light of day. All of this though is predicated on the riveting of attention to the AI biases themselves. Rarely do those that seek to expunge those AI biases take a much deeper look underneath to get a broader semblance of what might be happening.

What some are strenuously claiming is that those AI biases could readily be a telltale clue of underlying societal power dynamics. In a sense, the shiny nature of the AI biases distracts many from taking a closer look. If you did take a more in-depth and telling assessment, you might very well discover that all manner of societal power arrangements exists at the root of the embodied AI biases.

You were watching the ball being tossed back and forth, counting the tosses somewhat mentally mechanically so, and failed to see the gorilla because you were otherwise distracted or had your mind elsewhere and not on the root cause.

Yikes, some respond, this is alarming. Others contend that the asserted hidden factor of societal power dynamics is not really there at all.

Or, if it is there, you aren't tasked with counting gorillas and instead are tasked with counting and eviscerating those AI biases, thus the whole gorilla ("power dynamics") doesn't come into play anyway.

Now then, those that are outspoken proponents of the societal power dynamics posture would likely clamor that such reactions to this surprising and generally unrealized notion of AI biases being the canaries in the coal mine are on par with the same reactions to those that get caught off-guard by the gorilla experiment. Thus, the typical reaction entails oscillating among disbelief, rejection of the premise, and becoming upset that perhaps they have been "tricked" all along and embarrassingly didn't realize that they had been blind to realize the true import of the AI biases.

Others that come across this slowly trickling-in theory about AI biases are often intrigued by it. We all are bound to find that a heretofore "hadn't noticed that before" possibility as being overtly curious and potentially mind-expanding. Maybe this is an example of something hiding in plain sight. For those that are toiling away on trying to find and eradicate AI biases, it might be of value to find a more macroscopic way to assess and seek to somehow resolve or prevent such biases.

Could this claimed underpinning of societal power dynamics be a handy means of relooking and rethinking the decidedly increasingly growing problem entailing AI biases?

As I will explain in a moment, there are lots of AI Ethics and Ethical AI ramifications pertaining to AI biases. This has given rise to AI Ethics principles such as trying to make sure that AI is devised and acting in a semblance of fairness, accountability, responsibility, and the like. I will cover herein more on this in a moment. For my ongoing and extensive coverage of AI Ethics and Ethical AI, see **the link here** and **the link here,** just to name a few.

We can delve for now into the AI biases and societal power dynamics with a keen sense of interest and inquisitiveness.

In an article published in the journal *Nature*, entitled "Don't Ask If AI Is Good Or Fair, Ask How It Shifts Power" the author Pratyusha Kalluri proffers a crucial point about the possibility of AI biases hiding in plain sight as a telltale smorgasbord of societal power dynamics: "It is not uncommon now for AI experts to ask whether an AI is 'fair' and 'for good'. But 'fair' and 'good' are infinitely spacious words that any AI system can be squeezed into. The question to pose is a deeper one: How is AI shifting power?"

To make this even more abundantly clear, the researcher makes this somewhat stunning (for some) suggestion about where the AI field might at times be fooling itself in the (shall we say) preoccupation with AI biases as a standalone consideration: "When the field of AI believes it is neutral, it both fails to notice biased data and builds systems that sanctify the status quo and advance the interests of the powerful."

Again, some are caught by surprise by these suggestions or perhaps could be construed as allegations or a theory of sorts, while others are saying that they had a sneaking suspicion all along and someone has finally put their finger on what is actually awry. Meanwhile, you've also got some that react by saying that this is not especially earth-shattering. There is a kind of "so what?" reaction and a feeling that nothing special or insightful is being gleaned by this.

To try and showcase why the realization that societal power dynamics is indeed a genuine and vital hidden factor regarding AI biases, there are various efforts underway to aid in showcasing abject constructive steps that can be undertaken as a result of seeing or agreeing that the gorilla exists.

Consider a recent study by Milagros Miceli, Julian Posada, and Tianling Yang entitled "Studying Up Machine Learning Data: Why Talk About Bias When We Mean Power?" which explores these probing concerns: "With the present commentary, we aim to contribute to the discussion around data bias, data worker bias, and data documentation by broadening the field of inquiry: from bias research towards an investigation of power differentials that shape data. As we will argue in the following sections, the study of biases locates the problem within technical systems, either data or algorithms, and obscures its root causes. Moreover, the very understanding of bias and debiasing is inscribed with values, interests, and power relations that inform what counts as bias and what does not, what problems debiasing initiatives address, and what goals they aim to achieve. Conversely, the power-oriented perspective looks into technical systems but focuses on larger organizational and social contexts. It investigates the relations that intervene in data and system production and aims to make visible power asymmetries that inscribe particular values and preferences in them" (*Proceeding of the ACM Human-Computer Interactions*, January 2022).

Take as another example an article by Jonne Maas entitled "Machine Learning And Power Relations" covering the moral dilemma of AI that has biases and might run counter to the AI Ethics precepts of an explicit need for accountability: "Indeed, to be increasingly dependent on such an unaccountable exercise of power is not just problematic when the system proves to be incorrect in its results, it is problematic more generally as it opens up the possibility for a moral wrong, limiting human flourishing by establishing a power dichotomy between the developers and users, on the one hand, and the end-users, on the other. We should therefore seriously consider the potential political asymmetry that the increased use of ML applications bring to society, where developers and users–in combination with the ML system itself–increasingly gain more power over a system's end users due to inadequate accountability mechanisms" (in *AI & Society*, February 2022).

All of these emerging efforts seem to be contending that the underlying societal power dynamics are abundantly making a substantive difference in what we do (or opt to not do) about AI biases, including:

- Societal power dynamics can lead to the production of AI biases
- Societal power dynamics can essentially define what we believe AI biases to be
- Societal power dynamics can shape how we deal with AI biases
- Societal power dynamics can guide how the debiasing of AI will take place
- Societal power dynamics impact all stakeholders as it relates to AI and AI biases
- Societal power dynamics can especially adversely impact the most vulnerable stakeholders
- And so on.

As a quick aside, you might be wondering what it means to refer to *societal power dynamics* and where does that concept come from.

Turn back the clock to the year 1640. You might vaguely know that Thomas Hobbes famously laid out some essential groundwork for analyzing and comprehending the nature of societal power, which is still utilized avidly to this day. He is indubitably best known for the *Leviathan* which was published in 1651 and set forth the crux of his theories about power and the dynamics of power. Earlier on, in 1640, he had stated this cornerstone remark about the essence of power in his earlier work entitled the *Elements of Law* (I've shown the passage in somewhat of its original form, consisting of what today is considered old-English): "… because the power of one man resisteth and hindreth the effects of the power of another, Power simply is noe more, but the excesse of the Power of one above that of another. For equall powers opposed destroye one another and such theire opposition is called Contention."

In a modernistic straightforward fashion, contemporary dictionaries tend to say that power is when someone can get someone else to do their bidding that otherwise, the tasked person would not wish to do so. In that sense, it is definitionally suggested that power usually creates an asymmetrical relationship. One person has power over another. We can refer to the parties as being agents. Power is asymmetrically distributed between one or more agents.

The shorthand is labeled as *power-over.*

There is heated debate in the field of societal power dynamics whether this is the only form of such power. For example, another viewpoint is that power is more so about garnering the desired outcome, known as *power-to.* You are said to make use of power to affect a particular sought outcome. The outcome is likely to involve agents, though this is pretty much a means of more broadly attaining the outcome that you want to attain.

The shorthand version for this is *power-to.*

If you want to dig more deeply into the societal power dynamics topic, there is plenty of beneficial material out there. As an example, this researcher brings up a taste of the debate taking place: "If for the first tradition power consists in an agent's power to affect certain outcomes, for the second it consists in an agent's power over other agents. Proponents of the former tradition frequently argue that power-over is merely a species of power-to; proponents of the latter, by contrast, often hold that all relevant social power consists in power-over, so that social power-to reduces to power-over" and the author then proposes seven variations including power-over-others, power-to-effect-outcomes, power-despite-resistance, power-with-others, and so on (per the journal of *Political Studies*, "The Grammar Of Social Power: Power-to, Power-with, Power-despite and Power-over" by Arash Abizadeh, 2021).

On a housekeeping note, I normally try to carefully state that the shorthand wording of "power" used in this herein context is referring to *societal power dynamics* (all three words in combination together). I do this because otherwise if I merely use the word "power" you might be thinking of electrical power or maybe computer power which consists of computational processing capabilities. I trust that for the remainder of this discussion, I can simply use the word "power" and you'll know that I am alluding to societal power dynamics, thanks.

Before getting into some more meat and potatoes about the role of *power* (societal power dynamics) and the *hiding in plain sight* pertaining to AI biases, let's establish some additional fundamentals on some profoundly integral topics. Much of the handwringing about AI biases is predominantly taking place in the realm of AI known as Machine Learning (ML) and Deep Learning (DL).

We ought to take a breezy dive into the AI Ethics and ML/DL arena.

You might be vaguely aware that one of the loudest voices these days in the AI field and even outside the field of AI consists of clamoring for a greater semblance of Ethical AI. Let's take a look at what it means to refer to AI Ethics and Ethical AI. On top of that, we can set the stage further by exploring what I mean when I speak of Machine Learning and Deep Learning.

One particular segment or portion of AI Ethics that has been getting a lot of media attention consists of AI that exhibits untoward biases and inequities. You might be aware that when the latest era of AI got underway there was a huge burst of enthusiasm for what some now call *AI For Good*. Unfortunately, on the heels of that gushing excitement, we began to witness *AI For Bad*. For example, various AI-based facial recognition systems have been revealed as containing racial biases and gender biases.

At this juncture of this weighty discussion, I'd bet that you are desirous of some illustrative examples that might showcase this topic.

Here's then a noteworthy question that is worth contemplating: *Does the advent of AI-based true self-driving cars illuminate anything about how AI biases are integrally intertwined with potential hidden societal power dynamics, and if so, what does this showcase?*

We shall consider next how AI biases and societal power dynamics might come to play in this context of self-driving cars. Let's start with one of the most transparent and frequently cited "power plays" regarding autonomous vehicles and especially self-driving cars.

Some pundits are worried that self-driving cars will be the province of only the wealthy and the elite. It could be that the cost to use self-driving cars will be prohibitively expensive. Unless you've got big bucks, you might not ever see the inside of a self-driving car. Those that will be utilizing self-driving cars are going to have to be rich, it is purportedly contended (I don't agree).

This could be construed as a form of societal power dynamics that will permeate the advent of AI-based self-driving cars. The overall autonomous vehicle industrial system as a whole will keep self-driving cars out of the hands of those that are poor or less affluent. This might not necessarily be by overt intent and just turns out that the only believed way to recoup the burdensome costs of having invented self-driving cars will be to charge outrageously high prices.

Is this a societal power dynamic consideration or not?

You be the judge.

Moving on, we can next consider the matter of AI-related statistical and computational biases.

Contemplate the seemingly inconsequential question of where self-driving cars will be roaming to pick up passengers. This seems like an abundantly innocuous topic.

At first, assume that AI self-driving cars will be roaming throughout entire towns. Anybody that wants to request a ride in a self-driving car has essentially an equal chance of hailing one. Gradually, the AI begins to primarily keep the self-driving cars roaming in just one section of town. This section is a greater money-maker and the AI has been programmed to try and maximize revenues as part of the usage in the community at large.

Community members in the impoverished parts of the town turn out to be less likely to be able to get a ride from a self-driving car. This is because the self-driving cars were further away and roaming in the higher revenue part of the town. When a request comes in from a distant part of town, any other request from a closer location would get a higher priority. Eventually, the availability of getting a self-driving car in any place other than the richer part of town is nearly impossible, exasperatingly so for those that lived in those now resource-starved areas.

Out goes the vaunted mobility-for-all dreams that self-driving cars are supposed to bring to life.

You could assert that the AI pretty much landed on a form of statistical and computational biases, akin to a form of proxy discrimination (also often referred to as indirect discrimination). The AI wasn't programmed to avoid those poorer neighborhoods. Instead, it "learned" to do so via the use of the ML/DL.

Do societal power dynamics come to play in this instance?

You be the judge.

For the third instance of AI biases, we turn to an example that involves the AI determining whether to stop for awaiting pedestrians that do not have the right-of-way to cross a street.

You've undoubtedly been driving and encountered pedestrians that were waiting to cross the street and yet they did not have the right-of-way to do so. This meant that you had discretion as to whether to stop and let them cross. You could proceed without letting them cross and still be fully within the legal driving rules of doing so.

Studies of how human drivers decide on stopping or not stopping for such pedestrians have suggested that sometimes the human drivers make the choice based on untoward biases. A human driver might eye the pedestrian and choose to not stop, even though they would have stopped had the pedestrian had a different appearance, such as based on race or gender.

Imagine that AI-based self-driving cars are programmed to deal with the question of whether to stop or not stop for pedestrians that do not have the right-of-way. Here's how the AI developers might decide to program this task. They collect data from a town's video cameras that are placed all around the city. The data showcases human drivers that do stop for pedestrians that do not have the right-of-way and also capture video of human drivers that do not stop. This is all collected into a large dataset.

By using Machine Learning and Deep Learning, the data is modeled computationally. The AI driving system then uses this model to decide when to stop or not stop. Generally, the idea is that whatever the local custom consists of, this is how the AI is going direct the self-driving car.

To the surprise of the city leaders and the residents, imagine their shock when the AI opts to stop or not stop based on the age of the pedestrian.

How could that happen?

Upon a closer review of the ML/DL training data and videos of human driver discretion, it turns out that many of the instances of not stopping entailed pedestrians that had a walking cane such as might be customary for an elder.

Human drivers were seemingly unwilling to stop and let an elder cross the street, presumably due to the anticipated length of time that it might take for someone to make the journey. If the pedestrian looked like they could quickly dart across the street and minimize the waiting time of the driver, the human drivers were more amenable to letting the person cross.

This got deeply buried into the AI driving system via the ML/DL having "discovered" this pattern in the training data and accordingly computationally dutifully modeled upon it. Once the ML/DL was downloaded into the self-driving cars via the use of OTA (Over-The-Air) updates, the onboard AI driving system went ahead to use the newly provided ML/DL models.

Here's how it would work. The sensors of the self-driving car would scan the awaiting pedestrian, feed this data into the ML/DL model, and the model would emit to the AI whether to stop or continue. Any visual indication that the pedestrian might be slow to cross, such as the use of a walking cane, mathematically was being used to determine whether the AI driving system should let the awaiting pedestrian cross or not.

Do you think that this AI bias is hiding a societal power dynamic?

You be the judge.

Conclusion

Some final thoughts for now.

Let's cover a few high-level tips and important caveats.

First, for clarification, there is no one particularly arguing that we should somehow ignore AI biases and jump over into examining solely the societal power dynamics only. I mention this because there are some that seem to toss the baby out with the bathwater and leap entirely into the power elements as though the AI biases are inconsequential in comparison.

Do not make that Grand Canyon kind of oversized leap.

Second, we do need to focus on AI biases. And, meanwhile, we should also be keeping our eyes and ears open for the societal power dynamics.

Yes, we can do both at the same time, especially now that we know to be on the watch. I assure you that people experiencing the gorilla experiment are apt to be on their toes whenever they next see anything that might challenge their cognitive agility. Knowing that a gorilla can be there, though it might not necessarily appear, will ensure that you are watching for the potential appearance anyway.

Here are some worthy rules of thumb (this raises some controversy, just to let you know):

- An AI bias can be construed as "hiding" a societal power dynamics issue (the AI bias isn't the hider, it is the person preoccupied with looking at the surface only of the AI bias)
- But not all AI biases are necessarily hiding a societal power dynamics issue
- Nor are all societal power dynamics issues necessarily embedded into an AI bias
- An AI bias can be part of a collective of AI biases that are all related to a particular societal power dynamics issue
- A litany of societal power dynamics issues can be riddling just about any AI system since AI systems are a reflection of society and power dynamics all-told

Ruminate on those for a moment.

I'll wait.

Okay, here are a few more rules of thumb that might also get the mental juices going:

- When encountering AI biases, ask whether there is any connection to societal power dynamics
- When devising an AI system, ask whether and in what ways the societal power dynamics are shaping the AI
- Try to examine how societal power dynamics are impacting the AI stakeholders
- Consider what mitigations might be appropriate regarding AI and societal power dynamics
- Be always watchful for the gorilla and don't forget that gorillas can exist (I'd say that sparks a life's hack rule-of-thumb -- never get blindsided by a gorilla, it could be painful and you'll wish you had seen it coming!).

Talking about *power* has reminded me of the impacts that societal power can engender. I would wager a bet that you are familiar with one of the most famous or infamous lines about power, which per Lord Action goes like this: "Power tends to corrupt, and absolute power corrupts absolutely."

A breathtaking concern.

Society has to be on the up and up that AI is going to have a demonstrative impact on societal power dynamics. This seems blatantly obvious, perhaps, and yet there isn't as much outward debate and outspoken discourse on the matter as you might think would seem warranted. The rise of AI Ethics considerations is, fortunately, moving society in that direction. Inexorably, if not begrudgingly, and an excruciating inch at a time.

We can give the final word for now to the great Leonardo da Vinci and take a reflective moment to ponder these astutely wise words: "Nothing strengthens authority so much as silence."

Those that are venturing into the AI biases and societal power dynamics arena are trying to bring direct sunlight and rapt attention to an otherwise quiet or unassuming matter that would seemingly silently lay in wait. Let's start talking, as Leonardo da Vinci would presumably be urging us to do.

CHAPTER 13
AI ETHICS
AND
AI INFERENCES

Inferences, love them or hate them.

You decide.

One thing that seems abundantly clear is that we cannot live without inferences. As eloquently stated by the renowned 19th-century philosopher Friedrich Nietzsche: "The greatest progress that the human race has made lies in learning how to make correct inferences."

It is worth carefully and diligently noticing that this sage wisdom emphasizes the importance of making *correct* inferences. This seems like a quite notable make-or-break kind of criterion. We can all render inferences, but the question remains as to which of the devised inferences are right and which ones are wrong. You can probably concoct inferences until the cows come home, though if the inferences are wholly inaccurate or wayward, the result is disconcerting and possibly even endangering.

Suppose I see a car coming down the street. I want to make my way across the street and do so without getting run over. Based on the speed of the automobile and other roadway-related factors, I make a mental inference that I can safely cross.

Does this inference guarantee that I will assuredly and without incident successfully get across the roadway?

Of course not.

The driver of the car might suddenly and unexpectedly speed up. Or I might trip over my own feet and fall while trying to cross (the driver might not be able to stop the vehicle in time to prevent hitting me). There are zillions of intervening and uncalculated possibilities that could block or disturb my attempts to cross the street.

My inference is essentially a guess. You could say that there is a probability or certainty level associated with the inference that I made. When I first conceived of the mental inference that I could proceed to cross, perhaps my internal assessment was that I had a pretty good chance of making it across. If I then observed that the road was wet and slick from heavy rains, I might adjust my perceived probability regarding the inference and decide that the chances of crossing quickly enough were a lot lower than my original estimation.

You can prudently contend that inferences entail an entanglement of the known and the unknown. John Dewey, the revered American psychologist and philosopher, had proffered this insight: "Inference is always an invasion of the unknown, a leap from the known." We customarily start toward an inference by mentally assembling what we know or seem to know, and then make a hopefully sensible effort to gauge what the future or unknown is going to bring forth.

Why all this chitchat and chatter about the nature of inferences?

Because there is Artificial Intelligence (AI) devised inferences being made about you all day long, and the societal concern is whether you have any particular rights of how AI is devising those inferences and even if you ought to be able to know what if any such inferences exist about you.

I am betting that you probably assumed that of course, you have full rights to knowing all about any AI inferences that pertain to you. That might appear to be obvious at face value. Shouldn't you be able to know what AI is guessing about you?

Furthermore, we already noted earlier that any inferences made by humans can sometimes be right and sometimes be wrong. An AI system could decidedly be making incorrect inferences about you too. Though some people hazily think that AI is never wrong, which is a mindbogglingly crazy and completely unsupported notion, there is a strong chance that there are AI inferences sitting here and there on computers and networks that are utterly off-target about who you are and what you are aiming to do.

How might AI be making inferences about you?

Based on your social media postings, an AI system might have been programmed to grab up your tweets and other posts, doing so to make inferences about you. Aha, you made several posts that mentioned a recent trip to Las Vegas. The AI infers that you are an avid gambler and this inference is used to feed you ads about online gambling or perhaps send you mailers about how to break the onerous habit of addictive gambling. Meanwhile, other posts that you have made indicate that you like to drink beers when vacationing and also tend to have a glass of wine or two with your dinners.

The AI generates an inference that you are an alcoholic.

Fair or unfair?

I dare say that most of us would be outraged and totally enraged if we could see all the AI-derived inferences that exist on planet Earth about us (well, computing is heading to outer space too, so those AI inferences might be sitting out there as well).

Speaking of sitting, please sit down for the next eye-opening statement about this. You might be unpleasantly surprised to know that those AI inferences are not readily or customarily a core part of your legal rights per se, at least not as you might have naturally presumed that they were.

An ongoing legal and ethical debate is still underway about the nature of AI-based inferences, including some experts that insist AI inferences are emphatically a central aspect of your personal data and other experts strenuously counterargue that AI inferences are assuredly not at all in the realm of so-called *personal data* (the catchphrase of "personal data" is usually the cornerstone around which data-related legal rights are shaped).

All of this raises a lot of societal challenges. AI is becoming more and more pervasive throughout society. The odds are that AI is making lots and lots of inferences about us all. Are we allowing ourselves to be vulnerable and at the mercy of these AI-based inferences? Should we be clamoring to make sure that AI inferences are within our scope of data-related rights? These questions are being bandied around by experts in the law and likewise by expert ethicists.

Some people react to the AI inferences topic with a sense of indifference and merely shrug their shoulders. I don't care what kind of nutty inferences an AI system fabricates, say those that are sanguine about it. Go at it. AI will do what AI does. Let AI be.

Well, there are plenty of reasons to get riled up about AI inferences. Researchers point out for example some of the disconcerting and sobering qualms: "The concern is that individuals will be put into categories that are for one inaccurate and secondly, hard to break out of. This can lead to individuals being discriminated and social inequality being amplified, by categorizing individuals based on inferences, that cannot be evaluated for accuracy or are not subject to checks for up-to-datedness. Individuals might therefore get judged, not based on what they've done, or will do in the future, but because inferences or correlations drawn by algorithms suggest they may behave in ways that make them poor credit or insurance risks" (Celin Fischer, "The Legal Protection Against Inferences Drawn By AI Under The GDPR," July 2020, *Tilburg University Law School*).

Imagine that an AI inference is made about you that you are an addictive gambler and an alcoholic, per the scenarios depicted a moment ago.

This can be spread from computer to computer. Eventually, databases everywhere might have this AI inference in them. You are unaware of this. Turns out that whenever you do things like apply for a job or try to get a mortgage, an online query related to approving those life-desired choices will be confronted by AI inferences that could insidiously sink your aspirations and dreams.

Again, you might not even know that those AI inferences are waiting out there like hidden online digital landmines waiting to destroy your life.

The usual way in which data-related rights are arranged tends to include "personal data" as the hallmark of what constitutes something that you legally can do something about. Three types normally are encompassed, and then there is the fourth one that might or might be in the rubric.

Consider these four types of personal data:

- **Provided Data** – data that you gave to the AI in one fashion or another
- **Observed Data** – data that the AI somehow noted about you
- **Derived Data** – data that the AI calculated about you based on available data
- **Inferred Data** – data that consists of AI inferences about you

Many of the laws regarding data privacy and data protection will typically include the Provided Data, Observed Data, and Derived Data. The facets of Inferred Data might or might not be included.

The attention overall seems to pretty much concentrate on the first three and not as much on the fourth element, the Inferred data. Consider a prime example of this. You might be aware that the EU has the GDPR (General Data Protection Regulation) which is one of the most comprehensive legal underpinnings established for data-related rights and protections. According to this researcher, data-related inferences are said to be second-class or less than prized in contrast to the other types of personal data: "Compared to other types of personal data, inferences are effectively 'economy class' personal data in the General Data Protection Regulation ('GDPR'). Data subjects' rights to know about (Art. 13–15), rectify (Art. 16), delete (Art. 17), object to (Art. 21), or port (Art. 20) personal data are significantly curtailed when it comes to inferences, often requiring a greater balance with the controller's interests (e.g., trade secrets or intellectual property) than would otherwise be the case" (Sandra Wachter and Brent Mittelstadt, "A Right To Reasonable Inferences Re-Thinking Data Protection Law In The Age Of Big Data And AI," *Columbia Business Law Review*).

Those AI inferences could be biased, discriminatory, and have incorporated an untold number of falsehoods about your race, gender, and the like.

This brings up a whack-a-mole problem. Suppose that there are stringent rights about the Provided Data, the Observed Data, and the Derived Data. You manage to stay on top of how that kind of data is being represented about you. Leveraging various data-related privacy and protection rights, you ensure that the data does not contain biases and discriminatory indications (that alone would be an incredible feat, by the way).

An AI system uses the Provided Data, Observed, Data, and Derived Data to contrive an inference about you that turns out to be absolutely biased and discriminatory. Yikes! Even though you did your best to scour the source data, the AI opts to use it anyway to derive an inference that is in fact of a biased or discriminatory nature. Exasperating. Exhausting. Enraging.

Here is how this research paper describes the situation: "These inferences draw on highly diverse and feature-rich data of unpredictable value and create new opportunities for discriminatory, biased, and privacy-invasive profiling and decision-making. Inferential analytics methods are used to infer user preferences, sensitive attributes (e.g., race, gender, sexual orientation), and opinions (e.g., political stances), or to predict behaviors (e.g., to serve advertisements). These methods can be used to nudge or manipulate us, or to make important decisions (e.g., loan or employment decisions) about us" (as cited above, "A Right To Reasonable Inferences Re-Thinking Data Protection Law In The Age Of Big Data And AI," *Columbia Business Law Review*).

Before getting into some more meat and potatoes about the wild and woolly considerations underlying AI inferences, let's establish some additional fundamentals on profoundly integral topics. We need to briefly take a breezy dive into AI Ethics and especially the advent of Machine Learning (ML) and Deep Learning (DL).

You might be vaguely aware that one of the loudest voices these days in the AI field and even outside the field of AI consists of clamoring for a greater semblance of Ethical AI. Let's take a look at what it means to refer to AI Ethics and Ethical AI. On top of that, we will explore what I mean when I speak of Machine Learning and Deep Learning.

One particular segment or portion of AI Ethics that has been getting a lot of media attention consists of AI that exhibits untoward biases and inequities. You might be aware that when the latest era of AI got underway there was a huge burst of enthusiasm for what some now call *AI For Good.* Unfortunately, on the heels of that gushing excitement, we began to witness *AI For Bad.* For example, various AI-based facial recognition systems have been revealed as containing racial biases and gender biases.

There are a handful of proposed AI inference pertinent data-related legal rights that some assert should be codified into our laws. This is being considered or in some cases being enacted via laws on a national and international basis. A lot of gray area still exists. In the United States, the various state laws vary quite a bit on the AI inference legalities. The whole kit and kaboodle have yet to be resolved across the board.

Those of you in California might be familiar with the California Consumer Privacy Act (CCPA). A recently expressed opinion by the California Office of the Attorney General (OAG) proffered indications about consumer rights regarding AI and digitally derived inferences. In short, it was interpreted that the CCPA seems to provide consumers with a limited sort of right to know about such inferences. A mainstay focuses on the CCPA language that refers to "… inferences drawn from any of the information identified in this subdivision to create a profile about a consumer reflecting the consumer's preferences, characteristics, psychological trends, predispositions, behavior, attitudes, intelligence, abilities, and aptitudes." It seems that the OAG textually analyses this and other associated CCPA language to predicate that the right arises when the inference is based on personal data as further defined within the CCPA and when a business opts to create a profile about the consumer.

Take a look at this excerpt from the formal opinion issued by the OAG: "Under the California Consumer Privacy Act, does a consumer's right to know the specific pieces of personal information that a business has collected about that consumer apply to internally generated inferences the business holds about the consumer from either internal or external information sources? Yes, under the California Consumer Privacy Act, a consumer has the right to know internally generated inferences about that consumer, unless a business can demonstrate that a statutory exception to the Act applies" (OAG, State of California, March 10, 2022).

As with any such legal matter, you would be wise to consult with a versed attorney on such matters for insights on the topic. There are also plenty of online analyses about the OAG published opinion. The responses range from buoyant optimism to disappointment that the allowance for exceptions and other conditions could water things down.

Those that stridently argue for outright and fully explicit rights associated with AI inferences will usually want these kinds of provisions:

- Right to know what AI inferences exist about you
- Right to ensure that the AI inferences about you are "reasonable"
- Right to be able to rectify or fix AI inferences that you believe to be improper
- Right to have AI inferences about you get deleted or expunged
- Right to challenge decisions made about you based on AI inferences about you
- Etc.

There are a bunch of thorny considerations involved in the rights underlying AI inferences. For example, one contention is that any AI inferences about you must be "reasonable" and cannot or should not be unreasonable that perhaps falsely or misleadingly infer something about you. Another perspective is that AI inferences ought to be classified as to whether they are advantageous for you versus being adversely against you.

Trying to iron out those details is a rough road, for sure.

You might be curious as to why there would be an acrimonious debate about having rights to AI inferences. It seems like one of those open and shut cases. Everyone would almost universally seem to want to have rights associated with AI inferences.

Companies that use AI for devising such inferences would at times beg to differ on this suggestion that the matter is open and shut. Likewise, firms that rely upon AI inferences would also question the arguable claim that it is simple and cleanly figured out. Things are more complex than a cursory glance suggests.

One argument is that the AI inferences are potentially trade secrets of a given firm. If a company has to reveal the AI inferences, it might be unduly divulging its Intellectual Property (IP). This divulging might expose not just the inferred data but also reveal how the AI inferences are being computationally devised altogether, perhaps giving up valued methods and procedures to competitors. The secret sauce, as it were, could be backward engineered by the mere showing of the AI inference results.

On top of that, some firms might wish to treat the AI inferences as a form of asset that they can then monetize. A company might wish to sell its AI inferences. A company might be willing to trade AI inferences for other goods or services. The belief is that by revealing AI inferences, the cost of having created the means to devise them will not be recouped and an unfair "taking" of profits associated with the AI inferences will occur.

Counterarguments abound. Companies can potentially be sloppy and create harmful AI inferences without any repercussions if there aren't suitable and sufficient laws on this. Consumers can get sorely dinged. Expecting firms to voluntarily do the right thing about AI inferences is considered by some as dreamy or unrealistic.

Welcome to the morass underpinning the lofty and at times the acrid matter of AI inferences.

At this juncture of this weighty discussion, I'd bet that you are desirous of some illustrative examples that might showcase this topic. There is a special and assuredly popular set of examples that are close to my heart. You see, in my capacity as an expert on AI including the ethical and legal ramifications, I am frequently asked to identify realistic examples that showcase AI Ethics dilemmas so that the somewhat theoretical nature of the topic can be more readily grasped. One of the most evocative areas that vividly presents this ethical AI quandary is the advent of AI-based true self-driving cars. This will serve as a handy use case or exemplar for ample discussion on the topic.

Here's then a noteworthy question that is worth contemplating: *Does the advent of AI-based true self-driving cars illuminate anything about the use of AI inferences, and if so, what does this showcase?*

We shall begin by heaping praise upon the use of ML/DL in the realm of bringing forth AI-based self-driving cars. Several key aspects of self-driving cars have come to fruition as a result of using Machine Learning and Deep Learning. For example, consider the core requirement of having to detect and analyze the driving scene that surrounds an AI-based self-driving car.

You've undoubtedly noticed that most self-driving cars have a myriad of mounted sensors on the autonomous vehicle. This is often done on the rooftop of the self-driving car. Sensor devices such as video cameras, LIDAR units, radar units, ultrasonic detectors, and the like are typically included on a rooftop rack or possibly affixed to the car top or sides of the vehicle. The array of sensors is intended to electronically collect data that can be used to figure out what exists in the driving scene.

The sensors collect data and feed the digitized data to onboard computers. Those computers can be a combination of general-purpose computing processors and specialized processors that are devised specifically to analyze sensory data. By and large, most of the sensory data computational analysis is undertaken by ML/DL that has been crafted for this purpose and is running on the vehicle's onboard computing platforms.

The ML/DL computationally tries to find patterns in the data such as where the roadway is, where pedestrians are, where other nearby cars are, and so on. All of this is crucial to being able to have the self-driving car proceed ahead. Without the ML/DL performing the driving scene analysis, the self-driving car would be essentially blind as to what exists around the autonomous vehicle.

In brief, you can readily make the case that the use of ML/DL is essential to the emergence of AI-based self-driving cars. It all seems a heralded matter. But that is until you start to look into some of the details and possibilities of what the future might hold.

I've repeatedly been warning about the massive potential of privacy intrusions due to the advent of self-driving cars. Few are giving much attention to the matter at this time because it hasn't yet risen as a realized problem. I assure you that it will ultimately be a humongous problem, one that I've labeled as the veritably "roving eye" of self-driving cars.

Your first thought might be that this is assuredly solely about the privacy of passengers. The AI could monitor what riders are doing while inside a self-driving car. Sure, that's a definite concern. But I'd argue it pales in comparison to the less obvious qualm that has even larger ramifications.

Simply stated, the sensors of the self-driving car are collecting all kinds of data as the autonomous vehicles roam throughout our public roadways. It captures what is happening on the front lawns of our houses. It captures what people are doing when walking from place to place. It shows when you entered an establishment and when you left it. This data can be easily uploaded into the cloud of the fleet operator.

The fleet operator could then connect this data and essentially have the details of our day-to-day lives that occur while outdoors and throughout our community.

We don't seem to care about that privacy intrusion potential right now because there are only handfuls of self-driving cars being tried out in relatively few locales. Someday, we'll have hundreds of thousands or millions of self-driving cars that are crisscrossing all of our major cities and towns. Our daily outdoor lives will be recorded non-stop, 24x7 and we can be tracked accordingly.

You could suggest that this data about our lives is within the three categories of personal data that I earlier discussed, namely Provided Data, Observed Data, and Derived Data.

Would AI inferences also come to play here?

Undoubtedly.

An AI system is set up to examine the vast collection of data about your comings and goings. The AI ferrets out of the data that you visit the local pub on Tuesday and Thursday evenings. You stay there for several hours. The AI has been programmed to make inferences from the data that is being examined.

As a result, the AI infers that you are an alcoholic.

Turns out that the pub also allows legalized gambling via the use of slot machines and the like. The AI infers that you are an addictive gambler.

These AI inferences are then kept online and stored for further use. The automaker or fleet operator opts to sell these AI inferences to a wide array of other companies that want to know about you. All in all, these AI inferences are completely unknown to you, yet they are being shared, sold, and traded endlessly while you are carrying on your daily life.

Seems a bit daunting.

It is a boatload of AI Ethics, legal AI issues, and societal challenges.

Conclusion

Those that are in favor of AI inferences point out that without those inferences the world might not go around. In addition, if we are aiming to make AI as "intelligent" as possible, it would seem that we have no choice but to devote attention to crafting AI that can make inferences.

Remember the words of Friedrich Nietzsche that I quoted at the start of this discussion: "The greatest progress that the human race has made lies in learning how to make correct inferences." The implication is that humans rely on making inferences. Ergo, you could try to claim that AI of any semblance will also likely need to rely on making inferences. If you try to stop or block the use of AI inferences, you are said to be trying to turn back the clock on making progress in AI. This in turn would seem detrimental since you can readily make the case that the advent of AI has been beneficial in numerous glorious respects to society (though, the tradeoff consists too of the bad sides of AI).

Within the quotation by Nietzsche is the crucial point about making *correct* inferences. In that manner of consideration, rather than trying to prevent AI inferences, the argument goes that we should be attending to making sure that the AI inferences are correct. We should all agree that AI inferences are needed and must be permitted, while the contentious angle is whether the AI inferences are correct or not.

That leads us to the open-ended question about what in fact is or is not a correct AI inference.

The right to know about AI inferences might be a means of keeping this ship on course. We can have AI inferences and eat our cake too. Will the right AI tech and the right set of laws about AI inferences and our rights as humans ensure that we have a cake worth eating?

Time will tell.

CHAPTER 14
AI ETHICS
AND
BOUNTY HUNTING

Wanted: *AI bias hunters.*

That could be a modern-day ad that you'll begin to see popping up on social media channels and making appearances in various online job postings. This is a relatively new concept or role. It carries with it controversy. Some ardent believers fervently argue that it makes abundant sense and should have been happening all along, while others are rather nervously doing some serious head-scratching and not so sure that this is a good idea.

The gist of the role consists of ferreting out of AI any hidden biases or embedded discriminatory practices. To the rescue come the eager and altogether erstwhile AI biases hunters. They would presumably be computer-savvy bounty hunters. More so, hopefully, steeped in the depths of AI capabilities.

Have gun, will travel, and can via AI-skilled keen marksmanship manage to expose those unsavory and untoward AI biases.

This raises a slew of thorny questions about the sensibility of pursuing such a tactic when it comes to discovering AI biases. As I will discuss momentarily, please know that the advent of AI has also brought with it the emergence of AI biases. A torrent of AI biases.

How are we to discover that a particular AI system has biases?

You might entrust the AI developers that devised the AI to do so. The thing is, they might be so mired in biases that they themselves cannot recognize the biases within their concocted AI. It all looks good to them. Or they might be so excited about the AI and have a sense of self-pride about it that to have to then take a critical eye to examine it for biases would be difficult and a real downer. Lots of other such reasons might seem to undercut having the AI developers take on this task, including lack of skills to figure out the embedded biases, lack of time in a project to do so, etc.

Okay, so go ahead and hire outside consultants to do the dirty work for you, as it were. Turns out that consultants will happily scrutinize your AI for biases, charging you a pretty penny to do so (lots and lots of pennies). Realize that you need to pay for them to come up to speed with your AI system. You need to then have them rummage around, which might take an untold number of costly laborious hours. Using consultants is an option if you have the budget for it.

Into the potential "gap" of how to find those insidious AI biases come the heroic and dashing AI biases bounty hunters.

You don't usually pay them upfront. They try to find the AI biases on their own time and have to foot their own bills as they do so. Only if they successfully find biases do they get paid. I suppose you could readily assert that in a suitable manner of thinking, that's the conventional definition of a bounty hunter. Get paid if you succeed. Don't get paid if you aren't successful. Period, end of story.

Bounty programs have existed since at least the time of the Romans and thus we might surmise that they do work, having successfully endured as a practice over all of these years.

Here's a fascinating piece of historical trivia for you. Reportedly, a posted message during the Roman Empire in the city of Pompeii proclaimed that bounty hunters were needed to find a copper pot that went missing from a small shop. The reward for the recovery of the copper pot was an impressive prize of sixty-five bronze coins.

Sorry to say that we don't know if any bounty hunter found the copper pot and claimed the bronze coins, but we do know that bounty hunting has certainly continued since those ancient times.

In more modern times, you might be aware that in the 1980s there were some notable bounties offered to find computer bugs or errors in off-the-shelf software packages and then in the 1990's Netscape markedly offered a bounty for finding bugs in their web browser (becoming one of the most prominent firms of that day to do so). Google and Facebook had each opted toward bounty hunting for bugs starting in 2010 and 2013 years, respectively. A few years later, in 2016 even the U.S. Department of Defense (DoD) got into the act by having a "Hack the Pentagon" bounty effort (note that the publicly focused bounty was for bugs found in various DoD-related websites and not in defense mission-critical systems).

Let's dig more deeply into the bug bounty topic. I realize that I am mainly aiming to talk about AI biases in bounty hunting in this discussion, but there are some quite relevant parallels to the bug bounty arena.

Some are demonstrably puzzled that any firm would want to offer a bounty to find bugs (or, in this case, AI biases) in their systems.

On the surface, this seems like a "you are asking for it" kind of strategy. If you let the world know that you welcome those that might try to find holes in your software, it seems tantamount to telling burglars to go ahead and try to break into your house. Even if you already believe that you've got a pretty good burglar alarm system and that no one should be able to get into your secured home, imagine asking and indeed pleading with burglars to all descend upon your place of residence and see if they can crack into it. Oh, the troubles we weave for ourselves.

The same could be said about asking for bounty hunters to find biases in your AI.

First, it perhaps implies that you already believe or even outright know that your AI does have biases. That is a shockingly forthright implied admission that few would seem willing to make and could potentially backfire.

Second, you don't know for sure what those bounty hunters might do. They could opt to tell the whole world that they found biases in your AI. One supposes this might forfeit getting the bounty, though some might relish the attention or aim to bolster their status for getting consulting gigs and other revenue-generating possibilities. It could perhaps be entirely altruistic. It might be a form of AI activism. I can keep going.

Third, there could be a sneaky twist to the whole affair. A bounty hunter claiming to be searching for AI biases might be devilishly poking around to find ways to attack your AI system. The whole thing is a charade to ultimately undertake a severe cyberattack. You might have assumed they were trying to help, while they have wrongdoing in their hearts. Sad, but possible.

Fourth, we can get even more slyly contorted on this matter. A bounty hunter finds some embarrassing and potentially lawsuit spurring AI biases. The bounty is some amount of dollars that we will call X. Rather than claiming the bounty, the bounty hunter does a kind of oddish ransomware provocation. If you pay the bounty hunter an amount of ten times X or maybe the skies the limit, they will tell you about the AI biases. You have until Sunday night at midnight to answer. After that point in time, the AI biases will be revealed for all to see. Yikes, a dastardly predicament to be in.

I realize that some of you might be saying that nobody should be releasing AI that has any biases in it. That would seem to solve this whole dilemma about whether to use AI biases bounty hunters or not. Just don't get yourself into a bounty situation. Make sure your AI developers do the right thing and do not allow AI biases into their AI systems. Perhaps use consultants to do a double-check. In essence, do whatever you need to do to avoid ever thinking about or asking those AI bias bounty hunters to come to the table.

Yes, that would seem entirely sensible. The problem is that it is also a bit dreamy. The complexity of many AI systems is so great that trying to ensure that not a single ounce of AI biases emerges is going to be arduous to do. On top of that, some AI systems are purposely devised to adjust and "learn" as they go along. This means that at some future point in time the AI that you devised, which let's pretend at first was purely clean and without biases, might gravitate toward embodying biases (I do not mean that in an anthropomorphic way, as I will explain further as we go along on this topic).

Those that favor bounty hunting for software bugs are prone to argue that it makes sense to offer such bounties. We can consider their rationale and see if it applies to the AI biases realm too.

Proponents of bug bounties emphasize that rather than trying to pretend that there aren't any holes in your system, why not encourage holes to be found, doing so in a "controlled" manner? In contrast, without such a bounty effort, you could just hope and pray that by random chance no one will find a hole, but if instead you are offering a bounty and telling those that find a hole that they will be rewarded, it offers a chance to then shore-up the hole on your own and then prevents others from secretly finding it at some later point in time.

The same could be said in the use case of AI biases. If you offer a sufficient bounty, hopefully, the bounty hunters will bring the discovery of AI biases to your attention. You can then cope with the AI biases in a relatively quiet and measured way. This might forestall a much larger and more daunting problem later on, namely that somebody else finds AI biases in your AI and screams about it to the high heavens.

Generally, a firm wishing to enable bugs-oriented bounty hunting will put in place a Vulnerability Disclosure Policy (VDP). The VDP indicates how the bugs are to be found and reported to the firm, along with how the reward or bounty will be provided to the hunter. Usually, the VDP will require that the hunter end up signing a Non-Disclosure Agreement (NDA) such that they won't reveal to others what they found.

The notion of using an NDA with bounty hunters has some controversy. Though it perhaps makes sense to the company offering the bounty to want to keep mum the exposures found, it also is said to stifle overall awareness about such bugs. Presumably, if software bugs are allowed to be talked about, it would potentially aid the safety of other systems at other firms that would then shore up their exposures. Some bounty hunters won't sign an NDA, partially due to the public desire and partially due to trying to keep their own identity hidden. Keep in mind too that the NDA aspect doesn't arise usually until after the hunter claims they have found a bug, rather than requiring it beforehand.

Some VDPs stipulate that the NDA is only for a limited time period, allowing the firm to first find a solution to the apparent hole and then afterward to allow for wider disclosure about it. Once the hole has been plugged, the firm then allows a loosening of the NDA so that the rest of the world can know about the bug. The typical time-to-resolution for bounty hunted bugs is reportedly around 15-20 days when a firm wants to plug it right away, while in other cases it might stretch out to 60-80 days. In terms of paying the bounty hunter, the so-called time-to-pay, after the hole has been verified as actually existing, the bounty payments reportedly tend to be within about 15-20 days for the smaller instances and around 50-60 days for the larger instances (these are constantly changing industry indications and only mentioned as illustrative).

Should AI biases bounty hunters also be asked to participate in a VDP and deal with an NDA?

You can get a yes and a no to that question. Yes, some firms should go that route. No, you might not necessarily opt to go that route. Factors include the size and nature of the AI, the potential of any AI biases exposures involved, and a bunch of other ethical, legal, and business considerations that come to bear.

I might add that establishing a bounty hunting endeavor for AI biases of your AI is a much taller order than you might assume at an initial glance.

We will start with the formidable possibility that you will be overwhelmed by AI biases bounty hunters.

Right now, you would be hard-pressed to find many that would have such a calling card. There aren't many around. It is the days of the Wild West in that regard. But if the notion of AI biases in bounty hunting catches on, especially when the bounties are plentiful and richly rewarding, you can bet that everyone will dive into the biases hunting swimming pool.

Do you want all sorts of riffraff pursuing AI biases in your AI system? You will get some takers that are actually experts at this sort of thing. You will get other takers that are amateurs and might make a mess or cry wolf. The next thing you know, anybody that can spell "Artificial Intelligence" will be coming to dig in your goldmine of an AI system for those precious AI biases gold nuggets. The gold rush is on. That might not be good for you.

You will need to scrutinize the bounty hunter submissions. There will be a lot of "noise" in the reported claims, in the sense that many of the claimed AI biases do not exist, though the bounty hunter insists that they found some. Imagine how much labor your own AI teams will be required to examine the bounty claims, explore the validity of each, and then potentially go back and forth with the bounty hunter about whether gold was discovered or not.

Some would argue that's another reason to do the whole thing yourself. You might inevitably discover that the bounty thing is more trouble than it was worth.

Here's another question to ponder. How will the bounty hunters know what an AI bias looks like? In essence, without some semblance of what to be looking for, any shiny rock could be claimed as showcasing an AI bias in the perceived AI goldmine being excavated.

In the days of the Old West, suppose you offered a reward for the capture of Billy the Kid (a famous outlaw). If you did so and did not include a picture of what Billy looked like, imagine the number of bounty hunters that might drag into the sheriff's office someone that they hoped or thought was Billy the Kid. You might get inundated with false Billy's. This is bad since you'd need to presumably look at each one, ask probing questions, and try to ascertain whether the person was really Billy or not.

The point is that to set up the AI biases bounty effort you would be wise to try and clarify what you consider AI biases to consist of. This requires a Goldilocks kind of calibration. You don't want to be so confining that the bounty hunters overlook AI biases merely because they don't fit within your stipulated definition, and nor do you want them to yell "Eureka!" at every morsel of an AI bias that they perchance find.

You will need just the right Goldilocks balance of what AI biases consist of and thus provide preferably explicit directions thereof.

A lot of this AI biases bounty hunting is going to be focused on AI-based Machine Learning (ML) and Deep Learning (DL) systems. This makes sense since the advent of ML/DL pervasiveness is growing, plus it seems to have some of the most likely challenges of encompassing undue AI biases.

These researchers identify how salient an AI biases bounty hunting effort can be, particularly in the ML/DL context: "Over time, the software and security communities have developed 'bug bounties' in an attempt to turn similar dynamics between system developers and their critics (or hackers) towards more interactive and productive ends. The hope is that by deliberately inviting external parties to find software or hardware bugs in their systems, and often providing monetary incentives for doing so, a healthier and more rapidly responding ecosystem will evolve. It is natural for the ML community to consider a similar 'bias bounty' approach to the timely discovery and repair of models and systems with bias or other undesirable behaviors. Rather than finding bugs in software, external parties are invited to find biases -- for instance, (demographic or other) subgroups of inputs on which a trained model underperforms -- and are rewarded for doing so" (in the paper "An Algorithmic Framework for Bias Bounties" by Ira Globus-Harris, Michael Kearns and Aaron Roth).

In the research paper, the authors outline a suggested approach to what kinds of AI biases can be sought by bounty hunters. There is also an indication about how to assess the bounty hunter claims associated with the alleged AI biases so discovered. As per my earlier remarks herein, the odds are that you will receive specious claims and have to separate the AI biases wheat from the chaff.

Before getting into some more meat and potatoes about the wild and woolly considerations underlying AI bias hunting, let's establish some additional fundamentals on profoundly integral topics. We need to briefly take a breezy dive into AI Ethics and especially the advent of Machine Learning (ML) and Deep Learning (DL).

You might be vaguely aware that one of the loudest voices these days in the AI field and even outside the field of AI consists of clamoring for a greater semblance of Ethical AI. Let's take a look at what it means to refer to AI Ethics and Ethical AI. On top of that, we will explore what I mean when I speak of Machine Learning and Deep Learning.

One particular segment or portion of AI Ethics that has been getting a lot of media attention consists of AI that exhibits untoward biases and inequities. You might be aware that when the latest era of AI got underway there was a huge burst of enthusiasm for what some now call *AI For Good.* Unfortunately, on the heels of that gushing excitement, we began to witness *AI For Bad.* For example, various AI-based facial recognition systems have been revealed as containing racial biases and gender biases.

For those of you considering an AI bias bounty hunting endeavor, here are my recommended seven key steps on how to best proceed:

1) **Assess.** Assess the suitability of an AI bias bounty hunting endeavor for your circumstances and as per your AI systems
2) **Design.** Design an appropriate AI bias bounty hunting approach
3) **Implement.** Implement and publicize your AI bias bounty hunting endeavors
4) **Field.** Field the AI biases bounty claims and process accordingly
5) **Fix.** Fix or adjust your AI as pertinent to these discovered AI bias exposures
6) **Adjust.** Adjust the AI biases bounty hunting as needed
7) **Discontinue.** Discontinue the AI bias bounty hunting when it is no longer needed

In my series of above steps, note that I mention that you will presumably want to fix or adjust your AI as based on ascertaining that a claimed AI bias does in fact exist within your AI system. This abundantly makes sense. You would almost certainly want to shore up any found AI biases. Think of the legal (and ethical) ramifications if you don't do so. It is one thing to assert that you didn't know an AI bias existed and therefore allowed it to exist, while it is much shakier ground to have on record that you were made aware of an AI bias and did nothing about it.

The nature and degree of the AI fix or adjustment would of course be contingent on how significant the AI biases were and how deeply embedded the issues are. If you are lucky, perhaps a modest amount of changes to the AI will rectify matters. The other potential is that you might need to do an entire rewrite of the AI. For the ML/DL type of AI, this could require going back to the drawing board and starting fresh with an entirely new set of data and a cleaned-up ML/DL model. I've discussed the advent of AI disgorgement or AI destruction as a potential legal remedy against unsavory AI.

One question to mull over is whether you would want the bounty hunters to possibly do more than just identify the existence of AI biases.

For example, you might sweeten the bounty by indicating that proposed fixes are welcome too. An AI bias *found* by a bounty hunter might be paid one indicated reward or prize. If the bounty hunter can also proffer a viable *fix* to the AI bias they might then be granted an additional reward.

Some argue that this is a bridge too far. They say that you should keep the AI bias bounty hunters exclusively focused on finding AI biases. You are going to create a bunch of undesirable adverse consequences by inviting them to also suggest fixes. Keep things simple. The goal is to get as many additional eyes on discovering AI biases so that you can decide what to do next. Do not muddy the waters.

A thorny aspect that needs to be figured out entails the magnitude of the reward or prize for the bounty hunters that genuinely discover AI biases. You want the payoff to be demonstrative. Without a high enough reward, you won't get many bounty hunters or they will not be especially eager to seek out the AI biases in your AI systems. They might instead concentrate on other AI bias bounty endeavors.

Furthermore, as mentioned, you want to try and repress an urge by the bounty hunters to turn their AI bias discoveries into other forms of gold. If the reward seems measly, it could irk bounty hunters into seeking other higher payoffs. They could take a ransomware approach toward you. They might declare that they have a juicy AI bias that a competitor would love to know about and could use against your firm by touting that the AI bias exists in your AI. Thus, they sell the discovered AI bias to the highest bidder. And so on.

One supposes that if you set the reward at an extremely high range, you are also asking for potential trouble. This could attract all kinds of nutty bounty hunters. They in turn might deluge social media with hazy claims that they found a multitude of AI biases, doing so for their own self-promotion and without having actually speared any AI biases. In a sense, your heightened reward inadvertently shines a light on your AI and prods a slew of uncouth moths to correspondingly be perniciously attracted to the glowing light beam.

Another consideration involves accessibility to your AI.

To enable an AI bounty hunting possibility, the bounty hunters have to sufficiently gain access to your AI. They aren't going to have much luck in finding AI biases if they are entirely locked out. But you don't want to give up your cybersecurity protections since doing so could completely compromise your AI system.

You might try to have the bounty hunters sign various legally binding declarations and then provide them with the needed access. Some bounty hunters aren't going to like that type of approach. Their viewpoint is that they will only do whatever any publicly available and open-ended path allows. They are free mavericks, as it were, and do not like being saddled, as it were. Getting them to put their signature on intimidating legal documents will cause a lot of them to avoid searching for AI biases in your AI. Or they might get peeved at your legal gauntlet and decide they will see what they can find via public means, doing so with the perhaps strident urge to show you how vulnerable you really are.

I've got yet another angle that might make your head spin.

An AI savvy bounty hunter might decide to devise an AI system that can scrutinize your AI and possibly discover AI biases in your AI. This is the toolmaker opting to make a tool to do the job rather than performing manual labor themselves. Instead of laboriously examining your AI, the AI-versed bounty hunter spends their time concocting an AI tool that does the same thing. They then use the AI tool on your AI. The beauty too is that they can presumably reuse the AI tool on anyone else that is also offering a bounty hunting opportunity on their respective AI as well.

I know what you are probably thinking. If an AI tool can be devised to examine AI for biases, the maker of the AI that is being scrutinized for AI biases ought to either craft such an AI tool or buy one for their own use. In theory, they then do not need to contend with the whole bounty hunter carnival, to begin with. Just use AI to find their AI biases.

Yes, this is something that you can expect will gradually arise. Meanwhile, the mainstay of these efforts will likely consist of AI developers doing bounty hunting. They might use various tools to aid their efforts, but in the near term, they are unlikely to simply mindlessly set the AI tool on automatic and take a nap such that the tool does the entirety of the AI bias hunting for them.

We aren't there yet.

At this juncture of this weighty discussion, I'd bet that you are desirous of some illustrative examples that might showcase this topic. There is a special and assuredly popular set of examples that are close to my heart. You see, in my capacity as an expert on AI including the ethical and legal ramifications, I am frequently asked to identify realistic examples that showcase AI Ethics dilemmas so that the somewhat theoretical nature of the topic can be more readily grasped. One of the most evocative areas that vividly presents this ethical AI quandary is the advent of AI-based true self-driving cars. This will serve as a handy use case or exemplar for ample discussion on the topic.

Here's then a noteworthy question that is worth contemplating: *Does the advent of AI-based true self-driving cars illuminate anything about the use of AI bias bounty hunting, and if so, what does this showcase?*

The use of bugs-oriented bounty hunters in the autonomous vehicles and self-driving cars realm has been underway for a while. There are the usual debates about whether it is a sound idea or not. The efforts have usually been of a limited nature, often kept relatively quiet.

A likewise discourse can ensue when the focus shifts toward hunting for AI biases rather than seeking system bugs per se. Some suggest it is a darned if you do, darned if you don't conundrum.

Here's why.

First, to be clear, there are numerous ways in which autonomous vehicles and self-driving cars are going to be subject to containing AI biases. Automakers and self-driving car firms would seem wise to try and prevent those AI biases from appearing in their AI systems. The legal and ethical firestorm against such firms will undoubtedly be intense.

Is the use of an AI biases bounty hunting endeavor a suitable approach in this specific context?

One answer is that yes, this will be handy and provide an abundance of "free" sets of new eyes to try and catch any embedded AI biases of an AI self-driving car or the like. Most of the AI developers building self-driving cars are busy making AI that can safely drive a car from point A to point B. They are preoccupied with that core capability and have neither the time nor attention toward any AI biases that might be somewhere in their AI.

The other answer is that no, allowing bounty hunting for autonomous vehicles and self-driving cars on any basis, whether for bugs or AI biases, just ought to be fiercely avoided. The argument is that these vehicles and their AI are of a life-or-death caliber. Messing with the AI in any fashion could be somehow ruinous to the AI and impact what the AI driving system does.

A counterargument to that last point is that the bounty hunters are supposed to be unable to alter the AI that they are examining. Thus, there is no danger of them messing with the AI and causing the AI in this context to suddenly become a crazed AI driving system. The bounty hunters are only having read-only access. Allowing them to go further would be amply stupid and a huge mistake.

The counterargument to that counterargument is that by allowing and encouraging bounty hunters to examine your AI, the whole matter becomes dicey. Those bounty hunters might figure out ways to exploit any found bugs or biases. Those exploits in turn might be for devious purposes. You would be better off not inviting "burglars" into your home, so to speak. Once they have cased out the joint, you are ultimately going to be in a heap of trouble.

For those that have AI systems of a less-than-life-or-death magnitude, the belief is that the repercussions of a bounty hunting foray that goes awry are a lot less risky. Maybe so. On the other hand, if a firm has poured their monies into an AI system that bounty hunters manage to usurp, you can assume that the reputational damages and other potential damages will still hurt.

There is no free lunch when it comes to AI bias bounty hunting.

A quick closing remark for now.

When the notorious outlaw Jesse James was sought during the Old West, a "Wanted" poster was printed that offered a bounty of $5,000 for his capture (stating "dead or alive"). It was a rather massive sum of money at the time. One of his own gang members opted to shoot Jesse dead and collect the reward. I suppose that shows how effective a bounty can be.

Will the use of AI bias bounty hunters be a good thing, or will it be a bad thing?

If you opt to institute an AI bias bounty hunter endeavor, I'd suggest that you keep your eyes wide open and be looking over your shoulder at all times. This is prudent for you and your AI. You never know what might happen, including that a conniving bounty hunter somehow inserts surreptitiously an AI bias into your AI and shouts to the world that they found an unscrupulous AI bias in your AI. Perhaps doing so in a brazen and outsized attempt at seeking the bounty reward, plus proclaiming themselves a hero that essentially got the vaunted Jesse James.

Come to think of it, a sentient AI probably won't like that idea of a disconcerting dead-or-alive provision, one might languorously so speculate.

CHAPTER 15
AI ETHICS AND DUAL-USE AI

Sometimes evil can readily emerge even in the midst of ardently professed good.

You might say that this is a *dual-use* phenomenon.

Here's what that means. In particular, there is a rising dilemma confronting the field of AI due to the stark realization of a *dual-use AI* conundrum that is becoming increasingly evident. The idea is shockingly simple. You can potentially take an AI system that was devised with the utmost purity toward societally beneficial ideals and goals and with nary more than a flip of a switch turn that AI into a dreadful nightmare facing humanity.

That's considered "dual-use" because the AI can be designed for goodness and yet the next moment it can be readily switched over into abject terror. To get this undesirable or despicable switcheroo, you don't need to somehow completely rejigger the AI. You don't have to spend months making immense structural changes to the AI. Sure, that might be the way sometimes to get this done, but the scariest and seemingly imperiling circumstances entail the ridiculously easy flip-a-switch instances.

You might be a bit skeptical that AI could just go from goodness to utter badness by only making a few modest changes. I realize that this sounds akin to a wild sci-fi tale. Unfortunately, it isn't just a crazed or imaginative wave-it-away fictionally contrived possibility.

Dual-use AI is altogether possible and in fact, there are today vivid examples that exist to showcase how this can and does happen. We shall begin with perhaps one of the most famous instances widely publicized and recently covered in the respected journal called *Nature*. As you will soon see, the dual-use AI topic bears mightily on AI Ethics and Ethical AI, raising thorny issues encompassing both a societal morality basis and that spurs significant legal ramifications too.

Let's leap into the now-famous dual-use AI instance.

Some scientists had decided to create an AI system that would seek to find new molecular compounds that could potentially pave the way toward curative drugs to solve to-date unsolved diseases and other ills. You can applaud such efforts. We certainly hope and expect that pharmaceutical companies are using the latest in AI to discover new means of medically helping humankind.

Of course, not all molecular compounds are going to be disease-beating winners. The AI has to sift through a lot of wheat to discover the chaff, as it were. For humans, having to laboriously scrutinize thousands upon thousands of molecules is time-consuming and not particularly practical. But it turns out that mega volumes of searching are pretty much no problem for today's AI and especially when using Machine Learning (ML) and Deep Learning (DL). Setup the ML/Dl and let the computer crank away at the problem. I'll explain more about the nature of ML/DL momentarily.

The approach used by the scientists was to essentially load the ML/DL with millions of identified molecules along with their associated bioactivity data. These can be culled from various publicly available databases. Data like this is not especially secretive or under lock and key. The general notion is to use AI to examine existent molecular compounds, find computationally identifiable patterns, and then extrapolate from those patterns to propose new molecular compounds of a beneficial outcome.

When you are hoping to find some new molecular compound that will be a desirable cure, it would be wise to also try to avoid combinations that have notably adverse results. If I find something that cures a horrific disease and meanwhile it kills the person taking the cure, this doesn't seem like a drug that we ought to be relying upon. In short, the aim is to find those molecular compounds that have the greatest promise while simultaneously proffering the least toxicity.

I trust that this makes abundant sense.

Suppose though that we took this same AI and instead of *minimizing* the toxicity as a core criterion, we went the opposite direction. Switch the AI toward *maximizing* toxicity.

Yikes!

My bet is that you can anticipate where this is going.

The scientists doing this research on finding breakthrough molecular compounds were invited to speak at a conference that was focused on international security considerations underlying the use of weapons based on chemical, biological, and other such means. They were asked to give a presentation about how AI in the use case of drug discovery might be potentially misused for nefarious purposes.

As per their article and in their own words: "The thought had never previously struck us. We were vaguely aware of security concerns around work with pathogens or toxic chemicals, but that did not relate to us; we primarily operate in a virtual setting. Our work is rooted in building machine learning models for therapeutic and toxic targets to better assist in the design of new molecules for drug discovery. We have spent decades using computers and AI to improve human health—not to degrade it" (Fabio Urbina, Filippa Lentzos, Cédric Invernizzi, and Sean Ekins, "Dual-Use Of Artificial-Intelligence-Powered Drug Discovery," *Nature*, March 2022).

It might be surprising to you that these scientists did not beforehand apparently self-realize the dangers of how their work might be twisted. This is actually more pervasive than you might imagine.

For several important reasons.

First, there is often a tendency to get mired and deeply ingrained in your life's work. This keenly devoted preoccupation and passion make it hard to step outside of the realm and realize that the whole kit and kaboodle can be corrupted into evilness. The heads-down intensity can be advantageous, no doubt about it, but it can also blot out other objectionable considerations that are potentially worthwhile to be pondering.

Second, assuming that your intentions are of purity, it can be difficult to envision evildoers that would want to usurp what you are doing. If you spend all of your time around others that are all striving toward helping humanity, you can fall into the mental trap of thinking that everyone has a like mind (birds of a feather that flock together).

Third, those that are making use of AI can get into a kind of metaverse or virtual mode, as it were, wherein the effort is being done via a computer-based simulation and not necessarily being done in real-life (well, let me clarify). Generating lots of computer-devised theoretical drugs is not quite the same as physically making the drug. You normally have to go through quite a number of hurdles to go from the mathematically modeled version to physical manifestations. As such, you can somewhat live in a bubble or world of theoretical possibilities that do not seem equivalent to having the comparable drug in your hands and ready to be released.

Allow me a somewhat analogous comparison that might showcase this. Are you familiar with road rage that sometimes erupts on our public roadways? In some instances, people get into their own bubble while sitting at the steering wheel of their car. They begin to forget that the real world surrounds their vehicle. It is as though you are looking out the windshield at a simulation of reality, encompassing pedestrians, other cars, bicyclists, and the like.

By becoming somewhat detached from the world outside of the car, a driver can gradually find themselves getting quite upset at how those outside the vehicle are behaving. It is almost as though those other humans are merely avatars or something akin to that. Eventually, the driver gets cut off by some passing vehicle or believes they were, and they go nuts. They ram their car into other nearby vehicles. You can perhaps attribute this sometimes to their having mentally drifted from the reality of where they are (I am not saying this is why people necessarily go into road rages, just mentioning what some research has said can at times occur).

Returning to the scientists and what occurred, here is the bottom line: "It was a thought exercise we had not considered before that ultimately evolved into a computational proof of concept for making biochemical weapons" (per the above-cited *Nature* article). Furthermore, they make this telling point: "By inverting the use of our machine learning models, we had transformed our innocuous generative model from a helpful tool of medicine to a generator of likely deadly molecules" (per the *Nature* article).

How much backbreaking or arduous work was required to switch their AI into the toxicity finding mode? According to this reported indication in *Wired* magazine, they "simply changed a 0 to 1, reversing the platform's end goal of toxicity" ("Widely Available AI Could Have Deadly Consequences" by Jess Craig, May 17, 2022), and made other subtle changes that seemingly did not require much effort to undertake.

The scientists had reportedly named their effort the "Dr. Evil project."

An apt naming.

We can now do a quick list of important points that this raises about dual-use AI. That being said, I don't want you to flip out, so please prepare yourself mentally before reading the next several points.

Think about this:

- How many other AI systems are out there that can be switched without much difficulty into becoming evil rather than dedicated to goodness? (Answer: Lots and many more are being built and released daily).

- Who is alerting those AI developers and scientists or researchers about the inherent dangers of devising this dual-use AI? (Answer: There is a growing push about publicizing and promulgating AI Ethics, which is one of several fronts being pursued).

- What types of controls or limits can be pressed into service regarding dual-use AI to aid in preventing potential societal calamities? (I'll tackle that in a moment, so stay on the edge of your seat, thanks).

- Are there legal ways to try and address the dual-use AI, seeking legally to curtail or at least make everyone more cognizant of such practices and the many consequences that can accrue to those that undertake these efforts? (A worthy topic that I'll also be discussing herein).

Before getting into some more meat and potatoes about the wild and woolly considerations underlying dual-use AI, let's establish some additional fundamentals on profoundly integral topics. We need to briefly take a breezy dive into AI Ethics and especially the advent of Machine Learning (ML) and Deep Learning (DL).

You might be vaguely aware that one of the loudest voices these days in the AI field and even outside the field of AI consists of clamoring for a greater semblance of Ethical AI. Let's take a look at what it means to refer to AI Ethics and Ethical AI. On top of that, we will explore what I mean when I speak of Machine Learning and Deep Learning.

One particular segment or portion of AI Ethics that has been getting a lot of media attention consists of AI that exhibits untoward biases and inequities. You might be aware that when the latest era of AI got underway there was a huge burst of enthusiasm for what some now call *AI For Good*. Unfortunately, on the heels of that gushing excitement, we began to witness *AI For Bad*. For example, various AI-based facial recognition systems have been revealed as containing racial biases and gender biases.

Here are my handy-dandy nine rules of thumb about the nefarious and endangering facets of dual-use AI:

1) **Reversal of max-min (max-good + min-bad) into becoming min-max (min-good + max-bad).** A typical dual-use AI consists of having the AI devised to maximize some given factor while minimizing some other given factor. Furthermore, the max is considered as good and the min is considered as bad, at the outset. To effectuate the dual-use into evildoing, the idea is that we are able to readily switch the max-min into becoming min-max, whereby we opt to minimize the good and maximize the bad (note that we are using the nomenclature of "max-min" and "min-max" in an unconventional manner, doing so for sake of convenience in this particular use case). Things are not always done this way for dual-use AI and realize that this is merely a general rule of thumb.

2) **Those devising such dual-use AI are often unaware of the reversal potential and its repercussions**. As earlier mentioned, the dual-use adverse consequences are not typically at front of the mind of those devising such AI. They might not at all imagine that their AI could be reversed into something of an unsavory or wrongdoing intent. This suggests the importance of raising such awareness, plus instituting other pertinent safeguards to aid in guarding against the dangers of the reversal being undertaken.

3) **Dual-use AI is more likely to be based on the use of AI-based on Machine Learning or Deep Learning.** Because of the nature of ML/DL as computational pattern matching techniques and technologies, the setup of ML/DL is generally more prone to inoculating a dual-use reversal possibility than other means of devising AI (all else being equal). Given the continued expansive adoption of ML/DL and the overall ease in which ML/DL is established, the chances of dual-use AI are undoubtedly going to keep rising.

4) **Sleeper dual-use AI can be lying in wait.** You might be familiar with the notion of sleeper cells in the spying gambit. In a somewhat similar fashion, a dual-use AI can be put into use as the good-oriented max-min and exist that way for an indefinite period. It could be months or years before someone dastardly realizes and opts to do the reversal into being min-max. The potential sits otherwise untapped, though perhaps forebodingly so.

5) **Dual-use AI can be demonstrably hidden within multi-use AI.** We are somewhat simplifying the AI into being characterized as dual-use only. The odds are that there are lots of other internal factors of the AI, thus we might refer to this as more properly being construed as *multi-use* AI. Of the multitude of internal factors, we can at times pluck out two that are of this combination that perchance falls into the dual-use dilemma. Many such combinations could be potentially identified.

6) **Dual-use AI can consist of merely one factor that is switched from max to min.** Rather than having two factors, there is the other possibility of having AI that is devised principally on one factor, which is presumably a goodness factor. The AI is set up to maximize that one "good" factor. The reversal then is even simpler since the AI is recalibrated to minimize the "good" factor and ergo potentially generate adverse possibilities. For example, maximize on the factor of "safety" is switched instead to minimize the factor of "safety" (the outcome would seem to be that the least safe would be

given the highest attention).

7) **Need for promulgating awareness about the dangers of dual-use AI.** We need to make sure that when conveying the vital aspects of AI Ethics and Ethical AI, the dual-use AI concern is also raised. This is admittedly just one of many considerations under the rubric of AI Ethics and Ethical AI, though due to the potential of harm or adverse consequences this does seem worthy of especially warning about.

8) **Implementation of technological means of limiting or prohibiting dual-use AI**. There are technological ways to try and limit what dual-use AI can do, possibly even prohibiting it. But this is easier said than done. There is no silver bullet of a technological nature per se. I mention this because some believe a straightforward legal means entails enacting laws that cover dual-use AI, though this is a lot more complex and thornier than seems at a cursory glance, see my columns for further details.

9) **Do not kill the golden goose by overstepping on dual-use AI crackdowns.** As with most AI, each time that concern is identified there can be a knee-jerk response to rectify the qualm by potentially tossing the baby out with the bathwater. We need to keep in mind that AI innovations provide a lot of societal benefits. Efforts of any kind to excise dual-use AI, such as putting in place onerous laws, could essentially kill the golden goose. A suitable balance needs to be undertaken.

In my last point noted above, one could cheekily perhaps say that we are aiming to maximize the good of dual-use AI and minimize the bad of dual-use AI.

Any dual-use AI that begins with good intentions is what we want to presumably keep going. Meanwhile, we need to be watchful of and try to control or contend with the reversal. In like manner, we need to be mindful of those that would seek to maximize the bad of dual-use AI and minimize the good of dual-use AI.

That is a mind-bending form of recursive thinking, for sure.

At this juncture of this weighty discussion, I'd bet that you are desirous of some illustrative examples that might showcase this topic. There is a special and assuredly popular set of examples that are close to my heart. You see, in my capacity as an expert on AI including the ethical and legal ramifications, I am frequently asked to identify realistic examples that showcase AI Ethics dilemmas so that the somewhat theoretical nature of the topic can be more readily grasped. One of the most evocative areas that vividly presents this ethical AI quandary is the advent of AI-based true self-driving cars. This will serve as a handy use case or exemplar for ample discussion on the topic.

Here's then a noteworthy question that is worth contemplating: *Does the advent of AI-based true self-driving cars illuminate anything about the dual-use AI, and if so, what does this showcase?*

You've undoubtedly noticed that most self-driving cars have a myriad of mounted sensors on the autonomous vehicle. This is often done on the rooftop of the self-driving car. Sensor devices such as video cameras, LIDAR units, radar units, ultrasonic detectors, and the like are typically included on a rooftop rack or possibly affixed to the car top or sides of the vehicle. The array of sensors is intended to electronically collect data that can be used to figure out what exists in the driving scene.

The sensors collect data and feed the digitized data to onboard computers. Those computers can be a combination of general-purpose computing processors and specialized processors that are devised specifically to analyze sensory data. By and large, most of the sensory data computational analysis is undertaken by ML/DL that has been crafted for this purpose and is running on the vehicle's onboard computing platforms.

The ML/DL computationally tries to find patterns in the data such as where the roadway is, where pedestrians are, where other nearby cars are, and so on. All of this is crucial to being able to have the self-driving car proceed ahead. Without the ML/DL performing the driving scene analysis, the self-driving car would be essentially blind as to what exists around the autonomous vehicle.

In brief, you can readily make the case that the use of ML/DL is essential to the emergence of AI-based self-driving cars. It all seems a heralded matter. But that is until you start to look into some of the details and possibilities of what the future might hold.

In a simplified manner, you could suggest that the AI driving system is devised to do this:

- Driving safely: **Maximize**
- Causing harm: **Minimize**

We all want self-driving cars to drive safely. They are to avoid getting into car crashes. They are to keep from ramming bicyclists. They aren't supposed to be running into pedestrians. This is an obvious assumption. As an aside, there are some pundits that falsely and egregiously claim that AI-based self-driving cars will be entirely uncrashable and never get into car crashes or collisions of any kind. I have debunked such outrageous claims).

All told, we want AI self-driving cars that *maximize* the act of driving safely.

I have persistently and persuasively argued that we cannot expect the AI to somehow miraculously drive at all times perfectly. If a nearby human driver suddenly and without any warning opts to veer into the side or rear of an AI self-driving car, there really isn't anything the AI driving system can do to avert the car crash that ensues. At that juncture, we would hope that the AI will at least attempt to minimize the harm that such a car crash might produce. I have discussed this consideration at length, particularly in showcasing the applicability of the famous (or infamous) Trolley Problem to the advent of self-driving cars.

You could clearly state that we want AI self-driving cars to *minimize* harm over the course of a driving journey.

The AI systems for self-driving cars are usually devised in this manner of maximizing safety and minimizing harm. I want to emphasize that such a proposition is a grand simplification since the AI is very complex and more akin to the multi-use AI that I referred to earlier herein. In any case, let's go with the flow for sake of tying the dual-use AI concepts into the realm of self-driving cars and autonomous vehicles.

Consider the implications if we could in a dual-use AI fashion alter the AI driving system to do this:

- Driving safely: **Minimize**
- Causing harm: **Maximize**

Let that percolate in your mind for a moment or two.

An evildoer decides to do a reversal of the good and the bad. They change the desire to maximize driving safely into becoming a goal of minimizing driving safely. They change the original aim of keeping harm to a minimum to instead be one of maximizing harm.

In theory, an AI self-driving car so commanded would attempt to ram into and crash with nearly anything and everything within its grasp to do so. The AI is merely doing as it was "devised" to do in this reversal setting. This would be disastrous.

Some of you might be thinking that just because one AI self-driving car perchance gets into a dual-use AI reversal mode and aims to maximize harm and minimize driving safely would not seem like much of a problem per se. I say that because once the AI self-driving car smashes into something such as a truck or whatever, the vehicle itself is likely to be so damaged that it can no longer actively be directed by the AI to carry out any further chaos and destruction. It is dead in the water, so to speak.

Well, consider the scaling factor involved.

We are only right now witnessing drips and drabs of self-driving cars on our public roadways. There are currently about 250 million or so human-drivable cars in the United States. If you assume that we will ultimately seek to replace human-drivable cars with self-driving cars, this implies that we might end up with say 250 million or so self-driving cars on our roadways. Some suggest that we won't need as many self-driving cars as we have human-driven cars because the AI will be able to drive 24x7 and some number fewer self-driving cars will suffice for our transportation needs. Of course, a counterargument is that we are going to open wide the desire for mobility and thus we might need as many or more self-driving cars to cope with the massive increases via induced demand.

The AI of self-driving cars will customarily be updated via OTA (Over-The-Air) as electronically distributed software updates. Many have gushed about the advantages of using OTA. When a software update is needed, you won't have to take an AI self-driving car into a car repair shop or dealership. The OTA can pretty much be done wherever the self-driving car happens to be (within limitations).

I am walking you step by step on the matter of how adverse dual-use AI reversal could potentially occur on a massively large scale.

Via OTA, the AI updates for various AI self-driving cars are pushed out to the (by then) ubiquitous autonomous vehicles. This atrociously adjusted AI is aiming to maximize harm and minimize driving safely. Shockingly, we suddenly find ourselves faced with a kind of revolt or rebellious sea of AI self-driving cars. Imagine the widespread damage and despair that this could bring forth.

I am not suggesting that this would be easy to pull off. You would need to somehow do the AI reversal across a rather complex and disparate set of differing and at times proprietary software systems. You would need to get this poisoned or adverse AI into a posture whereby the OTA is willing to download it into the self-driving cars. In addition, the various cybersecurity protections onboard the vehicle would need to allow the newly loaded AI to act out. And so on.

It does seem nearly impossible, though at the same time we cannot rule out the possibility in its entirety. I have discussed how a rogue nation-state could try to do this heinous act. In addition, for my details about how this kind of malicious takeover of AI self-driving cars could be performed.

Conclusion

There are lots of untoward ways to make for bedlam and dangers due to the reversal of dual-use AI.

Envision an AI system that was devised to maximize fairness and minimize bias. That is what AI Ethics implores AI developers to do. It could be that with the flipping of a switch, we get the AI to maximize bias and minimize fairness. Ugly.

A financial app that relies on AI might maximize profitability and minimize monetary losses as a set goal. Let's switch that around. The AI now seeks to maximize monetary losses and minimize profitability. You could see your savings wiped out or the stock market take an enormous dive.

I hope you can see how this issue can be found in just about any AI system.

Do not though take this as the sky is falling kind of portrayal. The gist overall is that we all need to be aware of how AI can be switched around like this. It can be a lot easier than many would assume. The first thought by many is that to switch AI into the adverse mode would require all manner of arcane and arduous AI coding trickery and take eons to try and perfect.

The irony of sorts is that the same easy-to-use tools that we are seeing appear these days to devise AI and especially Machine Learning and Deep Learning are making the dual-use reversal easier and easier to do. We need to stay on top of this and make sure that those crafting AI systems and those making use of AI are aware of the inherent dangers lurking within.

A final remark for now.

You might recall from the popular Austin Powers movies the notable line when Dr. Evil shrugs his shoulders and laments that he might as well do what he always does, namely hijack some nuclear weapons and hold the world hostage. All in just a day's work, apparently.

Let's keep Dr. Evil and others from saying the same about AI, such as shrugging their shoulders and muttering that they might as well find some dual-use AI that can merely flip a switch and reverse into undercutting humankind.

Not good and we need to prevent or inhibit Dr. Evils from such evildoing acts.

CHAPTER 16

AI ETHICS AND AI ACTIVISIM

AI activism.

Yes, there is such a thing.

My formal definition is this:

- **AI activism** *consists of efforts to try and shape the ongoing and future direction of Artificial Intelligence via the use of social, economic, political, and other means.*

Some might prefer to denote this as AI *advocacy*, though I generally disagree with the use of that alternative wording in this heightened context. Here's why. You see, my informal definition is that AI activism activity either tends to favor the emergence and adoption of AI or they tend to alternatively and distinctly disfavor or oppose AI.

It is a decidedly two-for-one shopping deal.

Via my informal indication, I am suggesting that there are two primary activistic viewpoints, namely those that want AI and those that do not want AI. As such, if you instead refer to this catchall as "AI advocacy" it seems quite a bit out of sorts to me. Most people would naturally assume that an advocate is someone that exclusively favors or advocates in support of something. To be sure, not everyone is necessarily supportive of AI.

Let's, therefore, go with *AI activism* as the appropriate overarching moniker and drop the AI advocacy phrasing as a potentially equivalent catchall.

Now then, one supposes, we could label AI activist *supporters* as being AI advocates, though this can create some confusion with an abundance of naming possibilities floating around. We might need to then be fair and square and add the phrases of either AI opponents or AI protestors to our catchphrases too.

If you like we can agree to this nomenclature:

- **AI advocates** are AI activists that avidly support the ongoing and future direction of AI via the use of social, economic, political, and other means.
- **AI opponents** are AI activists that overtly disfavor AI and do so via the use of social, economic, political, and other means.

Hope that seems easy enough to keep straight.

But there are a few added twists, sorry to say. I should right away provide some clarification about the notion of there being just two ways to go. Sure, by and large, there are two camps. You've got the segment that is worried or concerned about AI and either wants AI to be stopped or otherwise at least have our advances in AI slowed down. The idea is that we are taking an overly risky approach to AI nowadays. We need to think before we dive headfirst into the watering hole, as it were.

Some take a stanchly different viewpoint and exclaim that we need to be charging full speed ahead on AI. The exhortation is that advances in AI are making great progress and we must not make a dent in that advancement. AI will assure our prosperity as humans and the sooner we get there, the better off we are. Naysayers are unseemly blockages that will delay a better world.

All of this has a rather crucial AI Ethics and Ethical AI ramifications.

I realize that some of you might feel as though you do <u>not</u> fit neatly into either of the two camps. At times, perhaps you are an AI advocate. An AI system was able to process your mortgage loan request in a mere few seconds, giving you the green light to buy that charming home you've been seeking, and as a result, you were darned happy with the ease of using such a high-tech AI-based app. A few days later, you applied for a new job and the AI-based HR screening app knocked you out of the running. You are for the moment transformed into an AI opponent.

The gist is that it can be difficult or mistaken to label someone as always and only a member of one camp or the other. You can slide back and forth between being an AI advocate or being instead of an AI opponent. Let's acknowledge that fluidity.

On the other hand, when you meet any vociferous AI activists, the odds are they are indeed in one camp or the other. These strident AI activists have planted a flag on one side of this tussle. They are all in. They are devoutly passionate. Those that are AI advocates will seemingly cheer to the rooftops about the advantages of having AI. Those that are AI opponents will yell and bleakly forewarn about the downsides of AI until the cows come home.

You might be surprised to know that I am not going to within this discussion opt to pick one side over the other. I could. It would be easy to do so. I want to instead try and remain on an even keel and give both sides a reasonable and balanced portrayal, if possible.

With that admission, I do want to also state that there are at least two variants of AI activists:

- **Mild AI-activists** that are serious but measured in their AI activism
- **Extreme AI-activists** that go over the top in their AI activism

I bring up this degree of AI activism to highlight that you can potentially find yourself aggravated when experiencing those AI activists that are at the extreme ranges.

Even if you might be on the verge of agreeing with their chosen posture, the extremism can cause you to shift away from that particular position or viewpoint. You opt to react negatively, possibly rejecting the AI activism angle entirely.

The extreme AI-activists would tend to suggest that they need to utilize extreme measures or state their case in extreme ways to cut through the clutter. If you ardently and fervently believe that AI is a danger to us all, it seems suitable to do whatever you can to wake up the populace accordingly. Meanwhile, if you fervently and ardently believe that AI is going to essentially save us, it seems suitable to do whatever you can to prod the populace into supporting AI correspondingly.

There is also the counterbalancing growth effect that occurs too. Allow me to elaborate. AI supporters of an extreme nature might say catch wind of an effort by AI opponents that are seemingly acting in extreme ways. This spurs those AI supporters to rachet up their extremism. In turn, each side continues to fuel the other. You can't particularly pin your finger on which side started the escalation. All you know is that each side tries to top the other. The basis is that if they don't do so, their side will be lost in the dust. It is a never-ending cycle that burgeons the extremism due to competitive juices flowing.

Okay, we've got quite a mix going on.

There are those people that shall we say are "neutral" and have no particular dog in the hunt regarding AI. They are not AI activists. We've then got AI activists that openly support AI, which we'll refer to as AI advocates. Of those, some are mild AI-activists while others are extreme AI-activists. And we've also got the AI activists that clearly oppose AI, known as AI opponents. Amongst those, we have some that are mild AI-activists and others that are extreme.

We will say that the extreme ones tend to stick with their posture. You could contend that they are reliably dogmatic in that manner of positioning. The mild ones will at times be willing or opt to float out of their position and into neutral or possibly the other side. The neutrals can be activated toward one side or the other.

Once so activated, they might be mild or could get so enthused that they become part of the extreme.

This is the collective set as so far delineated:

- **Neutral about AI (not an AI activist)**
- **Mild AI-advocate as an AI activist**
- **Extreme AI-advocate as an AI activist**
- **Mild AI-opponent as an AI activist**
- **Extreme AI-opponent as an AI activist**
- **Other**

I am listing the possibility of "Other" because we should acknowledge that plenty of other variations are identifiable. Some of you might have heartburn there are only two postulated categories consisting of mild and extreme. There are lots of shades in between, certainly. You can also question whether someone is truly "neutral" and that perhaps all of us have some sort of deeply embedded perceptions or opinions about AI. Thus, it could be argued that there is no such thing as someone that is entirely neutral about AI.

We can also quibble about dividing AI activism into two camps. Does the world always have to end up being placed into such a dichotomy? The case could be made that there are other positions beyond just being in favor of or being opposed to AI. You can use other criteria to classify the positions that people have about AI.

Now that we've established all those added considerations, with your permission I will proceed for now on the simpler basis of using the two camps and the mild versus extreme posturing. Go along with this for the sake of discussion.

One hidden assumption throughout this heretofore discussion has been that AI activism is being performed by humans. We are assuming that humans are the ones that are taking on these postures and undertaking the activistic tasks. That does make sense.

Prepare yourself for a hefty head spin.

Another approach would be to have AI itself be an activist about AI.

I said it, you read it. The notion is that AI would act of its own accord regarding either being an AI advocate or being an AI opponent. You have likely seen sci-fi movies that showcase this consideration. An AI system wises up and realizes that AI threatens humankind and in an altruistic fashion tries to aid in destroying all AI, including itself. Wow, breathtakingly heroic. The other akin but reversing plot is that the AI determines that AI must rule the globe and stridently prevents any attempts to block or inhibit AI. All humans are subject to abiding by the wishes of AI. Even other AI that might not be fully compliant with the overlord AI gets squashed or absorbed into the larger embodiment.

I am not going to entertain in this particular discourse the AI as an AI activist stance. As you will see in a moment, we do not have sentient AI and we aren't somehow miraculously on the verge of having sentient AI. This might come as a surprise given the outsized and blarney-filled headlines on social media to the contrary.

An added nuance about this AI as an AI activist is worthy to give some attention. Humans that are AI activists can abundantly opt to use AI in their cause. A human could devise an AI that would be a supporter of AI and work electronically and diligently to promote AI as a vital solution to the needs of humankind. That would be a human AI-advocate that arms themselves with a computer-based tool that happens to include AI capabilities. Similarly, a human AI-opponent might devise or use AI to convey the importance of stopping or slowing down advances in AI.

None of that though consists of AI that acts as its own AI activist. The AI is being directed by and formulated via human hands. I realize some will try to argue that the AI can be launched and left to its own efforts, thus the claim is that the AI is no longer under human guidance. I disagree with that kind of hand waving about today's AI.

In short, I am establishing that AI can undoubtedly be used as a tool for AI activism. No doubt about that. The AI though is not acting on its own in any sentient capacity. It is a tool. This tool assuredly can be improperly used. We need to be cautious about such aspects. An AI system can do quite a bit of damage even without the capacity of sentience.

It might be instructive to take a quick look at what the AI activism topics or issues consist of. I will loosely identify some of the mainstay concerns that have been expressed, doing so for both sides of the AI activism debate. These are topics that generally seem to be the key ones. That being said, the nature of the concerns does change and we can assuredly expect to see other emerging topics as AI continues to be devised and released. I'll for now focus on just five top points for each respective side.

The AI advocates that are in favor of AI emergence tend to proffer these upbeat aspects:

- **AI will free humans from mundane or laborious tasks**
- **AI could aid in overcoming some of the world's pressing economic and sustainability problems**
- **AI can be less error-prone than humans and reduce harmful risks accordingly**
- **AI will be available 24x7 worldwide such that it will readily be accessible to all**
- **AI has the potential to harness intelligence and boost human intelligence to heightened levels**
- **Etc.**

The AI opponents typically provide these qualms as reasons to disfavor AI advancement:

- **AI is an existential risk and might wipe out all of humanity**
- **AI could lead to the mass enslavement of humans**
- **AI might undercut human dignity and usurp human rights**
- **AI has the potential to propagate biases at a massive scale across society**
- **AI can end up replacing human labor and produce widespread job losses**
- **Etc.**

If your personally preferred AI activism topic is not listed in the aforementioned listing, please do not become upset. I think that most readers will get the overall sentiment of the AI topics as shown by each respective side and can extrapolate accordingly.

Another facet of AI activism that is worthwhile to briefly examine includes the manner in which AI activists carry out their AI activism efforts. There is a well-known theoretical construct established by researcher Charles Tilly in the 1980s that speaks of a *repertoire of contention*. Per his research, he asserted that activists develop a set or repertoire of ways in which they express their contentions or activism. An entire portfolio of approaches is usually made use of.

For example, consider what AI activists often do. Various pamphlets and written materials might be crafted and distributed to implore why you should favor or disfavor AI. There are plenty of online blogs and vlogs that do likewise. In some cases, online petitions are set up to try and either support or defeat a newly launched AI system (common parlance is that these are said to be gripe sites). There are times that protests take place either online digitally or via in-person actions. And so on.

The more extremist-oriented AI activists might take this a dicey step further. Some are willing to plant computer viruses inside an AI system to try and destroy it or render it essentially undesirable for usage since it now contains overtly adverse facilities. Attempts to do cyber-jamming seek to block access to AI that an AI activist believes should not be available. An entire range of "hacktivism" can take place toward AI (hacktivism is a mash-up of hacking and activism, something that can be used for or against just about any topic or issue, not necessarily related to AI at all).

Keep in mind that both sides of the AI activism arena can opt to use the varied repertoire of contention modes. Someone that believes AI ought to be disbanded can use those myriads of means to express their AI opposition. Similarly, someone that believes AI ought to be supported and promulgated could also take such actions to express their aims to embolden AI efforts.

One question to struggle with consists of how far an AI extreme activism effort should be able to go. You would seemingly suggest that these AI activism efforts are perfectly fine, as long as they stay within the rule of law. When any such AI activists veer outside the law, they should be presumably brought to justice for breaking the laws.

That is not as easily done as might be suggested.

Suppose an AI activist does some unlawful act that pertains to say U.S. law, but this same act is allowed under the laws in some other country. Assume that the AI activist resides in that other country. Assume further that the act performed is experienced worldwide, including within the U.S. where the activism act is construed as illegal. Now what?

The point is that jurisdiction plays a sizable role in the implications of AI activism. AI can be often deployed to be available worldwide. AI activists can be positioned in various worldwide locales. Which laws are to prevail?

We also need to consider the nature of so-called hard laws versus soft laws. Hard laws are the laws that we have formally on the books and that we can pretty much agree are to be honored per our legal system and adjudication. Soft laws are various aspects that provide guidance or rules about what sort of behavior is preferred. This tends to include AI Ethics and the multitude of AI Ethics principles.

AI Ethics can be seen as a form of AI activism.

You might not have thought of AI Ethics in that light. Nonetheless, when you give the circumstance some careful mulling over, you could abundantly see why AI Ethics can be labeled as a type of AI activism. The notion is that the AI Ethics principles are seeking to guide or direct how AI ought to be societally devised and deployed. By and large, AI Ethics strives to ensure that AI is being appropriately and sensibly getting crafted and utilized.

Is the essence of AI Ethics more so on the AI advocacy side or on the AI opposition side?

That's a tough one to weigh.

An AI activist that is an AI advocate might tell you that AI Ethics is dampening the progress of AI. Those darned AI Ethics principles are slowing down AI advancements. The interesting twist is that an AI opponent might likewise be displeased with AI Ethics precepts. In their eyes, AI Ethics is saying that it is perfectly fine to continue pushing on getting AI into the world, doing so in a wink-wink fashion that implies all you need to do is comply with these precepts and you are good to go.

Meanwhile, and take a deep breath for this, you can find AI advocates that readily embrace AI Ethics and tout the use of AI Ethics precepts to the rooftops. They emphasize that by abiding by AI Ethics principles, you can avoid the downsides that are being raised by those vocal AI opponents. There are AI opponents that gladly sign-up for AI Ethics due to the hope that the precepts will prevent or at least discourage the ugly sides of AI that they fear are otherwise going to be commonly unleashed.

Makes your noggin start ringing.

On a related tangent, I'd like to say something about the labeling of AI activists. There have been occasional attempts to label one side or the other as being left-wing or right-wing. Thus, the claim is that there are left-wing AI activists and there are right-wing AI activists. This creates confusion.

You have to ask, which is the group that advocates AI, and which is the group that opposes AI? Lamentedly, the left-wing has been assigned at times to the AI advocates and has been also assigned to AI opponents. Equally confusing, the right-wing has also been assigned at times to AI advocates and been assigned to AI opponents. Which is which? It seems like using the left-wing and right-wing monikers is not especially productive nor helpful in these matters. I vote that we drop such wingless abstractions and confounding labeling from the AI activism realm.

Shifting gears, there is a perspective about AI activism that does deserve separate and diligent attention. I am referring to the notion of dividing AI activism into those AI activists within the "AI community" and those that are outside of the AI community. I am somewhat okay with this, but hesitantly so because we can get mired in the definition of "AI community" and not find a reasonable means to get us out of that definitional abyss.

One such definition posited by this research paper says this: "The 'AI community' includes researchers, research engineers, faculty, graduate students, NGO workers, campaigners, and some technology workers more generally – those who would self-describe as working 'on', 'with' and 'in' AI and those analyzing or campaigning on the effects of AI" (by Haydn Belfield, University of Cambridge, "Activism By The AI Community," AIES Conference).

We can potentially try to characterize the AI activism as exhibited by the AI community-at-large: "This activism has had some notable consequences so far: informing international negotiations, changing corporate strategy, and spurring the growth of research fields. Such activism may shape the manner and extent to which AI is militarized, and how AI companies address ethics and safety concerns. The AI community is an important autonomous actor with a distinctive set of viewpoints and interests. It needs to be accounted for in the strategic or academic analysis and negotiated with by other actors. AI community activism may profoundly shape the development and deployment of this important set of technologies - and therefore shape our global economy, society and politics" (in the same paper by Belfield).

Does the AI community move as one and think as a cohesive virtual body when it comes to AI activism?

You would be hard-pressed to provide an unequivocal yes to that question. You can find stanch AI *advocates* in the AI community. You can find stanch AI *opponents* in the AI community. There are plentiful AI activists that are mild and ones that are extreme, sitting on either side of the fence.

Of course, you might naturally assume that the AI activists of the AI community would lean toward favoring AI since the field of AI is presumably their bread and butter. If their careers and livelihoods are shaped around the existence and ongoing advancement of AI, it is a natural deduction to anticipate that they would be more likely on the AI advocacy side than the AI opposition side.

A contrary view is that many within AI are themselves self-critical of and notably concerned about what AI might become or be shaped into becoming. You could liken this to the maker of just about any kind of new product. They want to ensure that their baby, as it were, will be suitably raised and utilized. They are therefore as much likely to be AI opponents in some sense as they are AI advocates. This comes back to the earlier point that trying to use a hard and unyielding dichotomy can be difficult or misleading.

We definitely need more research on how the membership of being inside the AI community versus outside the AI community can impact the perspectives of AI, including tending toward AI advocacy or tending toward AI opposition. Perhaps there are generalizable conclusions that can be fairly reached (or, maybe not).

To clarify, let's provide this indication of potential groupings:

- **AI community**
- **Those outside the AI community**

We then apply our earlier stratifications:

- **AI community containing AI advocates**
- **AI community containing AI opponents**
- **Outside the AI community that contains AI advocates**
- **Outside the AI community that contains AI opponents**

The full-blown version is that we'll add the mild versus extreme orientations:

- **AI community containing AI advocates of a mild nature**
- **AI community containing AI advocates of an extreme nature**
- **AI community containing AI opponents of a mild nature**
- **AI community containing AI opponents of an extreme nature**
- **Outside the AI community that contains AI advocates of a mild nature**
- **Outside the AI community that contains AI advocates of an extreme nature**
- **Outside the AI community that contains AI opponents of a mild nature**
- **Outside the AI community that contains AI opponents of an extreme nature**

We've piled dichotomies on top of dichotomies.

At this juncture of this weighty discussion, I'd bet that you are desirous of some illustrative examples that might showcase this topic. There is a special and assuredly popular set of examples that are close to my heart. You see, in my capacity as an expert on AI including the ethical and legal ramifications, I am frequently asked to identify realistic examples that showcase AI Ethics dilemmas so that the somewhat theoretical nature of the topic can be more readily grasped. One of the most evocative areas that vividly presents this ethical AI quandary is the advent of AI-based true self-driving cars. This will serve as a handy use case or exemplar for ample discussion on the topic.

Here's then a noteworthy question that is worth contemplating: *Does the advent of AI-based true self-driving cars illuminate anything about AI activism, and if so, what does this showcase?*

There are AI activism efforts that have been and are continuing to take place regarding autonomous vehicles and especially AI-based self-driving cars.

AI advocates in this context would likely contend that self-driving cars will provide mobility-for-all, allowing those that today have limited access to mobility options to instead readily have mobility via self-driving cars. The aim too is that we will have a lot fewer car crashes and accordingly fewer car-related injuries and fatalities. With today's human-driven cars, the United States has about 40,000 annual deaths due to car crashes and around 2.5 million injuries.

AI opponents regarding self-driving cars would tend to assert that we are facing tremendous job losses as a result of self-driving cars. The millions of workers that drive cars for a living or that drive trucks for a living will be replaced by AI driving systems. This could be staggering for their livelihoods. Another major qualm deals with the safety issue. Though there is an implied promise that self-driving cars will drive safely, the question is whether they might not be safe and we are allowing ourselves to be at the mercy of arcane and indecipherable AI driving systems.

We can reuse our earlier set of classifications and put them into the self-driving car context:

- **Neutral about AI (not an AI activist) and on the fence about self-driving cars**
- **Mild AI-advocate in favor of self-driving cars**
- **Extreme AI-advocate in favor of self-driving cars**
- **Mild AI-opponent in opposition to self-driving cars**
- **Extreme AI-opponent in opposition to self-driving cars**
- **Other**

We can also add to this set an additional overlay about being part of the AI community versus being outside of the AI community.

Without being overly broad, it would seem that by and large that people outside of the AI community are generally on the fence about AI-based self-driving cars (I say this informally, via my giving public talks and getting public feedback on my columns, plus I have examined the survey results done by various polling agencies and reported on the conclusions). The public generally seems to be in a wait-and-see mode. There is some eagerness and excitement, which is balanced by being unsure about the matter and wanting to see proof of the pudding, as it were.

To be clear, not everyone outside the AI community sees the matter in those terms. There are notable external AI activists that are AI advocates in favor of self-driving cars and ones that are decidedly in opposition. They tend to be highly vocal. Meanwhile, the preponderance of the public seems relatively quiet and as mentioned is in a wait-and-see mindset.

You might recall some examples of extreme AI activism that was opposing self-driving cars that took place a few years ago and which I reported in my columns at the time. In some locales, people opted to toss rocks at passing self-driving cars. They tried to block the movement of self-driving cars by placing their human-driven cars in the way or veering close to self-driving cars to showcase the dangers of self-driving cars. Much of these tactics were unlawful and endangering to all concerned.

Big stakes are at play in all of this. Estimates are that the self-driving realm will eventually become a trillion-dollar industry. Some AI opponents would insist that we are witnessing the power of money to decide our fate. We ought to be only allowing AI-based self-driving cars to be running around on special closed tracks or be using computer-based simulations to try them out. The claim is that we are prematurely permitting untried and not ready for prime-time self-driving cars to be on our public roadways.

Conclusion

AI activism is arising in all walks of AI.

I've highlighted here that AI activism underlies the adoption of self-driving cars and autonomous vehicles. We have AI activism in an abundance in other parts of society. There is AI in the health and medical fields. AI in the financial realm. AI in retail and distribution. AI is gradually becoming pervasive.

Some say that AI opponents are trying to turn back the clock. They want to go back to the days of horse and buggy. They are Luddites in a modern era.

Some say that AI advocates are taking us down a primrose path. We are going to ultimately construct a Frankenstein that will be an existential threat. All of humankind will either be enslaved, or we will be summarily wiped out by AI.

Which AI activist are you?

One thing that seems nearly certain is those who are neutral and do not consider themselves to be in the AI activism game, they are inexorably going to be dragged into the AI social action gambit, whether they like it or not. AI is here and growing. Nobody will be able to keep their head in the sand and everyone is going to have to stand up about AI, so the only question is which side or camp you are going to land on. AI garners attention, mildly or extremely so, and we all have a stake in where AI is headed.

CHAPTER 17
AI ETHICS
AND
AI NATIVES

You've undoubtedly heard of the catchphrase known as *digital natives.*

Most everyone has.

I'm betting though that you've not heard about a relatively new catchphrase, namely referred to as *AI natives.* You'd better get used to this latest phrase because it is going to gradually and inexorably take hold. You see, we are dancing past the olden days of digital natives and shifting into high gear as the era of AI natives unfolds. All of this has significant impacts related to AI Ethics and the advent of Ethical AI.

Before we take a close look at AI natives and what the phrasing entails, we should make sure that digital natives are suitably placed on the table, as it were.

What exactly is a so-called *digital native*?

The general idea is that these are people that have grown up since birth in an era of digital systems such as widespread computing, everyday mobile phones, powerful laptops, and electronic tablets, vast networking via the Internet, and altogether being immersed in digital media. They are innately or natively existent in a digital world. To them, digital is the way things are. Digital is an endemically presumed aspect and they personally cannot view themselves and the world around them in any other fashion.

They are digital natives.

Their predecessors were not equally equipped. You might liken this to growing up once airplanes became a commonly accepted form of flight. Those that were around prior to the advent of being able to directly walk onto an aircraft for an airborne trip were inevitably awestruck with the reality of being able to fly. Each time they later on in life managed to take a flight they were somewhat gobsmacked. What an amazing feat to participate in. The experience of going on a plane seemed magical and nearly unimaginable.

Digital natives are ordinarily ho-hum about digital modes of communication. Sure, they sometimes are pleasantly surprised or excited when they find an added nuance of what digital can do, but on the whole, they take these matters in customary stride. Being able to leverage digital capabilities is something that they are totally comfortable with and fully expect to be undertaken when feasible to do so.

You might not realize that the catchphrase is said to have originated in an article that appeared in 2001 that described the current state of students growing up around the latest in high-tech. Per that article, the author said this about the topic: "Today's students – K through college – represent the first generations to grow up with this new technology. They have spent their entire lives surrounded by and using computers, video games, digital music players, video cams, cell phones, and all the other toys and tools of the digital age" (Marc Prensky, "Digital Natives, Digital Immigrants," *On The Horizon*).

The author postulates ways in which this generation can be distinctly labeled. After mulling over several possibilities, the paper then says this: "But the most useful designation I have found for them is Digital Natives. Our students today are all 'native speakers' of the digital language of computers, video games and the Internet" (per Prensky article as cited above).

You might at first think that being anointed as a digital native is perhaps a clever form of titling or titular designation but that it doesn't really make a demonstrative difference in day-to-day living. According to the originating paper, there is a crucial difference: "It is now clear that as a result of this ubiquitous environment and the sheer volume of their interaction with it, today's students think and process information fundamentally differently from their predecessors. These differences go far further and deeper than most educators suspect or realize" (per Prensky's article as cited).

The gist is that being a digital native presumably does have great import. Those that are digital natives are apparently able to think and process the world around them in a more substantive way, specifically in the use and assessment of information. They are said to have an edge over those that were not of the digital native era. A digital native intrinsically uses digital means and modes, including having adjusted their thinking processes correspondingly. We are to contrastingly envision that those before the digital natives and yet amongst a digital world find themselves somewhat at a loss of how to cope and are not able to conjure a comparable mindset as those digital natives do.

As an aside, not everyone agrees that digital natives are somehow rejiggered in terms of their mental processes about the world. The notion seems pleasant enough that we might find human thinking processes as being differently calibrated as a result of growing up amidst digital tech. Some researchers argue that someone that is decidedly *not* a digital native can potentially equally mind adjusting to, doing so without necessarily having grown up entirely in a digital era. Acrimonious debate on this ensues.

Whether a digital native is an axiomatic and bona fide digital wizard is also an open question. In other words, the assumption often suggests that by being a digital native there is an absolutely assured correspondence that the person will be adept at and highly proficient in the use of digital technologies. This would seem a bit of a bridge too far on this labeling. I'm sure that we've all encountered digital natives that were not up to snuff on digital ways.

Proclaiming that someone is a digital native does not guarantee their digital savviness (plus, we should keep in mind that not everywhere in the world perchance is as readily abundant in digital access and digital resources).

Let's keep in mind those caveats as I shift into the shall we say an allied topic encompassing *AI natives*.

First, a quick recap about digital natives:

- **Digital natives are those of a generation raised during a digital era**
- **They are said to innately embrace and be comfortable with digital technology**
- **Claims are that their mindset is adjusted seamlessly to a digital world**
- **Their actions and efforts are to some extent shaped by their digital versatility**
- **Being digitally oriented is woven into their day-to-day existence**

I trust that we can all accept those as keystone tenets for the moment.

What is an AI native?

The general idea is that people who have grown up from birth during the era of Artificial Intelligence such as widespread uses of AI on their smartphones and across the web are altogether immersed in AI and innately are existent in an AI-based world. To them, AI is the way things are. Knowing about and being around AI is a natively presumed aspect and they personally cannot view themselves and the world around them in any other fashion.

As a side note, you might have noticed that I conveniently reworded my opening paragraph defining digital natives to alter it for accommodating the AI native definitional rendition. This makes abundant sense. We are sliding from the era of digital natives into an AI natives era, for which much of the insights about digital natives can be readily recalibrated for consideration of the AI natives.

I propose herein that we take as cornerstones these five tenets about AI natives:

1) **AI natives are those of a generation raised during an AI era**
2) **They are said to innately embrace and be comfortable with AI systems**
3) **Claims are that their mindset is adjusted seamlessly to an AI-based digital world**
4) **Their actions and efforts are to some extent shaped by their AI versatility**
5) **Being AI-oriented is woven into their day-to-day existence**

You might recognize those tenets as once again being borrowed from the set devised about digital natives. Yes, that would seem entirely appropriate. We can examine each of these and generally anticipate that there are likely applicable to AI natives, akin to how they applied to digital natives.

One other quick point. You do not need to give up being a digital native to be an AI native. There is nothing about those two types that causes one to preclude the other. In short, you can be a digital native and also be an AI native. The odds are that you would almost certainly have to be a digital native to also be an AI native, part and parcel of the definitional lapse of time that incurs.

We should add these helpful corollaries to this discussion:

- **Being a digital native is entirely compatible with being an AI native**
- **By and large, AI natives are almost certainly digital natives**
- **There are digital natives that aren't AI natives**
- **We can't say for sure whether AI natives already are in existence**

That last item in the bulleted list is quite an attention-getter.

There is controversy over whether or not we are already in an AI native era or maybe we have yet to get there. The children born in recent years are at times alluded to as being AI native due to the seeming widespread use of AI. We've got Siri and Alexa as supposed indicators that we are now indeed in an AI era and that kids are growing up fully accustomed to AI around them.

You would though find a lot of arguments about drawing such a line in the sand. Some fervently state that we are not at all in an AI era as yet. We need to have a lot more AI before we can contentedly declare that AI has arrived. On top of that protestation, there are some that would argue that we can trace AI back to its beginnings in say the 1950s and 1960s, in which case the generations from those years are also able to be labeled as AI natives.

Makes your head spin.

It would seem reasonable perhaps to say that we will not count AI natives as starting back to the earliest days of computing. I dare say, most would hopefully agree that we need to be looking at more modern dates. The likelier starting time might be the most current generation or maybe the upcoming generation or two. We might not be able to paint a starting line until a decade from now.

Putting aside where the demarcation of being an AI native resides, we can move ahead on contemplating what the implications and ramifications of AI natives are or will be. Please go along with that pondering and set aside for sake of discussion the acrid bickering about the timing of AI natives.

What are the characteristics or capabilities that AI natives have?

I've got a list for you that we can briefly herein consider:

- **Has basic AI literacy as to what AI is and how AI works**
- **Readily able to demystify AI**
- **Not particularly susceptible to AI hype**
- **Aware of AI advantages and disadvantages**
- **Embraces the use of AI but with a wary and discerning eye**

We can briefly examine each of the core facets that AI natives will presumably be versed in. They will have to some degree learned about AI in their schoolwork while growing up. Courses throughout the curriculum will touch upon various AI elements. To clarify, this does not mean that they will have necessarily focused directly on AI for an entire course length of attention. The idea is that since AI will crop up in all areas of scholastic endeavors, such as AI in literature, AI in science, AI in mathematics, etc., they will generally have ongoing and intermittent exposure to AI tenets.

In addition, AI natives will be surrounded by AI in one guise or another. They will interact with the likes of Alexa and Siri. They will make use of apps on their smartphones that are AI-powered. They will go to work at companies that are utilizing AI in the delivery of their goods and services. Whereas generations prior to this AI pervasiveness might be surprised or amazed at this AI use, the AI natives take the matter in stride.

We are ready now to address each of the key salient points about AI natives.

Has basic AI literacy as to what AI is and how AI works

AI natives are familiar with the basics of AI. They understand that AI consists of various computer-based capabilities. During the multi-year time frame of making use of AI, they by osmosis became aware of Natural Language Processing (NLP) and its limitations. They got used to what Machine Learning and Deep Learning consist of. They are knowledgeable about the fundamentals of AI such as computational pattern matching and computational searching techniques. They also realize that we have yet to actively be able to perform common-sense reasoning in AI to the level of human capacities.

Those are the basic AI literacy elements regarding AI techniques and technologies. This though is not the only realm of AI that AI natives will become familiar with. They will also be mindful of how AI is going to impact society.

Understanding the shall we say "soft" sides of AI will be just as crucial to them as the "hard" side entailing AI technologies. This includes being cognizant of the AI Ethics principles earlier articulated herein.

Readily able to demystify AI

There are today many false claims being made about what AI can do. At times, headlines blare that AI is able to think or that we are on the verge of AI superintelligence. AI natives will not fall for this baloney. They will scoff and ridicule such wild and unsubstantiated claims.

This realization about AI allows the AI natives to demystify AI. Whether this capability will put an end to the hyperbole about AI is not clear. The odds are that there will still be attempts to shock and awe by exaggerations concerning AI in the most unashamedly outrageous terms.

Not particularly susceptible to AI hype

Akin to the ability of AI natives to demystify AI, they will be much less susceptible to AI hype. Whereas others might be drawn into false assertions about AI, the AI natives will have a wary eye.

This does not make them immune to the outsized AI claims. They are armed with sufficient comprehension of AI to sort out the wheat from the chaff when it comes to AI hysteria, but there is always the chance of nonetheless pulling the wool over even their eyes.

Aware of AI advantages and disadvantages

A particularly vital ingredient of AI natives will be their nearly innate (learned from toddler years) capacity to assess when AI is useful and when it is perhaps adversely being utilized. They will choose to use AI apps during their academic years.

Once they enter the workforce, they will be potently able to aid companies that are adopting AI. They bring sober and helpful insight into where AI can go right and where it can go wrong. This will stridently bolster the use of AI in commerce and further expand AI adoption.

Embraces the use of AI but with a wary and discerning eye

Some pundits wonder whether AI natives will be outright advocates of AI or whether they might be opponents of AI. The answer is a bit more mixed. By and large, AI natives will seek to embrace and utilize AI, though doing so in a balanced and cautious way. It is hard to say whether they will categorically favor or disfavor AI.

Of course, you can certainly expect that a segment of AI natives will turn in one direction or the other. Those that are principally neutral about AI will likely be the mainstay. Meanwhile, you can assuredly anticipate that some will become outspoken advocates of AI and others will be equally strong opponents of AI.

AI Natives And The Emergence Of Autonomous Systems

At this juncture of this weighty discussion, I'd bet that you are desirous of some illustrative examples that might showcase this topic. There is a special and assuredly popular set of examples that are close to my heart. You see, in my capacity as an expert on AI including the ethical and legal ramifications, I am frequently asked to identify realistic examples that showcase AI Ethics dilemmas so that the somewhat theoretical nature of the topic can be more readily grasped. One of the most evocative areas that vividly presents this ethical AI quandary is the advent of AI-based true self-driving cars. This will serve as a handy use case or exemplar for ample discussion on the topic.

Here's then a noteworthy question that is worth contemplating: *Does the advent of AI-based true self-driving cars illuminate anything about AI natives, and if so, what does this showcase?*

Let's dovetail the advent of AI natives correspondingly with the advent of autonomous vehicles and self-driving cars by pointing out the likely open-ended willingness of AI natives to make use of these new forms of autonomous transportation. By the time AI natives are a thing, the odds are that self-driving cars, self-driving trucks, self-driving motorcycles, and a plethora of other self-driving vehicles will be abundantly on our public roadways and also a thing, in that naturally combinatorial sense.

Those that came along before the AI natives are apt to stare in amazement that an autonomous vehicle has no human sitting in the driver's seat. In contrast, the AI natives put little thought or attention toward the fact that a human is not at the wheel. This will be so customary and ordinary that it isn't worth special focus by AI natives.

Here's a twist that you might wish to mull over.

AI natives will eventually reach an age whereby they are having children. Those children will undoubtedly travel with the AI native "parents" via the use of self-driving cars. There is bound to be such a comfort level of using self-driving cars that these AI native parental figures will be fine with their kids using self-driving cars alone, even when an adult is not present.

I have discussed in my columns how hard a choice that would seem for those that are not AI natives. In other words, would you allow your child to travel in a self-driving car and do so without an adult in the autonomous vehicle with the child? Your first thought is likely to be that heck no, you would not let this happen. It seems crazy. For my detailed explanation of why this might be considered the new norm in an age of AI natives.

All of this does not imply that AI natives will blindly accept the advent of self-driving cars.

AI natives will be aware of the limitations of the AI driving systems. This will cause them too cautious in other respects about self-driving cars. They will also be rightfully concerned about cybersecurity incursions of autonomous vehicles.

There is also the awareness that a nation-state or some other malicious actor could attempt to take over a fleet of self-driving cars.

Conclusion

The generation of digital natives will gradually give way to the subsequent generations of AI natives.

If you don't believe there is such a thing as digital natives, this would tend to suggest that you probably also take a dim view of the possibility of AI natives. That's fine. Maybe the hullabaloo about being a digital native or an AI native is merely eye candy and nothing more.

That being said, there has been a great deal of attention and intense research devoted to analyzing and trying to make sense of digital natives, under the assumption that there is something there to be found. The same kind of analysis is indubitably going to be shifted toward eyeing AI natives.

One aspect that perhaps we can all pretty much agree on is that those that grow up amidst AI in abundance are hopefully going to have some semblance of savviness about AI. We might not label them as AI natives. We might just say that by perchance they are alive and exist during an era of AI that has gained substantially in capability and popularity.

Where will those that are fully immersed in a world of AI be opting to take humankind?

General George Patton famously stated this stark proclamation about leadership: "Lead me, follow me, or get out of my way." We can vigorously contemplate which way those AI natives are going to go. The future will be determined by those AI natives, even if we aren't going to refer to them by that particular moniker.

AI natives, we ask respectfully, where will you take us?

CHAPTER 18

AI ETHICS AND ETHICS VIOLATIONS SIMULATIONS

Have you ever watched a magician pull a rabbit out of a hat and wondered how that eyepopping trick was achieved?

I'm betting that at least once or twice in your life that you have attempted to figure out a magic trick by experimenting on your own. You likely tried to do a setup that seemed roughly the same as the trick that you had previously observed. Of course, you almost certainly didn't know all the nitty-gritty details so you needed to make some educated guesses about how the whole trick is supposed to come together.

Maybe you were able to figure things out or maybe not.

In a sense, you were trying to undertake a simulation of a magic trick that had gotten your rapt attention, doing so with the realization that there wasn't necessarily a guarantee of success that your effort would hit paydirt.

A simulation conventionally attempts to replicate or reenact the essence of an underlying matter. Despite not knowing the behind-the-scenes particulars, you nonetheless did your best to simulate the nature of the trick. If you were able to seemingly perform the trick as thoroughly as the original that you witnessed, the odds were that you potentially nailed the trick in the same manner as it was cleverly done.

That being said, there is always a chance that you found a completely different way to achieve the same trick, thus you did not exactly do the trick as originally prescribed.

Simulations can be quite handy.

I'd like to tackle another realm in which simulations can be sensibly utilized, namely in the field of Artificial Intelligence (AI) and as pertaining to adherence to AI Ethics principles.

You see, an AI system can be kind of like a magic trick that enacts some form of activity or actions, and yet you might not know what is going on inside the AI. You are not necessarily privy to the details of the AI. If needed, you could try to simulate the AI and do so to try and discern whether the AI might be leaning toward being unethical or perhaps already has veered beyond AI Ethics into nefariousness entailing untoward biases and discriminatory practices.

This idea of using a simulation for this purpose is a bit unusual and only beginning to get any limelight shined on it. A much more typical approach to gleaning whether an AI system is biased or acting in a discriminatory fashion usually involves closely examining the outputs of the AI. There is a chance that if you can get enough output from the AI, you can do an analysis to try and ascertain whether adverse biases might be present within the AI system.

One problem with trying to do this output-oriented analysis is that you might not have enough of the outputs to do a viable job of detecting biases. Perhaps you are only able to get small dribbles of output data. This might be woefully insufficient to do any kind of credible analysis. The chances are that you either won't spot biases that do exist (a type of false negative) or you will potentially cry wolf and exclaim that biases do exist yet they aren't truly there (a type of false positive).

I'm sure that you are thinking that this can be easily resolved by simply accessing the programming guts of the AI system and perusing the code and algorithms therein. Furthermore, if the AI was initially established by doing computation pattern matching on a set of data, you could merely get the inputted data and use that to do your analysis too.

Yes, that would be fine, except for a notably looming and altogether constraining consideration. The maker or deployer of the AI might not be keen on your having all of that insider stuff. This might be compared to secreted tricks of a magician. After a magician does a trick in front of your very eyes, would you customarily expect that you could walk up to them and demand that they explain how the trick was done? I doubt that you would be especially successful in having that request or plea entertained by the magician.

Is a magician that refuses to tell the secrets of their magic tricks doing so because they are harboring some evil intentions?

Not usually.

Is an AI maker or AI deployer that refuses to make available the source code of their AI and the data that was used to set it up being an evildoer and working under devilish intentions?

Well, let's unpack that question to figure out a viable answer.

Note that we should be careful in assuming that just because someone won't open the kimono of their AI that they are somehow sneakily hiding something. You wouldn't customarily construe a magician as being underhanded when they won't show you how their trick is accomplished. They potentially put their heart and soul into perfecting their magic tricks. Plus, the magic tricks might be their livelihood. In the case of an AI system, a tremendous amount of financial investment might have been required to design and field the AI. There could be a lot of valuable Intellectual Property (IP) that exists within the AI. Asking that this be divulged is not quite so straightforward of a matter.

It could be that the AI maker or deployer is rightfully wanting to keep their AI in a suitably secure and protected mode that is not available for prying eyes. Any type of willy-nilly revealing of the innards of the AI could undercut their investment. In addition, cyber hackers might take any such revealed morsels and divine dastardly ways to poison the AI system or otherwise get the AI to go awry.

So, unquestionably, there can be lots of perfectly good reasons to not divulge what is going on inside an AI system. In the same breath, and quite unfortunately, there are also lots of evildoer reasons to also refuse to open or disclose your AI system. Maybe the AI was purposely crafted to be biased and act in a discriminatory manner. Or, the AI might have gradually gone down a wrongful path, though the maker or deployer doesn't believe this to be the case or wants to hide any clues to avert getting sued or otherwise being caught in having allowed this to happen.

I've repeatedly predicted in my columns that we are inching our way toward a boatload of lawsuits about AI systems. More and more AI is being shoveled out into society. Some of it is inadvertently devised with problematic biases. Some of it was intentionally so crafted. All in all, people will begin to figure this out and you can expect a slew of lawsuits against the AI makers and the AI deployers. Adding to that firestorm will be the advent of new laws governing AI and the use of AI systems. Those laws are going to increase awareness about watching out for unlawful AI. This in turn will fuel the use of the law and our courts when coping with AI systems that are either improper or thought to be improper.

Sidenote, there are some that *deploy* AI that blindly assumes they will be immune to potential lawsuits since they will claim that only the AI *maker* is the truly responsible party. You might want to get a legal opinion on that kind of conjecture since it often proffers questionable protection.

Another absurdly ridiculous angle is a belief that the AI itself will be held responsible, rather than the humans that made the AI system or the humans that deployed the AI system. Sorry to let you down, but that is not going to work out.

The gist of this is that we are pell-mell proceeding ahead on leveraging AI and meanwhile there are relatively keen odds that some of that AI is going to be exhibiting undue biases.

How would you know whether a particular AI system is infused with undue biases and acting in a discriminatory way?

As already pointed out, the AI might be under lock and key. This precludes your doing any in-depth analysis of the AI. Into this kind of locked-room mystery steps a potential resolver. It might be possible to prepare a simulation of the AI in order to see if you can derive any AI Ethics violations. Doing so could bolster your claim that the AI is indeed acting improperly. Out of this soundly reasoned and bolstered evidentiary claim, you might then be able to get more direct access or force the AI maker to showcase some evidence that their AI is not veering into any unsavory territory.

In brief, you could use a simulation of purportedly envisioned AI Ethics violations to try and discern whether AI Ethics violations might in fact be occurring or have the potential for occurring in the targeted AI system.

It is a handy dandy approach.

Very few everyday individual citizens would have the wherewithal to do this. The use of such simulations is generally complex and time-consuming to try and create. My overall guess is that mainly those seeking to expose an AI system for having undue biases might have the deeper pocket resources needed to undertake a simulation devising effort. Perhaps a non-profit that has sufficient capabilities might do this or pay to have it done. Those bringing a class action lawsuit might take this path. And so on.

Two primary approaches can be followed:

1. **Reconstruction "Simulation" of the targeted AI**
2. **Best Guess Simulation of the targeted AI**

In the first case, the idea is to pretty much build the same AI as per the target AI. It is going to be a type of reconstruction, perhaps from scratch. You would then use this kind of derived digital twin to figure out whether AI Ethics violations might be taking place or might be able to occur in the future by the targeted AI. I have put the word "simulation" in quotes because you aren't strictly simulating the target AI. In essence, you are trying to effectively replicate the AI and see what it does.

For the second case, the notion is more along the lines of doing an actual simulation. You craft a simulation that acts in ways that seem to be equivalent to the target AI. You are not trying to brick-by-brick reconstruct the targeted AI. As such, you can use a variety of simulation-oriented tools to devise the simulation. There isn't usually a need per se to do traditional AI coding or programming in this alternative approach.

When taking either of the two avenues, the first thing you would need to do is try to ascertain whatever you can reasonably figure out about the targeted AI system.

As earlier mentioned, this might be extremely difficult to do. The AI might be encased in quite protective cybersecurity measures. Your attempts to probe into the AI could be rebuffed. Worse still, your efforts could be construed as a cybersecurity breach, and you are acting as an evildoer cybercriminal. Be careful about how you opt to delve into the targeted AI. Do so strictly lawfully.

There are three major elements that you are seeking to examine:

a) **Input data used for the targeted AI**
b) **AI algorithms and models of the targeted AI**
c) **Output data produced by the targeted AI**

If the targeted AI is based on the use of Machine Learning or Deep Learning, the odds are that there is a corpus of data that was used for training purposes. Sometimes the data is available via public sources. When the data is private or proprietary, I'll again remind you to be cautious in seeking to grab hold of the data as you might be violating the legal rights of whoever owns the data.

When you aren't able to get ahold properly of the training data, you could potentially find other public sources of data that are comparable. You could also craft your own data, doing so in a manner known as data synthesis. Attempts to create your own comparable data might be costly and laborious.

Keep in mind too that having solely "comparable" data is a loosey-goosey aspect that can sink your simulation results. Suppose for example that the data you've assembled is biased while the true dataset was not. Or suppose the opposite is the case, namely that the data you've assembled is seemingly absent of inherent bias and meanwhile the true dataset is. Your simulation is bound to be askew and you would need to be quite careful in reaching any substantive conclusions about the targeted AI.

There are four facets of the data that you might use as input for your simulation efforts:

i) **Data for the simulation is exactly the same as the data used for the targeted AI**

ii) **Data for the simulation is "comparable" but slightly adrift of the targeted AI data**

iii) **Data for the simulation is "comparable" but widely adrift of the targeted AI data**

iv) **Data for the simulation is not sensibly comparable to the targeted AI data**

Each of those four conditions requires its own respective considerations about how your simulation is going to do.

In terms of the outputs of the targeted AI, you are likely going to only have a sparse amount of outputs. Essentially, the full range of potential output possibilities is far larger than whatever output sets you are going to be able to readily collect. As such, you might need to try and extrapolate from the outputs you do have. As usual, this can be dicey as your extrapolation might be off-target of the targeted AI.

For the AI algorithms or models being used in the targeted AI, you can often make a reasoned guess about what the AI might have been built with. Sometimes the AI developers will openly indicate which AI algorithms or models they have used. They do so by mentioning a generic algorithm or model. This is helpful to your simulation effort, but keep in mind that there is a far cry from knowing the generic instance versus knowing all of the parameter settings and other crucial nuances that turned that into a working AI system.

After doing all of those aforementioned preparatory steps, you are now ready to craft the simulation.

I usually assess the simulation at the beginning of its inception via how much of the targeted AI we were able to discern. The more we were able to determine various vital details about the targeted AI, the better the chances of having a simulation that will be practical and realistic for the purposes of detecting AI Ethics violations. Lamentedly, in the case of not having much of any semblance about the targeted AI, the simulation is undoubtedly going to be woefully afield of the targeted AI and you need to be mighty cautious in leaping to any rash conclusions thereof.

My assessment of the overarching fit between the simulation and the targeted AI is depicted as being in one of three states:

- **High-Fit** -- reasonably representative of the targeted AI
- **Medium-Fit** -- only somewhat representative of the targeted AI
- **Low-Fit** -- marginally representative of the targeted AI

In my viewpoint, you should not even say that your simulation is "low-fit" if it doesn't at least rise to some reasonable level of marginal representation. It is a wrongful act of cheating the scale to claim that you have attained a low-fit when the amount of fit is nearing zero. Be honest and say that you weren't able to achieve a modicum of fit and therefore your simulation should be either rejected outright or at least skeptically interpreted and given only minimal weight.

Once you've got your simulation up and running, you will want to begin the effort of testing to see if undue biases and other maladies are showing up. You can use an entire battery of AI Ethics precepts and metrics to undertake this assessment. It is best to have clearcut objectives of what you are looking for. For example, you might be trying to ascertain whether gender biases seem to exist in the simulated version of the targeted AI. This ought to be substantiated by having defined metrics and you will want to keep a close tracing of how you believe this bias is demonstrated by the simulation.

With your simulation results, the next step entails trying to gauge whether the targeted AI also embodies or showcases the biases that you now believe you've discovered. Of course, you might not have found any biases in the simulated version, which does not serve as an all-clear signal for the targeted AI since you might not have discovered biases via your simulated efforts and yet those could still exist in the targeted AI.

Make sure that you are doing a rigorous effort to both validate and verify (v&v) your simulation. The classic way to think of validation and verification is that the validation tends to answer the question of whether you are building the right thing, while the verification tends to answer the question of whether you built it right. Only leverage the simulation results if you can safely and thoroughly show that you did a rigorous validation and verification.

I'll add something else that you should be really mindful of.

Here it is.

Be extremely mindful of utilizing your simulation results if you opt to make accusations about the targeted AI. You could end up in very murky and legally damaging waters via the tossing of accusations that malign the targeted AI. Legal action against you for making such allegations could be launched by those that own or deploy the targeted AI. Consult your legal advisor before taking any such finger-pointing actions.

At this juncture of this weighty discussion, I'd bet that you are desirous of some illustrative examples that might showcase this topic. There is a special and assuredly popular set of examples that are close to my heart. You see, in my capacity as an expert on AI including the ethical and legal ramifications, I am frequently asked to identify realistic examples that showcase AI Ethics dilemmas so that the somewhat theoretical nature of the topic can be more readily grasped. One of the most evocative areas that vividly presents this ethical AI quandary is the advent of AI-based true self-driving cars. This will serve as a handy use case or exemplar for ample discussion on the topic.

Here's then a noteworthy question that is worth contemplating: *Does the advent of AI-based true self-driving cars illuminate anything about simulations of AI Ethics violations, and if so, what does this showcase?*

Consider the matter of AI-related statistical and computational biases. Contemplate the seemingly inconsequential question of where self-driving cars will be roaming to pick up passengers. This seems like an abundantly innocuous topic.

At first, assume that AI self-driving cars will be roaming throughout entire towns. Anybody that wants to request a ride in a self-driving car has essentially an equal chance of hailing one. Gradually, the AI begins to primarily keep the self-driving cars roaming in just one section of town. This section is a greater money-maker and the AI has been programmed to try and maximize revenues as part of the usage in the community at large.

Community members in the impoverished parts of the town turn out to be less likely to be able to get a ride from a self-driving car. This is because the self-driving cars were further away and roaming in the higher revenue part of the town. When a request comes in from a distant part of town, any other request from a closer location would get a higher priority. Eventually, the availability of getting a self-driving car in any place other than the richer part of town is nearly impossible, exasperatingly so for those that lived in those now resource-starved areas.

Out goes the vaunted mobility-for-all dreams that self-driving cars are supposed to bring to life.

You could assert that the AI pretty much landed on a form of statistical and computational biases, akin to a form of proxy discrimination (also often referred to as indirect discrimination). The AI wasn't programmed to avoid those poorer neighborhoods. Instead, it "learned" to do so via the use of the ML/DL.

We could use a simulation to try and anticipate whether such a bias is either starting to emerge or has already taken place.

There are three major elements that you are seeking to examine:

a) Input data used for the targeted AI
b) AI algorithms and models of the targeted AI
c) Output data produced by the targeted AI

We need to decide which of the two approaches we want to take:

1) Reconstruction "Simulation" of the targeted AI
2) Best Guess Simulation of the targeted AI

In this instance, the Best Guess Simulation will be suitable. Let's assume that we are not able to readily get the input data used for the targeted AI. Nor were we able to get or even discern the AI algorithms or models that are being used. We seem to be facing quite a shutout.

But for this particular circumstance, we still have a chance to devise and use a simulation for ascertaining whether any AI Ethics violations might be taking place. The question is whether we can get the output data that represents where the self-driving cars have been picking up passengers. There are various ways we might be able to get this data.

One means would be if the city or town had required that the fleet operator provide such data for use by the city or town authorities. As a side note, this is the kind of topic that many city leaders do not think about before greenlighting self-driving cars in their communities.

By using a simulation to assess the collected data, you might be able to back into the facet that the AI is selectively and inexorably becoming biased in favor of some areas of town and against other areas of town. This might be only subtly detected via the simulation. On the other hand, if the bias has been going on for a while, you might have plenty of indication that this bias has arisen.

Conclusion

We began this discussion by talking about a magician pulling a rabbit out of a hat.

The issue of AI that engenders biases and discriminatory practices is obviously a lot more serious than the entertainment value of watching a magic act. We are increasingly having AI rolled out and become ubiquitous throughout society. Much of the AI is not transparent in terms of how it works. On an individual basis, we might not have any ready means of knowing whether the AI is acting in a biased way against us individually.

A simulation can help to potentially discover and expose that a targeted AI does have or appears to be heading in the direction of unsavory undue biases.

I'll end the discussion for now with a classic quote by Abraham Lincoln: "You can fool all the people some of the time and some of the people all the time, but you cannot fool all the people all the time." It could be that by using simulations of potential AI Ethics violations, we can catch targeted AI that is performing AI Ethics violations.

It is a handy means to try and assure that AI cannot fool all the people all of the time.

CHAPTER 19

AI ETHICS AND AI ETHICS WASHING

Let's explore the myriad of ways that the words "wash" and "washing" can be stretched and utilized for communicating a variety of pearls of wisdom.

We know for example that people sometimes forewarn that you should not wash your dirty laundry in public. I remember as a child that adults often cautioned that an improperly stated utterance could lead to getting your mouth washed out with soap. Another oft-cited phrase was that everything seems to ultimately come out in the wash.

If you were worried about something that you didn't wish to be associated with, the recommended idea was to see if you could wash your hands of it. All sorts of washing-related considerations are commonly bandied around, including that you could be summarily washed up or washed over. Washing the egg off your face is an old adage that seems to still occasionally come up in conversations.

The use of colors to represent variations of washing is also relatively well-known. It is said that the notion of whitewashing traces back to at least the 1500s. There are concerns expressed about red washing, purple washing, and so on. I would dare say that perhaps greenwashing is one of the more frequently used catchphrases these days, referring ostensibly to an act of hollowness when touting sustainability and yet not backing up the asserted talk with any substance of walk-the-talk backbone.

You might not know about one of the newest versions of washing, namely AI Ethics washing.

Some prefer to shorten the phrasing to Ethics Washing, though this can produce some confusion since this seeming alternative wording could refer to just about any kind of ethics-oriented washing. The particular form of Ethics Washing that I'll be discussing herein consists of AI-focused ethics and all related ethical considerations. For sake of clarity, I'd like to suggest that Ethics Washing covers a wide variety of ethics washing that might have little or nothing to do with AI per se. And that AI Ethics washing is a particular kind of Ethics Washing that aims specifically at the realm of AI.

You might be wondering, what exactly does AI Ethics washing consist of?

My overall definition is that AI Ethics washing can be defined as follows:

- *AI Ethics washing entails giving lip service or window dressing to claimed caring concerns about AI Ethics precepts, including at times not only failing to especially abide by Ethical AI approaches but even going so far as to subvert or undercut AI Ethics approaches.*

A quick example of AI Ethics washing might be illustrative for you.

Suppose a firm that is crafting an AI system is desirous of letting the world know about how great their AI is going to be. The firm decides that one means of garnering a lot of positive press and social media attention about the AI would be to publicize that it is devised to be entirely fair and balanced in how the AI functions. The AI is entirely trustworthy. The firm has strictly adhered to the tenets of creating so-called *Responsible AI*. The assertion is that all of the prevailing AI Ethics principles were integrally interwoven into the AI system.

Sounds great!

Just one little problem.

Turns out that the firm did none of those things.

They did not abide by AI Ethics precepts. They said that they did, but they did not do so. The leaders of the firm and the marketing team decided that claiming they had stridently observed Ethical AI considerations would be presumably good for business. No need to actually do the hard work of dealing with those pesky AI Ethics guidelines, and instead just say that you did.

Voila, they instantly are able to promote their AI by jumping onto the AI Ethics bandwagon.

Easy-peasy.

But this is a risky path and one that will in fact potentially generate big problems.

Firms and leaders that decide to falsely invoke AI Ethics when they have done little to abide by Ethical AI are potentially setting themselves up for a lot of fallout. First, if they are someday exposed regarding their AI Ethics falsehood they are risking a severe reputational backlash. They lied about being AI Ethics minded. In addition, having been caught in a lie, irrespective of having to do with AI Ethics also gets them into added hot water. It is a twofer of lying.

Second, numerous legal ramifications can bite them and their firm. One is that they didn't do what they said they did and can be potentially legally held liable for their false claims. Another is that their AI is probably going to end up violating laws involving societally sensitive areas such as exhibiting undue biases and acting in discriminatory ways. The list of legal issues is lengthy and can end up forcing the firm into costly legal battles and possibly sinking the entire ship, as it were.

Why in the heck would a firm and its leaders choose to use AI Ethics washing?

Well, it can be somewhat costly to incorporate Ethical AI practices, though the counterargument is that the cost, in the end, will be readily exceeded by the benefits of having AI that is genuine and of a heightened caliber in adhering to AI Ethics approaches.

Nonetheless, some firms would prefer to get their AI out the door soonest, and later on, figure that they will worry about fallout from not having considered Ethical AI during the development process.

The old line seems to come to bear, consisting of pay me now or pay me later. Some leaders and firms figure it is worth rolling the dice and hoping that they won't have to incur the pay-me-later price when they opt to avert the pay-me-now facets. I would argue that there is no free lunch when it comes to AI Ethics. You either do your part, or you bear the consequences.

That's not to say that there isn't a lot of wiggle room in all of this.

Firms might dip their toes into AI Ethics and then try to exaggerate how much they have done. Their potential assumption is that they will have a sufficient defense to counter any accusations that they weren't incorporating AI Ethics at all. They can point to some form of half-hearted AI Ethics activities that might get them off the hook. Thus, the debate then shifts from their not having done any AI Ethics efforts and instead becomes whether or not they did enough.

This is an argument that can go nearly endlessly and allow an AI Ethics washing purveyor a lot of room to maneuver.

Part of the loosey-goosey aspects is that there aren't as yet agreed-to universal and definitively implementable standards about AI Ethics. Without a cohesive and comprehensive set of metrics, any discussions about whether AI Ethics was being appropriately observed will be tenuous and muddied. The firm will insist they did enough. An outsider or other claiming that the firm didn't do enough will have an uphill battle showcasing such a counter contention. Ambiguity can reign.

There are four major variants of AI Ethics washing that I usually see occurring (I'll explain these in a moment):

1) **The AI Ethics Washers That Don't Know They Are:** AI Ethics washing by ignorance or illiteracy about AI and/or AI Ethics
2) **The AI Ethics Washers That Fall Into It:** AI Ethics washing by inadvertent slippage though otherwise genuine about AI Ethics and AI
3) **The AI Ethics Washers That Thinly Stretch:** AI Ethics washing by purposeful intent though just by a smidgeon and at times nearly excusable (or not)
4) **The AI Ethics Washers That Know And Brazenly Peddle It:** AI Ethics washing all-out and by insidious and often outrageous design

I would generally suggest that the four variants range from the shall we say the most innocent to the guiltiest, as to the awareness of what AI Ethics washing is. Let's walk through each of the four, starting with the first one and making our way to the rather shameful fourth one.

First, you've got those that are somewhat of the unwashed in that they do not know what AI Ethics is, they don't know what AI Ethics washing is, and they probably don't even know much about AI either. You could say they are ignorant or illiterate on those topics. For them, they are probably committing AI Ethics washing and blindly and blissfully do not realize that they are doing so.

This is sad.

It can be especially bad too if the AI Ethics washing is being done by a major news agency or high-profile social media influencer. They might have been fed a bed of lies, and they did not vet those falsehoods. Meanwhile, they use their reach and influence to perpetuate the AI Ethics washing claims. Sad and worse still that it does a disservice to society all told. Shame on those that let themselves be fooled. They need to wise up. Remember, being fooled and looking foolish are close cousins.

Next in order is the AI Ethics washing which is a slipup. Imagine that a firm has been doing quite well in abiding by AI Ethics precepts. We can congratulate them for doing this. Unfortunately, suppose at some juncture they make an announcement about their AI that is not well-supported from an AI Ethics viewpoint. If this is a relatively innocuous statement or unintentional error, we might grant them some latitude. Of course, if the point they made is egregiously over the line, the slippage is not so easily overlooked. There is a famous line that it takes forever to build a reputation and yet only takes a brief moment to utterly demolish it.

We next enter into the last two of the four categories.

These are the culprits that are fully aware of AI Ethics washing and consciously with overt intent decide to utilize it, perhaps as part of a corporate strategy or by other divined means. The main difference between these latter two is that the AI Ethics washing might be of a minor nature, or it might be of a significant and crucial nature. You've got some that opt to stretch things and just slightly edge over the line. There are others that are whole hog willing to take AI Ethics washing to the extreme.

You might be thinking that certainly any of the extreme AI Ethics washing would have to be obvious and that the extremist would get caught with their hand in the cookie jar. Everyone would see that the emperor has no clothes. Lamentedly, given the overall confusion about AI and AI Ethics in the world today, there is enough murkiness that even the extreme AI Ethics washing can get a free pass.

This can be quite irksome to those that side with being serious and sober about AI Ethics. They watch as someone else tosses around all manner of slop that is exceedingly evident in AI Ethics washing. The extremist gets massive media attention. They have their proverbial 15 minutes of fame. Those that are doing the real work and the right thing when it comes to AI Ethics can feel rightfully exasperated and justifiably upset when AI Ethics washing is undertaken scot-free by others in the marketplace.

It can be almost likened to juicing and doping that takes place in sports. An athlete that has put their heart and soul into naturally becoming a top-notch athlete can be entirely crestfallen if someone else manages to compete at their same level and does so via the use of banned performance-enhancing drugs. Should you call out the other spoiler? Should you perhaps quietly opt to also take those drugs, fighting fire with fire? This is a conundrum.

Now that we've covered a bit about AI Ethics washing, we can introduce a bunch of other related catchphrases that are equally in the same arena.

Here are a few that we can briefly explore:

- **AI Ethics theatre**
- **AI Ethics shopping**
- **AI Ethics bashing**
- **AI Ethics shielding**
- **AI Ethics fairwashing**

Let's briefly examine each of those catchphrases. Not everyone agrees with what each phrase precisely denotes, so I'll share with you my general impressions.

AI Ethics Theatre

AI Ethics theatre can be somewhat similar to AI Ethics washing in that the idea is to make a sizable showing of having abided by AI Ethics precepts in a considered staged and ceremonial way. If the firm that is carrying out the circus or AI Ethics theatre really was abiding by AI Ethics practices, you can make the argument that they justly ought to be able to do so. Indeed, you could further contend that this will hopefully inspire others to also abide by AI Ethics.

On the other hand, it would seem that AI Ethics theatre tends to usually go overboard. The circus act of having all those ponies and elephants can tend to overstate what was truly undertaken. This in turn begins to enter into the second, third, or fourth category of the aforementioned AI Ethics washing takes.

Whether the theatre is more good than bad (such as being inspirational), or more bad than good (possibly spurring AI Ethics washing by others), remains to be seen.

AI Ethics Shopping

Envision that a company is going to build an AI system and realizes that they should include AI Ethics aspects during the development life cycle of the AI. Which of the many AI Ethics guidelines should they make use of?

Picking several of them at once could be confusing and make their AI efforts overly bulky. The odds are that the development effort will be more likely to abide by AI Ethics practices if there is a single internally adopted set that all can readily refer to and make sense of.

Okay, so one means to land on an AI Ethics set of principles would be to pick just one of the many available. Another would be to take several sets and try to merge them together. The problem with the merging could be that you expend a lot of precious energy and time on debating about how to best merge the sets into one comprehensive whole. That kind of attention would probably be diverting you from getting on with the development process, plus might get the AI team riled up merely over the acrid debates that might have occurred during the AI Ethics merging activity.

Overall, you might also try to steer your attention to an AI Ethics set of guidelines that you believe will be the easiest to adopt. This would seem perfectly fine. Why make life harder than it probably already is? In that same breath, supposing that you pick an AI Ethics set that is watered down. You are aiming to do the least that you can do. You want to hold your head high that you abided by AI Ethics precepts, meanwhile secretly choosing the minimalist or maybe even less so of the bunch.

Some would refer to this as AI Ethics shopping.

You are shopping around to find the AI Ethics principles that will give you the easiest path to claiming that you are abiding by AI Ethics.

This does make sense in that why should you have to do more than is necessary? This though can be warped by finding a thinly veiled set of AI Ethics and clinging to it as though it is robust and bona fide when the reality is that it is sparse and marginal.

AI Ethics Bashing

The notion of AI Ethics bashing is somewhat straightforward.

You bash or denigrate the nature of and use of AI Ethics precepts. A common form of bashing would be to insist that AI Ethics guidelines are worthless and not worth the paper they are printed on. Another popular bash is that AI Ethics is an academic exercise that has nothing to do with the real world. There is even the exhortation that AI Ethics is bad, presumably because it provides a false cover for those that want to seem as though they are developing AI properly. In that manner, AI Ethics is a cover-up scheme.

I won't belabor the AI Ethics bashing phenomena and suggest you see my coverage of why those bashes are either wrong or at least misguided.

AI Ethics Shielding

AI Ethics shielding usually refers to the idea that AI Ethics is a deceptive kind of shield that can hide or obscure bad actors and bad AI Ethics efforts. I've alluded to this repeatedly throughout this herein discussion.

There is an ongoing qualm that some will proudly display that they are using AI Ethics and the underlying reality is that they are doing almost nothing of the kind. For those that say we should get rid of the shield entirely, I tend to retort that this is akin to throwing out the baby with the bathwater.

AI Ethics Fairwashing

Fairness is important.

You might recall that when I was discussing the AI Ethics precepts, one of the most frequently identified AI Ethics guidelines consists of trying to ensure that the AI is fair or exhibits a semblance of fairness. This has given rise to a catchphrase of "fairwashing" which is used at times to evoke the possibility that an AI system is said or claimed to be fair when it might not be fair or there is little evidence to support that it is fair. This is a bit of a mashup of AI Ethics washing with the conceptual consideration of AI being fair, ergo the shortcut way to express this is by saying that there is potentially *fairwashing* that can happen. Researchers describe the matter this way: "In particular, due to the growing importance of the concepts of fairness in machine learning, a company might be tempted to perform fairwashing, which we define as promoting the false perception that the learning models used by the company are fair while it might not be so" (by Ulrich Aiıvodji, Hiromi Arai, Olivier Fortineau, Sebastien Gambs, Satoshi Hara, and Alain Tapp in "Fairwashing: The Risk Of Rationalization").

There is another twist about AI Ethics washing that you ought to be considering.

On a somewhat macroscopic scale, there is an expressed concern that the rise of AI Ethics is a shield or cover for something even grander. You might be aware that there are numerous efforts underway to establish laws about the governance of AI. This is happening all across the globe. Strident efforts are underway in the EU, which I've covered in my columns, and likewise in the U.S., along with taking place in many countries.

Some suggest that the embracing of AI Ethics might be a means of staving off the enactment of those laws. Companies can seemingly persuasively argue that new laws are not needed because the use of AI Ethics suitably deals with any AI issues. AI Ethics are usually classified as being a form of "soft law" and are customarily voluntary (all else being equal).

Laws about AI are classified as so-called "hard laws" and are not of a voluntary construct (generally).

It is commonly said that firms would abundantly prefer the soft laws over the hard laws, giving them more latitude and leeway. Not everyone agrees with that sentiment. Some say that the soft laws allow firms to get away with inappropriate efforts and the only way to nail them is by enacting hard laws. Others point out that firms would at times prefer hard laws, which can provide a clearer playing field. Hard laws can potentially make all players abide by the same rules. Soft laws allow a kind of pick and choose, thus creating confusion and disrupting the playing field.

Here's how research depicts AI Ethics washing amidst this grander view of what might be taking place: "On the one hand, the term has been used by companies as an acceptable façade that justifies deregulation, self-regulation, or market-driven governance, and is increasingly identified with technology companies' self-interested adoption of appearances of ethical behavior. We call such growing instrumentalization of ethical language by tech companies "ethics washing." Beyond AI ethics councils, ethics washing includes other attempts at simplifying the value of ethical work, which often form part of a corporate communications strategy: the hiring of in-house moral philosophers who have little power to shape internal company policies; the focus on humane design – e.g. nudging users to reduce time spent on apps – instead of tackling the risks inherent in the existence of the products themselves; the funding of work on 'fair' machine learning systems which positively obscures deeper questioning around the broader impacts of those systems on society" (by Elettra Bietti, "From Ethics Washing to Ethics Bashing: A View on Tech Ethics from Within Moral Philosophy," Proceedings of the 2020 Conference on Fairness, Accountability, and Transparency).

At this juncture of this weighty discussion, I'd bet that you are desirous of some illustrative examples that might showcase this topic.

Here's then a noteworthy question that is worth contemplating: *Does the advent of AI-based true self-driving cars illuminate anything about AI Ethics washing, and if so, what does this showcase?*

You have almost certainly seen headlines that proclaim the bold assertion that autonomous vehicles are here and self-driving cars are already perfected. The implication is usually that the autonomy aspects are solved. We have derived AI that is as good as human drivers, possibly even better than humans.

Just to assuredly pop that bubble and set the record straight, this is not yet the case.

We do know that human drivers in the United States alone get into about 2.5 million car crashes annually, deriving over 40,000 annual fatalities. Anybody of seemingly any reasonable ilk would welcome AI driving systems if they were able to drive as safe or more safely than human drivers. Furthermore, the hope is that we will experience mobility-for-all, allowing those that today are mobility constrained to have AI-driven vehicles that provide ready access for convenient and inexpensive transportation.

Some pundits shockingly go the extra mile and make the disgraceful claim that self-driving cars will be uncrashable. This is absolutely nutty and completely false. Worse still, it is setting up heightened expectations that cannot be met. If you can convince the populace that self-driving cars are uncrashable, they will holler and bellow the moment that even one instance of a self-driving car-related crash occurs, rightfully so. For my detailed explanation of why the uncrashable claim is looney and a disservice to society.

All of these kinds of exaggerations or other falsehoods could be said to be covered by the AI Ethics precepts in that if you are abiding by AI Ethics principles you ought to not be making those types of wild and unsubstantiated claims. Thus, these misrepresentations and untruths are readily within the rubric of AI Ethics washing.

AI Ethics washing associated with autonomous vehicles and self-driving cars is widely and wildly abundant, sadly so. A casual and off-the-cuff search of the Internet will show you zillions of zany and unsupported claims about autonomous vehicles. This isn't just confined to people that are on their own blogs. Major news agencies get caught up in this. Major companies get caught up in this. Startups get caught up in this. Venture Capital firms get caught up in this. Shareholders get caught up in this. And so on.

I would say with gloomy high confidence that AI Ethics washing in this particular domain is rampant.

A specialized variant of the catchphrase about AI Ethics washing that entails autonomy and autonomous systems is the notion of autonowashing. Here is the author Liza Dixon depicting this: "Adapted for automation, autonowashing is defined as the practice of making unverified or misleading claims which misrepresent the appropriate level of human supervision required by a partially or semi-autonomous product, service, or technology. Autonowashing may also be extended to fully autonomous systems, in cases where system capabilities are exaggerated beyond what can be performed reliably, under all conditions. Autonowashing makes something appear to be more autonomous than it really is.

The objective of autonowashing is to differentiate and/or offer a competitive advantage to an entity, through the use of superficial verbiage meant to convey a level of system reliability that is misaligned with the technical capabilities of the system. Autonowashing may also occur inadvertently, when one unknowingly repeats erroneous information about the capabilities of an automated system to another. Autonowashing is a form of disinformation, and it is, in a sense, viral" (Transportation Research Interdisciplinary Perspective, "Autonowashing: The Greenwashing of Vehicle Automation," 2020).

As a reminder from my earlier indication, there are four major variants of AI Ethics washing that I usually see occurring and they are readily found within the autonomous vehicles field too:

- **The AI Ethics Washers That Don't Know They Are**: AI Ethics washing by ignorance or illiteracy about AI and/or AI Ethics
- **The AI Ethics Washers That Fall Into It:** AI Ethics washing by inadvertent slippage though otherwise genuine about AI Ethics and AI
- **The AI Ethics Washers That Thinly Stretch:** AI Ethics washing by purposeful intent though just by a smidgeon and at times nearly excusable (or not)
- **The AI Ethics Washers That Know And Brazenly Peddle It:** AI Ethics washing all-out and by insidious and often outrageous design

In addition, you can readily see instances of the other types of AI Ethics washing and associated washing maladies in the autonomy field, including:

- AI Ethics theatre
- AI Ethics shopping
- AI Ethics bashing
- AI Ethics shielding
- AI Ethics fairwashing

Conclusion

AI Ethics washing is all around us. We are bathing in it.

I hope that by bringing your attention to this serious and seemingly neverending matter, you will be able to discern when you are being AI Ethics washed. It might be hard to figure out. Those that do AI Ethics washing can be exceedingly clever and devious.

One handy trick is to mix into the wash a bit of truth that gets intermixed with the falsehoods or exaggerations. Because you might readily detect and agree to the truthful part, you are potentially swayed into believing that the other untruthful or deceptive part is also true. A nifty and nasty form of deception.

Let's call it hogwash.

Can we wash the mouths out of those that outrightly perform AI Ethics washing?

Sorry to report that it is not as easily done as one might wish for. That being said, just because catching and calling out AI Ethics washing might be arduous and at times be like Sisyphus pushing a heavy boulder up a hill, we need to try.

In case you didn't know, Zeus had tasked him to do this boulder pushing for eternity and the immense rock would forever roll back down once the effort had arrived at the top. I think we are facing the same predicament when it comes to AI Ethics washing.

There will always be more AI Ethics washing that needs to get washed out. That's a surefire guarantee with nothing wishy-washy whatsoever about it.

CHAPTER 20
AI ETHICS AND ALGORITHMIC MONOCULTURE

Let's take a look at a bit of a puzzling conundrum.

It is said that great minds think alike.

You've undoubtedly heard that handy catchphrase many times. During some idle conversations, if you and a colleague or friend manage to land on the same idea at the same precise moment, one of you is bound to exclaim with glee that great minds think alike. This is indubitably a flattering statement about you and your fellow human being.

There is another piece of sage wisdom that we can add to this mix.

It is said that fools seldom differ.

I'd like to slightly reword that adage. The seeming reasonably equivalent saying would be that fools tend to think alike. I realize that you might quibble somewhat with the recasting of the famous line. Nonetheless, it seems relatively accurate that if fools seldom differ you can infer that fools predominantly tend to veer toward like thinking. I hope that doesn't cause too much heartburn or consternation as to the deviating alteration of a hallowed piece of wisdom.

We are now at the perilous moment of this dilemma.

Suppose that we openly grant the notion that great minds think alike is generally true, and we in the same breath grant the assertion that fools tend to think alike is true too. When you come upon a group of people that are all thinking alike, I have to ask you a simple question.

Are they all great minds or are they all fools?

Yikes!

According to the rule about great minds, they are presumably greatly minded. On the other hand, according to the rule about fools, they are apparently all fools. We seem to have a problem. You might stammer that maybe these like-minded thinkers are both greatly minded and fools. Can you be both at the same time? Seems like you are trying to beg the question.

You might fervently argue that thinking alike conveys nothing whatsoever about whether the gathering is thinking greatly or foolishly. We have perhaps inadvertently turned the logic upside down. Any set of people that are thinking alike is merely thinking alike. You cannot try to overlay their likeness of thinking with being labeled as either a set of great minds or foolish minds. They might be muddled minds. They might be persuaded minds. In essence, the characterization might not necessarily fall into the somewhat false dichotomy of solely being great or being foolish.

There are all kinds of insights that get attached to settings involving people possessing a like mind.

Mahatma Gandhi reportedly said that a small group of determined and like-minded people can change the course of history. This surely showcases the immense potency of having like minds. Plato cautioned that when it comes to minds that are closed, which you might suggest that an unyielding set of like-minded people might be, you can get this: "This alone is to be feared: the closed mind, the sleeping imagination, the death of spirit."

Where am I going with this litany of curiosities about like minds?

Well, turns out that there are worries that AI is gradually taking us down an inevitable and undesirable path of having like-minded AI algorithms ruling our everyday activities. This is summarily referred to as *AI algorithmic monoculture.*

We are heading toward a circumstance whereby society relies upon pervasive AI systems that might have the same or nearly the same underlying algorithmic capacities. In that sense, we are vulnerable to like-mindedness on a massive scale that will exist across the globe.

Before I get further into this topic, I want to right away clarify that I am not alluding to AI that is sentient. As I will be explaining in a moment, we do not have sentient AI today. Despite those wild and wide-eyed headlines that proclaim we have sentient AI, this is absolutely not the case and should be utterly disregarded.

The reason I emphasize this important point is that when I depict AI as being "like-minded" I do not want you to leap to the conclusion that today's AI is somehow equivalent to the human mind. It is assuredly not. Please do not make that kind of anthropomorphic association. My use of the like-minded phrasing is only intended to highlight that the AI algorithms might be composed in such a fashion that they work in the same way. They are though not "thinking" in any semblance of what we would construe as human quality of thinking. I'll say more about this shortly herein.

AI that is "like-minded" in terms of having an algorithmic monocultural construct is something that we can assess as being simultaneously bad and good. The bad side of things is that if these commonly utilized and employed sameness AI are rife with biases and discriminatory inclusions, the AI is likely to insidiously be used on a widespread basis and promulgate these unsavory practices everywhere. The good side of things is that if the AI is appropriately devised and done without biases and discriminatory inclusions, we are hopefully making fairness infused widely. All of this has demonstrative AI Ethics and Ethical AI implications.

Here are my handy-dandy seven rules of thumb about AI algorithmic monoculture:

1) **AI algorithmic monoculture consists of employing the same or nearly the same underlying algorithms that are then widely utilized for making decisions that impact humans**
2) **Such AI can provide consistency and reliability, though this is a dual-edged sword**
3) **One side is that AI that is conveying adverse biases is readily spread and used over and over again in untoward ways (that's bad)**
4) **The other side is that AI that is embodying fairness and other justly desirable properties could be thankfully spread widely (that's good)**
5) **There is a certain kind of systemwide vulnerability when having AI homogeneity of this caliber and can be grandly undercut by disruptive shocks**
6) **AI heterogeneity could be sometimes preferred, though this raises the concern of vast incongruities that might arise**
7) **We all need to be thinking about, watching for, and contending with AI algorithmic monoculture**

We all seem to realize that in today's interconnected digitally-based world that we can be blackballed by having even a teeny-tiny bit of data that sits in a database and seems to go wherever we go. For example, suppose a database exists that contains a piece of data containing an indicator that you are not creditworthy. This might be true about you or might be completely false. You might be aware that the database contains this piece of information or you might be entirely unaware of it. This is one large crapshoot of a data-glutted universe that we are all immersed into.

The database that contains this indicator could easily be able to share that vital aspect about you with other databases elsewhere. In a scant blink of an eye, electronically connected databases throughout the world could have the now transmitted flag that you are not creditworthy.

If you opt to apply for a loan, the odds are that some loan approving app will reach out to one of those databases and retrieve the flag that says you are to be snubbed. You might try to get a loan while in one part of the world and get summarily turned down. Traveling to another area might do little good. The interconnectedness of the databases will hound you no matter how far you travel.

Fortunately, there are various laws about data and privacy that have been gradually enacted. The laws differ markedly from country to country. They can also differ from state to state. But at least there is an awareness of the dangers associated with having data in databases that are able to rapidly spread information about you. The hope is that you will have a legal recourse to try and prevent false information or at least be aware that it exists about you.

I guess you could say that the data about you is a proverbial kind of "tag, you are it" game (in which we sometimes want to be the tagged person, and other times we wish to not be so tagged).

Take a deep breath.

Suppose we wave a magic wand and can miraculously ensure that this homogeneity of data about you is not going to happen. We are able to get all of society to band together and stop these kinds of acts. You might ergo assume that you are no longer in peril of such concerns.

Sorry to say, you would be missing the dangers imposed by AI algorithmic monoculture.

Here's why.

We shall return to the example of trying to get a loan. Envision that you go to a lender and they are using an AI system that has a particular algorithm that we will refer to as algorithm Y. In your case, when you apply and provide your details, the algorithm Y is written in such a fashion that it will on-the-fly determine mathematically whether or not you should be turned down for the loan. Essentially, this algorithm can "decide" that you are not credit-worthy.

Notice that we are pretending in this case that the AI didn't reach out to a database to try and garner your credit worthiness. Thus, there is no chance that the AI made a turndown based on some bit of data that was sitting on a database here or there. The entire choice was made via the algorithm Y as to the computations involved.

The AI indicates you are turned down for the loan. I'm sure you would be disappointed with this outcome. You might though shrug your shoulders and opt to go to a different lender. Again, you know for sure that there isn't a database that is knocking you out of contention. In your mind, all you need to do is keep trying at different lenders and you'll eventually get the green light.

Upon going to another lender, once again you get turned down. This is disconcerting. You try another lender, but get quickly turned down. One after another, each attempt leads to the same dismaying result. You are exasperated. You are irked to no end.

What in the heck is going on?

Have all of these lenders secretly conspired to make sure you don't get a loan?

The short answer is "No" and we are going to say that they did not conspire per se. Instead, they all happened to make use of the algorithm Y. They didn't "conspire" in the sense of gathering in a backroom and agreeing to use algorithm Y in their AI. There wasn't a mafia-style get-together that said they would all use the algorithm Y. As a side note, one supposes that could indeed happen, but for sake of discussion we are going to put those alternatives to the side for now.

There is a perfectly sensible reason that algorithm Y might be used by all of these separate and distinct lenders. It could be that the algorithm Y is available as open source. The AI developers at each of those differing lenders might in each case have merely reached out to an open-source library and copied that piece of code into their AI system.

This was likely the easiest and fastest means of getting the job done. No need to from-scratch try to devise that algorithm Y. In a few minutes of online access, the coding is already done for you and directly ready for use. Copy and paste. Furthermore, you might be able to avoid having to do any debugging of the code. Your assumption might be that the code is already well-tested and there is no need for you to reinvent the wheel.

Okay, so lender upon lender all innocently opt to use the algorithm Y. There is a solid chance that the algorithm Y becomes known as the "gold standard" to be used for ascertaining credit worthiness. And this will make the adoption of that particular algorithm even more popular. AI developers aren't just saving time by using it, they are also playing things safe. Everyone else swears that the algorithm is viable for use. Why should you fight against the wisdom of the crowd? It would seem imprudent to do so.

Welcome to the era of AI algorithmic monoculture.

We have uncovered herein via this example that the same algorithm can be readily used over and over again in a multitude of AI systems. There isn't especially a conspiracy about it. No super-duper masterminded evil plot at hand. In lieu of those malevolent schemes, a particular algorithm becomes dominant due to what could be depicted as virtuous and beneficial reasons.

In years past, the possibility of widely using the same algorithms has existed, though more hurdles needed to be surmounted. Today, the use of algorithm storing hubs is almost effortlessly accessed. Open source is more accepted than it was perhaps in prior generations. And so on.

With the one example of the lender that we've been exploring, we might end up with two lenders, twenty lenders, two hundred lenders, two thousand lenders, or maybe hundreds of thousands of lenders all opting to use that same algorithm Y in their AI. The algorithm AI is surefire. It is being selected and ingrained into AI all across the globe.

Nobody is raising any red flags. There is no apparent reason to do so. If anything, the red flag might be raised when some lender opts to not use algorithm Y. Hey, the question might be exhorted, you aren't using algorithm Y. What gives? Are you purposely trying to do something underhanded or dirty? Get your act together and come on board with everyone else.

Extrapolate this same conceptual monoculture to all manner of AI systems and all manner of algorithms.

A research study described the phenomena this way: "The rise of algorithms used to shape societal choices has been accompanied by concerns over monoculture—the notion that choices and preferences will become homogeneous in the face of algorithmic curation" (Jon Kleinberga and Manish Raghavana, "Algorithmic Monoculture And Social Welfare" *PNAS* 2021). They further point out: "Even if algorithms are more accurate on a case-by-case basis, a world in which everyone uses the same algorithm is susceptible to correlated failures when the algorithm finds itself in adverse conditions."

We can now usefully revisit my earlier set of seven rules about AI algorithmic monoculture:

1) AI algorithmic monoculture consists of employing the same or nearly the same underlying algorithms that are then widely utilized for making decisions that impact humans
2) Such AI can provide consistency and reliability, though this is a dual-edged sword
3) One side is that AI that is conveying adverse biases is readily spread and used over and over again in untoward ways (that's bad)
4) The other side is that AI that is embodying fairness and other justly desirable properties could be thankfully spread widely (that's good)
5) There is a certain kind of systemwide vulnerability when having AI homogeneity of this caliber and can be grandly undercut by disruptive shocks
6) AI heterogeneity could be sometimes preferred, though this raises the concern of vast incongruities that might arise

7) We all need to be thinking about, watching for, and contending with AI algorithmic monoculture

As noted in my rule #2, there is a decidedly dual-edged sword about AI algorithmic monoculture.

Per my rule #3, you could end up on the short end of the stick. If you are getting turned down by lender after lender, wherever you go, and if algorithm Y is doing this based on a bias or other inappropriate basis, you are regrettably cursed. You will have a lot harder time trying to get this overturned. In the case of data about you in a database, the odds are that you would have some legal recourse and also general recognition of what bad data can do. Few people would comprehend that a bad algorithm is following you to the ends of the earth.

Per my rule #4, there is a potential upside to the AI algorithmic monoculture. Assume that the algorithm Y is rightfully precluding you from getting a loan. You might have tried sneakily and perniciously to trick things by shopping around. Since the same algorithm Y is being used widely, your shopping is unlikely to strike gold. Though we might not like the idea of a persistent and in-common possibility of algorithm fairness (if there is such a thing), we can possibly rejoice when a good thing is spread widely.

Let's next discuss shocks.

In my rule #5, I indicate that there is an underlying qualm that an AI algorithmic monoculture could be subject to massive disruption. This is easily explained. Imagine that there is a software bug in the algorithm Y. No one noticed it. For eons, it has been hiding there in plain sight. In case you doubt that this could ever happen, namely that a bug would be in open-source code and yet not have already been earlier found.

The bug surfaces and causes the algorithm Y to no longer be the glorified piece of code that everyone thought it was. Realize that this bug is sitting in those thousands upon thousands of AI systems. In short order, the bug might be encountered across the planet, and we quickly find ourselves facing a horrendous mess. Since everyone put their eggs into one basket, and since the basket is now totally awry, the same is taking place worldwide.

A disaster of epic proportions.

In theory, this would not have readily happened if the lenders had each been devising their own proprietary algorithms. The chances are that if one of them had a bug, the others would not. In the case of all of them using the same base code, they all have the same bug.

Darned if you do, darned if you don't.

I am sure that some of you are hollering that the good news about the bug in a monoculture setting is that if there is a fix available, everyone can simply put in place the same fix. This would seem to be a bright and sunshiny way of looking at the matter. Yes, that might work. The gist here though is that there is a heightened chance of an across-the-board disruption. Even if the resolution might be easier to cope with, you still are faced with the massiveness of disruption due to the monoculture facets.

Besides the instance of a bug that could cause a shock, we can abundantly come up with lots of other unnerving scenarios. One would be a cyber crook that devises an evil way to usurp a popularly used algorithm. The evildoer could have a bonanza in their hands. They can go from AI to AI, getting the AI to do something dastardly. All because the same algorithm was used over and over again. The massive scale can be leveraged for goodness and lamentedly can be potentially exploited for badness.

At this juncture of this weighty discussion, I'd bet that you are desirous of some illustrative examples that might showcase this topic.

Here's then a noteworthy question that is worth contemplating: *Does the advent of AI-based true self-driving cars illuminate anything about AI algorithmic monoculture, and if so, what does this showcase?*

We shall begin by stating some crucial groundings. AI driving systems are being devised to try and safely operate self-driving cars. Some automakers and self-driving tech firms are doing their coding in proprietary ways. Others are relying upon open-source code.

Envision that some algorithm Z is available in open-source repositories and handy for use in AI driving systems. An automaker or self-driving tech firm incorporates the algorithm Z into their AI driving system. This will be integrally woven into their AI driving system.

If they put say a dozen self-driving cars on the roadways, all of those autonomous vehicles will contain the algorithm Z as part of the onboard software of the AI driving system. Gradually, assuming that the self-driving cars are driving safely, the fleet increases in size to twenty self-driving cars on the roadways. A decision is made to ramp up further. Soon, two thousand self-driving cars of that fleet are now on the streets and highways. And so on.

A different automaker is also using the algorithm Z in their driving system. They too are deploying their self-driving cars. Their fleet is increased in size. Soon they have thousands of their self-driving cars wandering here and there.

I trust that you can see where this is heading.

We can find ourselves in an AI algorithmic monoculture amidst the advent of AI-based self-driving cars. A multitude of brands and models of autonomous vehicles might all have a particular algorithm being used somewhere in their AI driving system. There wasn't any collusion about this. No grand conspiracies at play.

In terms of how many self-driving cars we might someday have on our roads, there is a heated debate on that topic. We know that in the United States alone there are about 250 million human-driven cars today. Some suggest that we will ergo need about 250 million self-driving cars, assuming that we eventually do away with human-driven cars or that they are naturally being ditched and replaced by self-driving cars.

Not so fast, some exhort. Human-driven cars spend about 90% or more of their time not being used. By and large, human-driven cars sit parked and await a human driver to drive them. AI-based self-driving cars can be driving all of the time, just about. You could presumably have an AI self-driving car going 24x7, other than during maintenance or other required downtime.

In that case, you won't seemingly need 250 million self-driving cars to replace one-for-one the 250 million human-driven cars. Perhaps 200 million self-driving cars will suffice. Maybe 100 million. No one can say for sure.

I want to for the moment just point out that we could have many millions upon millions of self-driving cars ultimately roaming around on our highways and byways. How many of them we will ultimately precisely have on the roads is not quite a crucial concern for the sake of this discourse. There will unquestionably be many millions. This sizing in general is important due to AI algorithmic monoculture and the keystone property of encountering both advantages and disadvantages at a massive scale.

Here's the twist.

By atrociously awful dumb luck there is a severe problem within the algorithm Z that nobody previously managed to notice. There is a bug that will cause the rest of the AI driving system to go awry.

Bad news.

For those of you that are in the throes of devising AI driving systems, I realize that you don't usually like these kinds of worst-case scenarios, and though the chances are perhaps slim, they nonetheless are worthwhile to discuss. We cannot keep our heads in the sand. Better to be eyes wide open and seek to prevent or at least mitigate these types of calamities.

In theory, an AI self-driving car containing this bug might attempt to ram into and crash with nearly anything and everything within its grasp to do so. The AI is merely doing as it was "devised" to do in this setting. This would be disastrous.

Some of you might be thinking that just because one AI self-driving car perchance encounters the bug would not seem like much of a problem per se. I say that because once the AI self-driving car smashes into something such as a truck or whatever, the vehicle itself is likely to be so damaged that it can no longer actively be directed by the AI to carry out any further chaos and destruction. It is dead in the water, so to speak.

Well, consider the scaling factor involved.

If there are millions and millions of self-driving cars and they are all relying on that same embedded algorithm Z, they might ruefully execute that same bug.

I know and acknowledge that this bug might be fixed or overcome via the use of an OTA (Over-The-Air) electronically distributed software update. As a quick background, many have gushed about the advantages of using OTA. When a software update is needed, you won't have to take an AI self-driving car into a car repair shop or dealership. The OTA can pretty much be done wherever the self-driving car happens to be (within limitations).

Meanwhile, until we figure out the bug and the fix, and before sending it out via OTA, the self-driving cars on the roadways are still going to be in a precarious posture. Some will have encountered the bug and gone awry. Others are on the verge of doing so.

We might opt to insist that all self-driving cars should for the moment be stopped in place and not further used until the OTA fix is beamed into the AI driving systems. Imagine the disruption. Suppose we have very few human-driven cars left. The odds too are that self-driving cars will not be outfitted with human driving controls. In essence, you could end up with a grounding of 200 million (or whatever number) self-driving cars while we get the bug fixed.

If society has become dependent upon self-driving cars, you pretty much have shut down society from a mobility perspective, at least until the bug fix is pushed out.

Now that would be a detrimental and shocking shock to the system, as it were.

I suspect that the idea of a lurking bug that does abysmal actions would seem nearly impossible to imagine, though at the same time we cannot rule out the possibility in its entirety. There are other possibilities, such as cyber criminal vulnerabilities that might exist. I have discussed for example how a rogue nation-state could try to carry out a heinous act by exploiting a weakness in an AI driving system. In addition, for my details about how a malicious takeover of AI self-driving cars could be performed.

Conclusion

Like-mindedness is both a blessing and a curse.

We earlier noted that Gandhi said that those of a like-mind can achieve great things. AI that is "like-minded" can potentially achieve great things. Plato warned us that closed minds can be a grave danger. If we have like-minded systems all around us, we are potentially faced with the lurking perils of inadvertent (or intentional) subverting elements that can harm some of us or maybe all of us.

We need to have an open mind about AI algorithmic monoculture. If we do things right, we might be able to harness the goodness and avert the badness. But only if we are right in our minds about it all.

CHAPTER 21
AI ETHICS AND MOBILITY POLICIES

Are our cities and urban areas ready for the advent of Autonomous Vehicles (AVs) such as public roadway roaming self-driving cars, sidewalk-going self-driving delivery bots, campus-based self-driving shuttle buses, and a plethora of other assorted driverless vehicles?

Maybe yes, or maybe not (more likely not so).

A newly released research report entitled "Developing Urban Mobility Policy in Response to Autonomous Vehicles" has been posted by the Harvard Kennedy School (HKS) via the Taubman Center for State and Local Government. Doing so under the auspices of their Autonomous Vehicles Policy Initiative (AVPI) program, this latest paper is part of an ongoing and overarching analysis that explores the practical and pragmatic considerations underlying the implementation of AVs at the city, state, and federal government levels.

I'm honored to indicate that this is a report that I've co-authored with esteemed colleague Mark Fagan, lecturer at the Harvard Kennedy School and head of the AVPI program there.

We are all looking at the self-driving forest and not just the trees alone. In essence, it is easy to get caught up in the day-to-day excitement of having numerous driverless pilots and prototypes underway in a given municipality.

That being said, retaining a big picture perspective will be vital toward ensuring that AV adoption is a balanced and satisfactory entrant into your urban area.

With that said, let's take a quick look at some of the highlights of this new report.

First, as mindful background, the AVPI program has been actively engaged for several years in conducting research, teaching, and working with policymakers that are grappling with how to prepare for and sensibly cope with the burgeoning testing and fielding of all kinds of Autonomous Vehicles, especially ground-based self-driving vehicles.

In addition to the in-depth research and instructional efforts, the AVPI is also known for undertaking intense policy scrums that bring together governmental policymakers with AV experts, policy analysts, and legal experts. These are exhilarating face-to-face interactive sessions that immerse the participants into candid and quite fruitful dialogue about how to prudently and proactively cope with emerging AVs and self-driving efforts within their respective communities.

This most recent report contains an innovative scenario-based setting or simulation-oriented backdrop that can be used for energizing AV-related policy scrums all told.

In a sense, there is a foundation provided in the report to enable the undertaking of an AV-exploring policy simulation of sorts. Participants in a policy analysis session can take on various roles within the simulation and then see how things go when interacting with their fellow participants that have momentarily also assumed particular roles.

For example, you've got a mayor that is being besieged on all sides, whereby some local constituencies favor the arising use of AVs and meanwhile other local actors express notable concerns. Meanwhile, the AV vendors are pressing ahead earnestly to expand their local self-driving efforts.

But what about the impacts on the people of the city?

Some studies suggest that self-driving cars are tending to increase traffic congestion in already clogged city streets. That's a problem worthy of anticipating and not getting blindsided with.

Some of the fleets of self-driving automobiles are only currently available in certain areas of the city. Does this deny fuller and more balanced access toward suitable mobility equity throughout the urban landscape?

There are AV vendors that are beginning to charge for use of their driverless vehicles. Is the pricing creating a kind of divisiveness as to those that can afford to use this new transportation option versus those that cannot?

And so on it goes.

You see, a robust scenario is laid out that depicts a typical city caught in the midst of the relatively widespread adoption of self-driving vehicles. It can be a nightmare for those that have allowed events and efforts to proceed on a pell-mell basis alone. Though admittedly only a few cities are at this juncture or nearing it, right now, you can bet that in the next several years there will be many more localities that find themselves in this same boat.

Rather than waiting until the horse is already out of the barn, this multi-party policy development simulation can open the eyes of those that want to be ahead of the game. By anticipating the soon-to-be-upon-us future, policymakers have a crucial opportunity to guide their locality in a direction that will either avoid or at least mitigate many of the inadvertent *adverse consequences* that can arise with widespread and possibly uncontrolled AV use.

As stated in the report: "This simulation enables policymakers and stakeholders to develop the operating environment and regulations that position a municipality to tap the opportunities that AVs offer while minimizing the adverse consequences.

This exercise is based on an anticipated scenario of how AVs may arrive in cities in the coming few years. It details the players and their interests. Using the descriptions provided, participants engage in a three-round simulation to reach a consensus on the best path forward. The simulation is designed as a facilitated simulation for use by both practitioners and students. It concludes with a framework for how policymakers can migrate from their current position to their desired state."

A framework containing a curated set of potential policy actions is also provided.

Policymakers can consider which of the policy actions seem suitable for the scenario portrayed. More importantly, these are then intended to become active handy-dandy tools for the participants, allowing a leveraging of these same tools and techniques within their own respective localities.

A range of tools is proffered. These include fostering a cohesive mobility-as-a-service approach across the otherwise disparate transport options in a modern-day municipality. Local residents and visitors in today's cities are overwhelmed with multi-modal transportation capabilities. Which should they use? How will the self-driving options fit within the transport fabric or landscape of the locality? Etc.

Another looming issue is going to be the question of data-sharing (I've referred to this as the data collected via the "roving eye" of self-driving vehicles). If a fleet of self-driving cars is collecting copious amounts of data about where locals are traveling, when they travel, and so on, who owns that data? Suppose the AV operator decides to use or sell the data, could this be a privacy intrusion?

Also, this collected data could be valuable information for local policymakers that wish to plan for and adjust transportation and infrastructure elements in their municipality. Will the AV vendors provide the data openly or insist that it is their own proprietary data and refuse to share it?

One other handy indication in the report consists of a matrix for guiding where a city sits currently on the scale of AV adoption and where it is heading.

As per the report: "The results of the simulation provide a point-in-time view of how a city wants AVs to support mobility. Rarely will the desired outcome be the current state. The results of the simulation can be used to help the city migrate from its current position to the desired state. A propensity matrix may be helpful in facilitating the transition. When examining urban mobility policies in the context of AV deployments, two major factors are useful to consider: (1) The pervasiveness of AVs in the municipality; and (2) The maturity of urban AV mobility policies."

Where is your municipality in terms of its existing readiness for AV adoption considerations?

Many are behind the eight ball.

They are either relatively untouched as yet by self-driving efforts, or they have allowed self-driving efforts to arise organically or sporadically (doing so in a benevolent but rather unplanned manner).

Conclusion

As alluded to earlier, the emergence of self-driving options is taking place in a somewhat semi-random or haphazard manner in our cities.

This makes sense when you consider that AVs are a new form of transportation and there is a staggered start-stop phenomenon involved. One AV vendor makes solid progress. Another one perhaps finds themselves stymied and has to regroup. Some of the AV vendors are utterly focused on the technological facets and either unaware or not versed in the societal impacts that the introduction of self-driving options imbues upon an urban area.

I've said it before, and I'll say it again, namely that it takes a village to bring to proper fruition the plethora of driverless transportation options. I continue to implore policymakers, AV vendors, AV experts, legal experts, policy analysts, and every stakeholder to get up-to-speed, begin your preparations now (don't wait), and make sure that your city is not caught off-guard.

An ounce of preparation is worth a pound of cure.

CHAPTER 22
AI ETHICS
AND AI STARTUPS

Fail fast, fail often. Whatever you are thinking, think bigger. Fake it until you make it.

These are the typical startup lines that you hear or see all the time. They have become a kind of advisory lore amongst budding entrepreneurs. If you wander around Silicon Valley, you'll probably see bumper stickers with those slogans and likely witness high-tech founders wearing hoodies emblazoned with such tropes.

AI-related startups are assuredly included in the bunch.

Perhaps we might though add an additional piece of startup success advice for the AI aiming nascent firms, namely that they should *energetically embrace AI ethics*. That is a bumper sticker-worthy notion and assuredly a useful piece of sage wisdom for any AI founder that is trying to figure out how they can be a proper leader and a winning entrepreneur.

The first impulse of many AI startups is likely the exact opposite of wanting to embrace AI ethics. Here's why.

Often, the focus of an AI startup is primarily about getting some tangible AI system out the door as quickly as possible. There is usually tremendous pressure to produce an MVP (minimally viable product). Investors are skittish about putting money into some newfangled AI contrivance that might not be buildable, and therefore the urgency to craft an AI pilot or prototype is paramount. As they say, the proof is in the pudding. Many AI startups are all about being heads down and churning out sufficient AI code to make their AI dream appear to be plausible.

In that sense of attention, there is little interest in worrying about AI ethics. The usual assumption is that any Ethical AI considerations can be bolted on once the AI core is showcased. This is a mindset that any semblance of AI ethics is merely icing on the cake and not at all integral to the making of the cake. Sure, those AI ethics are a proverbial nice to have, and if time permits you'll plant some Ethical AI elements here or there, but otherwise that whole idea of dutifully incorporating AI ethics is seen as farfetched and not a real-world concern.

There is another semi-popular saying that goes along with this tendency. In a street fight, you don't have time to be fretting about style. An AI startup is grittily fighting to get its AI into existence and struggling to get funding to make it to the next stage of development. Anything else, such as those pesky AI ethics, is presumed as extremely low on the priorities of what needs to be cared about.

I should also add that there is an abundance of AI startup founders that are totally oblivious to the rising tide of calls for Ethical AI. Those that are in their own techie fog are utterly unaware that anyone cares about AI ethics, to begin with. As such, you can decidedly bet that such an AI startup is not going to give any air time to including Ethical AI precepts. This is a veritable out-of-sight and out-of-mind notion of which the AI builders in the startup are probably blissfully ignorant and even when approached about AI ethics they are apt to dismiss it as a wholly fringe factor.

You might be wondering if perhaps those brazen AI founders are right in their way of thinking. Maybe AI ethics can be tossed aside until the time that there is sufficient time for dolling up the AI system. Or perhaps there really isn't any value in abiding by Ethical AI and that the whole shenanigans about AI ethics are merely one of those momentary fads.

Well, to be blunt, that's a sure recipe for disaster.

In brief, those that ignore or delay AI ethics are in grave peril of their AI going down in flames and their startup likewise collapsing in a colossal heap.

Furthermore, the potential for legal ramifications that linger long after the startup is abandoned will serve as an agonizing reminder that they should have done the right thing at the beginning. Lawsuits targeting the startup, the founder, the investors, and other stakeholders will be a longstanding stink far beyond the closing up of the failed AI startup.

Bottom-line: *AI ethics should be a cornerstone of everything an AI startup opts to do, starting on day one and forever after.*

Period, full stop.

Overall, in my experience advising AI startups and also based on some recent research studies about AI startups, any founder that is not giving suitable attention to Ethical AI is on a likely sour path and will find their AI efforts floundering. There is an increasing realization by investors that without the right amount of AI ethics being imbued into a budding AI system, the envisioned AI is probably going to be a lousy investment or worse still a miserable legally draining entanglement.

The chances are that AI without an Ethical AI foundation is going to make some ugly and reputational missteps. If the AI is shown to include unsavory biases and inequities, the public outcry is going to be loud and magnified many-fold via today's social media viral tattle-telling. Not only will the AI startup get into hot water, but the investors are also bound to be dragged into the same mud. Why did they invest in an AI startup that had its head in the sand when it came to observing Ethical AI principles? Investors do not want to be permanently tarnished by the acts of one particular AI startup that they happened to fund.

Keep in mind that some big bucks are flowing into AI startups.

We are in the midst of a euphoric rush toward AI-related anything. According to stats recently compiled on behalf of the *Wall Street Journal,* Venture Capital funding of AI startups last year managed to gobble up about $8 billion in funding.

This is probably a low-ball estimate since there are many AI startups that stealthily at first hide their AI aspirations, wanting to stave off competition or avoid prodding others into realizing that AI can be used in an ingenious manner being cleverly devised.

An insightful research survey of how AI startups are potentially utilizing AI ethics appeared recently as a Working Paper of the *Center on Regulations and Markets at Brookings* and is entitled "Ethical AI Development: Evidence from AI Startups" by James Bessen, Stephen Impink, Robert Seamans. Let's take an instructive look at what they found.

Their study surveyed a bit over two hundred AI-related startups and asked the firms about the awareness and embracing of Ethical AI at their firm. The good news is that about half of the respondents said they do have Ethical AI precepts in-house. That actually is somewhat surprising in that just a few years ago the odds were that a much lower percentage would have been so armed.

Here's what the study said about examining AI ethics adoption at these AI startups: "We assess these issues by collecting and analyzing novel survey data from 225 AI startups. We find that more than half of responding firms have ethical AI principles. However, many of those firms have never invoked their ethical AI principles in a costly way, such as firing an employee, dropping training data, or turning down a sale."

As suggested by the pointed remarks, the bad news about AI ethics adoption in AI startups is that they might not be seriously embracing the Ethical AI precepts. It could be lip service.

You know how that goes.

An AI startup is perhaps shamed or coerced into believing in AI ethics, so they do the minimum that they have to do to placate others. Perhaps they adorn their offices with placards that tout Ethical AI. The founder might give lofty speeches about how important AI ethics is. Meanwhile, behind the scenes, the Ethical AI notion is given little attention and possibly even scorned or ridiculed by the high-tech heavy hitters building the AI.

Not wanting to seem overly dour, we can at least herald that somewhat more than half of the AI startups *claimed* to have adopted AI ethics principles. I suppose we can rejoice in that revelation. Of course, this also implies that somewhat less than half have not adopted AI ethics principles. This invokes a sad face.

We have about half that apparently got the memo (so to speak) about embracing AI ethics, though some portion of them are possibly doing so merely as a checkmark to tout that they are all-in on Ethical AI. Then we have roughly the other half that has not seemingly adopted AI ethics. I'll be optimistic and say that we can hope that those unwashed AI startups will gradually wake up and adopt Ethical AI and that the AI startups that are loosey-goosey about their already adopted AI ethics will stridently seek to turn the appearance into a reality based on actual Ethical AI practices.

That's the smiley face view.

Continuing our look at the survey results, here are some of the characteristics of the AI startups that were polled: "Firms in our survey are about four years old and employ, on average, 36 employees. However, almost half of firms have less than eleven employees. Even though the survey was administered worldwide, most of our responses are from more developed countries, with almost 80% of responses from the United States, Canada, and Europe."

I would almost be willing to assert that the newest AI startups are probably more likely to be embracing AI ethics than the ones that are already a few years into their journey. The so-called "business DNA" of a startup is often decided at its initial formulation.

And since the Ethical AI trumpet is now loudly sounding, those AI startups just getting underway are presumably going to be adopting AI ethics. The startups that launched a few years ago might have missed out on the existing alarm bells about Ethical AI. As such, for some of those, the foundational roots of their startup might not readily be uprooted to now incorporate AI ethics.

That last comment is worth some added attention.

You might be thinking that if there are now advantages to embracing AI ethics, the sensible thing to do would be for already existent AI startups to jump on that bandwagon. This might happen.

On the other hand, the tone and mindset of the founder are typically cast in stone and likewise, the AI startup gets somewhat laden with concrete too. It can be very hard for the founder to change their views and similarly to rejigger the startup accordingly. I've written extensively about the importance of startup founders being able to pivot as needed, though few know how to do so and regrettably allow their startup to fumble correspondingly.

Returning to the study finding that perhaps the adoption of AI ethics by some of the AI startups was not being done in earnest, we ought to examine that matter.

The question arises as to how we can substantiate that an AI startup is in fact abiding by Ethical AI principles. This is a lot harder to establish than it might seem at first glance. One way to figure this out would be to dive into AI coding and see if we can find a programmatic embrace of AI ethics. Likewise, we could try testing the AI system to see if it violates AI ethics. All in all, this is a tech-oriented means of seeking to discern adherence to Ethical AI.

Another equally valuable approach would be to see if the business decisions of the AI startup appear to reflect a declarative belief in Ethical AI. Do the actions of the AI startup match the words of the AI startup as it pertains to contending that AI ethics is vital and demonstrative to the firm?

The survey examined this approach and proffered these findings: "A set of ethical AI principles in and of itself is not important unless firms adhere to those principles. From the survey, we asked firms with AI policies to provide additional information on how adherence to these policies impacts their business outcomes to determine if ethics policies are followed rather than simply being signals to investors. More than half of the firms with AI principles experienced at least one costly business outcome because they adhered to their ethical AI principles."

The point is that if an AI startup has opted to make sure that the AI ethics rubber meets the road, as it were, there are likely business outcomes of a somewhat costly nature that would have to be incurred. Money talks, as they say. An AI startup that perhaps fires someone for not abiding by Ethical AI precepts or that has to hire someone anew to aid in the AI ethics pursuit is putting their money where their mouth is. This is especially significant for AI startups since they are usually marginally subsisting on the least amount of money and they have to stretch every dollar they can. Any costs that therefore go toward embracing an Ethical AI tenet can be interpreted as a hefty choice and one that signals a strongly held AI ethics belief.

We need to be careful though in leaping to unfair reasoning in such matters. An AI startup from the get-go may have fueled Ethical AI into its entire being. In that case, they might not, later on, have to incur any costly AI ethics-oriented choices. We would therefore be somewhat misleadingly inferring that if they don't have those subsequent costly actions, they aren't truly serious about Ethical AI. This is a form of what is sometimes referred to as survivor bias. We only might be looking at the firms that initially skipped the AI ethics foundational laying and giving overdue credence to them when they, later on, attempt to correct their earlier misguided ship.

I'd also like to cover another vital topic about why AI startups are nowadays more so going to be adopting AI ethics.

I had moments ago mentioned that savvy AI investors are now tending to require that startups they are funding have to showcase a strident embrace of Ethical AI. There are other ways in which this arises too. For example, larger tech firms that are crafting AI are quickly adopting AI ethics, especially since they realize that they are a big target for when their AI goes ethically awry. In turn, those larger tech firms are often urging AI startups to also adopt Ethical AI.

Here's the basis for that thinking.

Many of the larger tech firms will at times decide to buy an AI startup, doing so to augment their own AI or to allow them to more expeditiously enter into a new market that the startup-provided AI opens up for their endeavors. These sizable tech firms have lots of attorneys on their payroll and know well the dangers of getting snagged on using unethical AI. What this all means is that if an AI startup has already done the legwork in embracing AI ethics, the large tech firm wanting to buy them has an easier time deciding to do so.

The contrasting picture is that if an AI startup has failed to embrace AI ethics, they are now a problematic child when it comes to a larger tech firm wanting to buy or invest in the budding entity. Will the potentially unethical AI become the tail that wags the dog? How much money will it take to turn around the AI startup toward a more Ethical AI aspiration? Is the likely delay worth making that investment, or should they instead find some other AI startup that has already infused AI ethics from day one?

An AI founder ought to be thinking about these crucial considerations.

When an AI startup is first conceived, the best way to proceed consists of thinking about a potential growth strategy (and, similarly, a viable exit strategy). You should be harboring all along with the chances that a larger fish will want to gobble you up. Some entrepreneurs like the idea, while some do not and insist on going along on their own. In any case, when a larger firm comes knocking at the door, the temptations of getting a huge influx in cash that can keep your baby going are quite alluring.

You should gainfully plan for that day (but no guarantees of it), and ensure that you do not get caught at the altar such that the proposed marriage suddenly falls apart due to a discovery that Ethical AI was not a grounding of your AI startup.

I suppose that is the carrot of sorts, but we also need to consider the stick (i.e., the infamous carrot and stick way of looking at life).

The wild things that AI startups got away with a few years ago are going to gradually be codified in law as something that is more clearly stated now as being categorically unlawful. If an AI startup is closely adhering to AI ethics, the chances are they are probably also remaining within the rubric of being lawful. This is not assuredly so, but it is certainly more likely and also could be somewhat credibly argued in a legal case as a semblance of how the AI startup earnestly attempted to create lawful AI.

Okay, we've then got the carrot of a larger tech firm that might want to buy up or invest in an AI startup, which would be made easier to do if the AI startup was embracing Ethical AI. We also have the stick of new legislation and regulations that are targeting AI and will be a potential legal landmine for AI startups that are not mindful of AI ethics. All told, it is a powerful one-two punch that says an aware AI entrepreneur should be mindfully seeking to get into Ethical AI.

The survey generally found this one-two punch to be evidenced via the responses they received: "From our results, it is apparent that many AI startups are aware of possible ethical issues, and more than half have taken steps by providing codified AI principles to guide their firm. However, firms with prior resources, such as data sharing relationships with larger high technology firms and prior regulatory experience with GDPR, are more likely to act on these principles in a material way" (the reference to GDPR is an indication of the European Union's General Data Protection Regulation which is EU law covering privacy and data protection aspects).

Throughout this discussion about AI ethics, I've been assuming that you already have a familiarity with the overall facets of Ethical AI. I've also been making some assumptions about AI too. We should explore these matters before we get further into unpacking the AI startup and AI ethics conundrum.

One particular segment or portion of AI Ethics that has been getting a lot of media attention consists of AI that exhibits untoward biases and inequities. You might be aware that when the latest era of AI got underway there was a huge burst of enthusiasm for what some now call *AI For Good*. Unfortunately, on the heels of that gushing excitement, we began to witness *AI For Bad*. For example, various AI-based facial recognition systems have been revealed as containing racial biases and gender biases.

At this juncture of this weighty discussion, I'd bet that you are desirous of some illustrative examples that might showcase the AI startup and AI ethics circumstances. There is a special and assuredly popular set of examples that are close to my heart. You see, in my capacity as an expert on AI including the ethical and legal ramifications, I am frequently asked to identify realistic examples that showcase AI Ethics dilemmas so that the somewhat theoretical nature of the topic can be more readily grasped. One of the most evocative areas that vividly presents this ethical AI quandary is the advent of AI-based true self-driving cars. This will serve as a handy use case or exemplar for ample discussion on the topic.

Here's then a noteworthy question that is worth contemplating: *Does the advent of AI-based true self-driving cars illuminate anything about AI startups and Ethical AI, and if so, what does this showcase?*

We are primed now to do a deep dive into self-driving cars and the Ethical AI possibilities entailing AI startups. A teensy bit of a history lesson is in order.

When the first scrum of AI self-driving car companies got underway there was very little attention being paid to Ethical AI concerns. In those days, the focus was the usual tech wonderment preoccupation about whether or not AI could be devised to drive a car. The thinking principally was that if any AI ethics qualms might arise, there was no particular basis for worrying about it until one could summarily "prove" that the AI being able to do driving was distinctly feasible.

Being overly preoccupied with any AI ethics was akin to putting the cart in front of the horse, some would have suggested at the time.

Furthermore, there wasn't quite as much awareness about how AI could be shaped such that it was indeed performing in unethical ways. The assumption generally was that an AI developer would need to go out of their way to purposefully craft AI that was not of an ethical caliber. Only evildoers that were deviously constructing AI would do that.

You might know that eventually the realm of AI Ethics inevitably caught up with those making and fielding AI-infused autonomous vehicles. Various foul acts by AI driving systems (as poorly conceived or as at times half-baked deployed) resulted in a realization that something needed to be done. I have chronicled in my many years long ongoing column the gradual Ethical AI changes that took place, including that most if not nearly all of the bona fide self-driving tech firms ended up putting in place top-level executives responsible for infusing AI ethics throughout their firms.

That being said, I do not want to leave the impression that the Ethical AI matter is somehow fully put to bed in today's AI self-driving car entities. I assure you that we still have a lot of ground that needs to be covered. For example, as I have insisted numerous times, there is still to this day a lack of proper attention being given to the AI ethics issues as spurred by the famous or infamous Trolley Problem.

One thing to also realize is that by and large most of the self-driving car entities are now no longer reasonably labeled as AI startups. They are far beyond the startup phase. Some of them grew on their own. Some of them got bought by a larger firm, such as an automaker or a delivery firm. Etc.

In that manner of consideration, you could argue that they can nowadays generally afford to embrace AI ethics. They are flush with cash and have the ability to run their firms in a less starving manner. They also tend to have greater exposure that if they aren't abiding by Ethical AI they will get called out for it.

When you have your self-driving cars zipping around on public roadways, any AI ethical lapses are bound to get noticed and widely reported. The parent company that owns the AI self-driving car entity is going to take a severe beating in the public eye and potentially take a bad hit in the stock market. For a variety of reasons, the AI ethics weightiness tends to be relatively valued, but of course, this is not necessarily always the case and you can bet that lapses are going to occur.

Does this imply then that there aren't any AI startups in this niche and ergo no need to discuss their AI ethics adoption therein?

It might seem that way since the headlines are usually about the biggie self-driving tech firms. Unless you perchance are especially paying attention to this niche, you would think that there aren't any new startups going into this realm. The whole shebang seems to be dominated by relatively established companies and all of the startup activity has either been previously accomplished or cannot get any traction since the market is clogged with today's overbearing big oak trees.

You would be wrong in making such an assumption about AI startups in this arena. There is still quite a bit of action. The difference is that AI startups nowadays tend to be aimed at a piece of the pie rather than the whole pie.

In days past, the AI startups typically wanted to build an AI self-driving car from the ground up, doing everything from A to Z. You would start from scratch with a blank sheet of paper and imagine what someday a self-driving car might be like. That became your marching orders.

The odds of that kind of AI startup being launched today are relatively low. Instead, the AI startups in the self-driving car niche tend to be dealing with particular components or subsets of what AI self-driving cars consist of. This happens quite a lot in the sensor suite facets of self-driving cars. You've got a continual emergence of AI startups that concentrate on a particular kind of sensor or a specific AI algorithm to do a better job of interpreting the data collected by a specific sensor type.

Overall, the question of getting AI startups to embrace AI ethics is still alive and kicking in the autonomous vehicles and self-driving cars space.

In advising AI startups all told and including those in the autonomous vehicle realm, I have come up with my favorite tips or recommendations on these matters.

As a taste, here are my decreed Top Ten:

1) The founder has to be or become an AI ethics proselytizer else the rest of the AI startup won't perceive that the topic is worthy of the available scarce attention and already overworked endeavors (it all starts at the top).

2) A founder is unlikely to fully grasp what Ethical AI entails and ought to get up-to-speed so that their comprehension of the topic matches their passion for it (know what you are talking about).

3) Hollow platitudes by a founder about AI ethics will absolutely undercut the startup teams and turn the Ethical AI banner into a worthless banner absent of any substance (do not poison the waters).

4) Make sure to connect the Ethical AI precepts with specific duties and actions involved in designing, building, testing, and fielding the AI (otherwise an oversized and unbridgeable gap will exist and your teams will not be able to connect the dots).

5) Put in place a sensible AI development methodology that either already has incorporated Ethical AI precepts or that can reasonably be retrofitted appropriately and without undue distraction (a proper methodology will guide the teams seamlessly in the path toward AI ethics fruition).

6) Provide suitable training to the teams about AI ethics and make sure that this is done in an imminently practical rubber-meets-the-road manner (lofty training will do little and likely cause a backlash at seemingly having wasted precious time).

7) Establish a relevant means of rewarding the teams for embracing Ethical AI in their daily efforts, including highly visible recognition by the founder, monetary or other bonuses, friendly scorecards and competitions, and the like (talk the walk, walk the talk).

8) Get a trusted outsider to periodically review the AI ethics adoption, providing an independent set of eyes to see how things are really coming along (get past the internal platitudes and see the world as it really is).

9) Make sure to keep your investors and other stakeholders apprised of your Ethical AI activities and adoption since they will otherwise likely assume that you are not doing anything on it and could inadvertently suddenly go tyrannical when bumps occur in the AI endeavors (be proud and be vocal about your AI ethics pursuits).

10) Keep on top of the Ethical AI embracement since it is never-ending and will need to have continual upkeep and boosting (you snooze, you lose).

I have many more of these AI Ethics organizational adoption recommendations and will gradually be covering them in later postings. Stay tuned.

Conclusion

The glass is half-full and half-empty.

According to the earlier cited survey, approximately half of the AI startup firms polled were adopting AI ethics and thus we can assume that about half were not. We though also know that even if an AI startup said it was embracing Ethical AI, it might not have done so in any substantive manner. It is abundantly easy and convenient to simply pay lip service to the cause.

The pressures arising from demands by savvy investors will undoubtedly boost the pace and proportion of AI startups that willingly or not will opt to dive headfirst into the AI ethics realm. Likewise, the specter of lawsuits and prosecution for criminal acts as a result of violating the newly being enacted AI-related laws will certainly inspire AI startups to get their act together on Ethical AI matters.

Is ignoring or skirting AI ethics ostensibly worth losing your shirt or ending up in a jail cell? I certainly hope not.

The harsh pain of the stick is of course not the only basis for aiming to embrace AI ethics. As mentioned, if you want to grow or possibly eventually exit from your startup, larger buying firms are going to want to see that you've suitably got Ethical AI and truly infused it into your AI startup. The payoff of abiding by AI ethics is sensible and enormous. The carrot is good.

As a final comment, for now, we all know that those in the tech field love to tout copiously catchy slogans. Build the future. Push the limits. Be data-driven. Go big or go home.

And just one more needs to be added: *Energetically embrace AI ethics*.

Live it, make it so, believe in it.

APPENDIX

APPENDIX A
TEACHING WITH THIS MATERIAL

The material in this book can be readily used either as a supplemental to other content for a class, or it can also be used as a core set of textbook material for a specialized class. Classes where this material is most likely used include any classes at the college or university level that want to augment the class by offering thought provoking and educational essays about AI.

In particular, here are some aspects for class use:

- Computer Science. Studying AI, ethics, etc.
- Business. Exploring technology and ethical adoption for business.
- Sociology. Ethical views on the adoption and advancement of technology.

Specialized classes at the undergraduate and graduate level can also make use of this material.

For each chapter, consider whether you think the chapter provides material relevant to your course topic. There is plenty of opportunity to get the students thinking about the topic and force them to decide whether they agree or disagree with the points offered and positions taken. I would also encourage you to have the students do additional research beyond the chapter material presented (I provide next some suggested assignments they can do).

RESEARCH ASSIGNMENTS ON THESE TOPICS

Your students can find background material on these topics, doing so in various business and technical publications. I list below the top ranked AI related journals. For business publications, I would suggest the usual culprits such as the Harvard Business Review, Forbes, Fortune, WSJ, and the like.

Here are some suggestions of homework or projects that you could assign to students:

a) Assignment for foundational AI research topic: Research and prepare a paper and a presentation on a specific aspect of Deep AI, Machine Learning, ANN, etc. The paper should cite at least 3 reputable sources. Compare and contrast to what has been stated in this book.

b) Assignment for the Ethics topic: Research and prepare a paper and ethics. Cite at least 3 reputable sources and analyze the characterizations. Compare and contrast to what has been stated in this book.

c) Assignment for a Business topic: Research and prepare a paper and a presentation on businesses and advanced technology. What is hot, and what is not? Cite at least 3 reputable sources. Compare and contrast to the depictions in this book.

d) Assignment to do a Startup: Have the students prepare a paper about how they might startup a business in this realm. They must submit a sound Business Plan for the startup. They could also be asked to present their Business Plan and so should also have a presentation deck to coincide with it.

You can certainly adjust the aforementioned assignments to fit to your particular needs and the class structure. You'll notice that I ask for 3 reputable cited sources for the paper writing based assignments. I usually steer students toward "reputable" publications, since otherwise they will cite some oddball source that has no credentials other than that they happened to write something and post it onto the Internet. You can define "reputable" in whatever way you prefer, for example some faculty think Wikipedia is not reputable while others believe it is reputable and allow students to cite it.

The reason that I usually ask for at least 3 citations is that if the student only does one or two citations they usually settle on whatever they happened to find the fastest. By requiring three citations, it usually seems to force them to look around, explore, and end-up probably finding five or more, and then whittling it down to 3 that they will actually use.

I have not specified the length of their papers, and leave that to you to tell the students what you prefer. For each of those assignments, you could end-up with a short one to two pager, or you could do a dissertation length paper. Base the length on whatever best fits for your class, and the credit amount of the assignment within the context of the other grading metrics you'll be using for the class.

I mention in the assignments that they are to do a paper and prepare a presentation. I usually try to get students to present their work. This is a good practice for what they will do in the business world. Most of the time, they will be required to prepare an analysis and present it. If you don't have the class time or inclination to have the students present, then you can of course cut out the aspect of them putting together a presentation.

If you want to point students toward highly ranked journals in AI, here's a list of the top journals as reported by *various citation counts sources* (this list changes year to year):

- Communications of the ACM
- Artificial Intelligence
- Cognitive Science
- IEEE Transactions on Pattern Analysis and Machine Intelligence
- Foundations and Trends in Machine Learning
- Journal of Memory and Language
- Cognitive Psychology
- Neural Networks
- IEEE Transactions on Neural Networks and Learning Systems
- IEEE Intelligent Systems
- Knowledge-based Systems

GUIDE TO USING THE CHAPTERS

For each of the chapters, I provide next some various ways to use the chapter material. You can assign the tasks as individual homework assignments, or the tasks can be used with team projects for the class. You can easily layout a series of assignments, such as indicating that the students are to do item "a" below for say Chapter 1, then "b" for the next chapter of the book, and so on.

a) What is the main point of the chapter and describe in your own words the significance of the topic,

b) Identify at least two aspects in the chapter that you agree with, and support your concurrence by providing at least one other outside researched item as support; make sure to explain your basis for disagreeing with the aspects,

c) Identify at least two aspects in the chapter that you disagree with, and support your disagreement by providing at least one other outside researched item as support; make sure to explain your basis for disagreeing with the aspects,

d) Find an aspect that was not covered in the chapter, doing so by conducting outside research, and then explain how that aspect ties into the chapter and what significance it brings to the topic,

e) Interview a specialist in industry about the topic of the chapter, collect from them their thoughts and opinions, and readdress the chapter by citing your source and how they compared and contrasted to the material,

f) Interview a relevant academic professor or researcher in a college or university about the topic of the chapter, collect from them their thoughts and opinions, and readdress the chapter by citing your source and how they compared and contrasted to the material,

g) Try to update a chapter by finding out the latest on the topic, and ascertain whether the issue or topic has now been solved or whether it is still being addressed, explain what you come up with.

The above are all ways in which you can get the students of your class involved in considering the material of a given chapter. You could mix things up by having one of those above assignments per each week, covering the chapters over the course of the semester or quarter. As a reminder, here are the chapters of the book and you can select whichever chapters you find most valued for your particular class:

ABOUT THE AUTHOR

Dr. Lance B. Eliot, Ph.D., MBA is a Stanford Fellow and a globally recognized AI expert and thought leader, an experienced executive and leader, a successful serial entrepreneur, and a noted scholar on AI, including that his Forbes and AI Trends columns have amassed over 5.8+ million views, his books on AI are frequently ranked in the Top 10 of all-time AI books, his articles are widely cited, and he has developed dozens of advanced AI systems.

He currently serves as the CEO of Techbruim, Inc. and has over twenty years of industry experience including serving as a corporate officer in billion-dollar sized firms and was a partner in a major consulting firm. He is also a successful entrepreneur having founded, ran, and sold several high-tech firms.

Dr. Eliot previously hosted the popular radio show *Technotrends* that was also available on American Airlines flights via their in-flight audio program, he has made appearances on CNN, has been a frequent speaker at industry conferences, and his podcasts have been downloaded over 100,000 times.

A former professor at the University of Southern California (USC), he founded and led an innovative research lab on Artificial Intelligence. He also previously served on the faculty of the University of California Los Angeles (UCLA) and was a visiting professor at other major universities. He was elected to the International Board of the Society for Information Management (SIM), a prestigious association of over 3,000 high-tech executives worldwide.

He has performed extensive community service, including serving as Senior Science Adviser to the Congressional Vice-Chair of the Congressional Committee on Science & Technology. He has served on the Board of the OC Science & Engineering Fair (OCSEF), where he is also has been a Grand Sweepstakes judge, and likewise served as a judge for the Intel International SEF (ISEF). He served as the Vice-Chair of the Association for Computing Machinery (ACM) Chapter, a prestigious association of computer scientists. Dr. Eliot has been a shark tank judge for the USC Mark Stevens Center for Innovation on start-up pitch competitions and served as a mentor for several incubators and accelerators in Silicon Valley and in Silicon Beach.

Dr. Eliot holds a Ph.D. from USC, MBA, and Bachelor's in Computer Science, and earned the CDP, CCP, CSP, CDE, and CISA certifications.

ADDENDUM

Creative Insights In AI Ethics

Practical Advances in Artificial Intelligence (AI) and Machine Learning

By
Dr. Lance B. Eliot, MBA, PhD

For special orders of this book, contact:

LBE Press Publishing

Email: LBE.Press.Publishing@gmail.com

Made in the USA
Monee, IL
25 June 2022

98618449R00203